DOING A RESEARCH PROJECT
PERFORMANCE ANALYSIS

The research project or dissertation is a core component of any degree programme in the rapidly developing discipline of sport performance analysis. This highly practical and accessible book provides a complete step-by-step guide to doing a research project. Showcasing the very latest research methods, it covers the whole research process, from identifying a research question and system development to data collection, data analysis and writing up the results.

Introducing the fundamentals of project planning and management, this book highlights the importance of research ethics and explains the differences between successful undergraduate and postgraduate projects. Full of expert advice and original insights that can be applied to theoretical and empirical research projects, it covers all the key aspects of conducting a degree-level research project, including:

- selecting a research topic and writing a research proposal
- working with a supervisor
- understanding research ethics
- implementing best practices for project management
- collecting, interpreting and presenting results.

Doing a Research Project in Sport Performance Analysis is an indispensable guide for any student, lecturer or practitioner working in sport performance analysis.

Peter O'Donoghue is a Reader in Sports Performance Analysis in the School of Sport at Cardiff Metropolitan University, UK. He is also the Programme Director of the BSc Hons Sports Performance Analysis degree. He has worked as a performance analyst in Gaelic football (inter-county level) and netball (junior and senior international levels as well as in the National Super League). Peter is a member of the International Society of Performance Analysis of Sport and General Editor of the *International Journal of Performance Analysis in Sport*.

Lucy Holmes is a Senior Lecturer in Sports Performance Analysis in the School of Sport at Cardiff Metropolitan University, UK. She is currently Programme Director for the MSc Sports Performance Analysis and MSc Professional Practice degrees. Her research interests include the use of technology in sport and education, the use of performance analysis and technology to provide feedback to athletes, and the use of performance analysis in assisting the development of sport-specific fitness assessments and training programmes. Lucy teaches courses on performance analysis and dance and also works as Lead Performance Analyst for Hockey Wales.

Gemma Robinson is a Senior Lecturer in Performance Analysis in the School of Sport at Cardiff Metropolitan University, UK. Her research interests include time-motion analysis, the assessment of injury risk and the analysis of technique. She teaches courses on performance analysis and research methods at both the undergraduate and postgraduate level.

Routledge Studies in Sports Performance Analysis

Series Editor
Peter O'Donoghue
Cardiff Metropolitan University

Routledge Studies in Sports Performance Analysis is designed to support students, lecturers and practitioners in all areas of this important and rapidly developing discipline. Books in the series are written by leading international experts in sports performance analysis and cover topics including match analysis, analysis of individual sports and team sports, technique analysis, data analytics, performance analysis for high performance management and various methodological areas. Drawing on the very latest research, and introducing key concepts and best practice, the series meets a need for accessible, up-to-date texts at all levels of study and work in performance analysis.

Available in this series:

An Introduction to Performance Analysis of Sport
Peter O'Donoghue

Data Analysis in Sport
Peter O'Donoghue and Lucy Holmes

Performance Analysis in Team Sports
Pedro Passos, Duarte Araújo and Anna Volossovitch

Doing a Research Project in Sport Performance Analysis
Peter O'Donoghue, Lucy Holmes and Gemma Robinson

DOING A RESEARCH PROJECT IN SPORT PERFORMANCE ANALYSIS

PETER O'DONOGHUE, LUCY HOLMES
AND GEMMA ROBINSON

Routledge
Taylor & Francis Group

LONDON AND NEW YORK

First published 2018
by Routledge
2 Park Square, Milton Park, Abingdon, Oxon OX14 4RN

and by Routledge
711 Third Avenue, New York, NY 10017

Routledge is an imprint of the Taylor & Francis Group, an informa business

British Library Cataloguing-in-Publication Data
A catalogue record for this book is available from the British Library

Library of Congress Cataloging-in-Publication Data
A catalog record for this book has been requested

ISBN: 978-1-138-66702-0 (hbk)
ISBN: 978-1-138-66703-7 (pbk)
ISBN: 978-1-315-61913-2 (ebk)

Typeset in Melior
by Apex CoVantage, LLC

CONTENTS

FIGURES

TABLES

ACKNOWLEDGEMENTS

The authors would like to express their sincere thanks to all of the people who helped us during the writing and production of this book. In particular, we'd like to thank William Bailey from Routledge and the reviewers of the book proposal for their constructive feedback.

PREFACE

In 2010, one of the authors of the current book (O'Donoghue) wrote a book entitled *Research Methods for Sports Performance Analysis*. At the time, there were very few books in the area of sports performance analysis; the main texts were those of Hughes and Franks (2008) and Carling et al. (2005). Hughes and Franks's *The Essentials of Performance Analysis of Sport* was the major reference book for those developing manual notation systems, as well as the main secondary source of research material in the area. Carling et al.'s book, by contrast, was aimed much more at a practitioner audience. O'Donoghue's (2010) book was, therefore, aimed at dissertation students in sports performance analysis. It covered the various stages of the research process, as well as underlying assumptions of research methods used in sports performance analysis. The main contributions of O'Donoghue's book were the discussion of the ontological and epistemological assumptions of sports performance analysis and a widening of the scope of sports performance analysis beyond notational analysis and biomechanics. However, O'Donoghue's book was written seven years ago, and there is a need for the current updated and more focussed book.

Sports performance analysis is becoming more popular throughout the world, with performance analysis support being provided to larger numbers of athletes and coaches using rapidly developing technology. Sports performance analysis has continued to grow as an academic discipline with modules and programmes being provided by a greater number of universities than before. Research in the area is truly international. This is evidenced by the list of chapter authors of McGarry et al.'s (2013) *Routledge Handbook of Sports Performance Analysis*, who come from

Europe, North and South America, Australia, Africa and Asia. The number and quality of papers published in the *International Journal of Performance Analysis in Sport* has also grown steadily since 2010. Given these developments, there was a strong rationale for an updated textbook on sports performance analysis research. At the time of writing, work had commenced on a series of books entitled Routledge Studies in Sports Performance Analysis. This series of books will cover all aspects of sports performance analysis; therefore, the current book did not need to be as broad as O'Donoghue's (2010) textbook. Instead, the book is a more focussed book on undertaking a research project in sports performance analysis. This makes it sound as though the current book is a subset of O'Donoghue's text, packaged into 75,000 words rather than 110,000 words. However there are three important new contributions that were not covered by O'Donoghue's earlier book.

Firstly, in Chapter 1 we distinguish between undergraduate and postgraduate projects, discussing national standards for quality and the 'step up' to masters level. The second main contribution is the review of recent research in Chapter 3. We deliberately reviewed research done since the *Routledge Handbook of Sports Performance Analysis* (McGarry et al., 2013) had been published. Chapter 4 makes the third contribution of the book. This chapter covers enterprise and development projects that were not addressed at all by O'Donoghue's (2010) book. Many students who are preparing to be professional performance analysts wish to undertake independent projects that are more vocational in nature than the traditional scientific studies done in research projects. Enterprise and development projects can be done by sports students in many universities and provide an attractive option for sports performance analysts. There was a clear need for these types of projects to be covered in a sports performance analysis textbook. The remaining chapters are more focussed and updated versions of different stages of the research projects in sports performance analysis. These are necessary for a book on research projects to be complete.

REFERENCES

Carling, C., Williams, A.M. and Reilly, T. (2005) *Handbook of soccer match analysis: a systematic approach to improving performance.* London: Routledge.

Hughes, M. and Franks, I.M. (2008) *The essentials of performance analysis: an introduction.* London: Routledge.

McGarry, T., O'Donoghue, P.G. and Sampaio, J. (2013) *Routledge handbook of sports performance analysis.* London: Routledge.

O'Donoghue, P.G. (2010) *Research methods for sports performance analysis.* London: Routledge.

CHAPTER 1

INTRODUCTION

OVERVIEW

This introductory chapter describes research projects and their role within academic programmes. The chapter is made up of three sections. The first section distinguishes research project work from the types of work done in other modules. The second section discusses how projects are assessed, which is typically through the final dissertation. Having established the 'goal post' of how the dissertation is being assessed, the chapter moves onto the third section, which distinguishes between different types of research projects that are done in various taught and research degrees.

RESEARCH PROJECT WORK

The specific requirements of your research project will be dictated by the programme and level that you are studying. All undergraduate and postgraduate programmes will require some element of research to provide evidence of autonomous working and alignment of theoretical concepts learnt with the application of knowledge to different areas.

Dissertation modules

A research project is typically a substantial piece of independent research involving academic and practical work leading to the production of

1

a dissertation. The dissertation reports on the research and is like a research paper except with a more expanded review of literature to add to the introduction. The research project is usually worth more than standard taught modules; at the authors' university, an undergraduate dissertation is worth 40 UK credit points (double the value of a standard taught module), and a postgraduate dissertation is worth 60 UK credit points (triple the value of a standard taught module). The volume of effort hours of work at the required level is 10 hours per credit point. Hence an undergraduate dissertation involves 400 effort hours of work, including background literature research, study design, project management activity, organisation of equipment and other resources, arrangements with participants, data collection, data analysis and writing up of the final dissertation report. When one considers that the research project is typically undertaken between mid-September and mid-March in Northern Hemisphere universities, students need to work over fifteen hours per week on average towards their research project.

Students will develop a breadth and depth of knowledge about a topic of interest that is not catered for within standard taught modules. This allows students to tailor their degree to their own requirements. Students with particular interests can pursue these through the dissertation. Students with set career aspirations can use the dissertation to advance relevant knowledge and ability. This can then appear on their curriculum vitae, providing evidence of specialist knowledge that distinguishes them from other graduates. Many students may reach the final stages of their degree programmes without having decided on particular career paths. Such students often undertake research projects in areas of interest which may coincide with areas where they achieve some of their higher marks. This is an effective strategy to achieve the best possible degree classification at the end of the programme. It may be possible for students to do dissertations in areas not covered in the standard taught modules they have chosen in final year. This allows students to keep the material covered in their degree programme as broad as possible. However, students undertaking projects in such areas may place themselves at a disadvantage to students doing dissertations in areas that they are covering in other modules. When a dissertation is done within one of the disciplines covered in a student's other taught modules, the underpinning knowledge from the standard taught module benefits the dissertation, and the in-depth dissertation work may benefit performance in the standard taught module as well. The option to do a dissertation in

2

an area outside those covered within standard taught modules is available, but students are often counselled to make sure they understand the disadvantages. Ultimately, students wishing to do a dissertation in an area outside their other module choices need to have the ability to do so.

Sports performance analysis is a special case when it comes to dissertation choices as many universities may not have modules in sports performance analysis. Indeed some universities may not have a specialist performance analysis lecturer. This should not rule out the possibility of interested students undertaking performance analysis dissertations, as lecturers in other disciplines can supervise sports performance analysis dissertations when needed.

The research project is not just a task that students do as part of an honours degree or higher degree. It is an opportunity to learn and develop through undertaking a substantial piece of independent research. The student undertakes background research, locating relevant material, synthesising it and summarising relevant academic debate in their area of interest. They improve their knowledge about the problem area that the project is concerned with, as well as about sports performance analysis in general. Indeed, they develop in-depth knowledge by answering a specific research question and may even contribute to knowledge; undergraduate student research is presented at the annual BASES (British Association of Sport and Exercise Sciences) student conference. The students develop time management skills during the project, working towards deadlines. They learn how to plan the project, ensuring that project tasks are scheduled along with other university work they are doing. They need to be organised and co-operate with participants, technicians and supervisors. The practical work of a sports performance analysis project typically involves system development, testing, data collection and analysis. The effort involved in these tasks also helps the student develop technical and intellectual abilities. Producing the final dissertation report helps the student develop scientific writing skills.

It is quite rare that supervisors will have actually done the exact study that their students undertake. This is unsurprising given the number of dissertation students that university staff supervise over the course of their careers. The supervisor should have expertise in the broad area of sports performance analysis or sports science in general. More importantly, the supervisor will have experience of undertaking and supervising research projects. The experience of the supervisor means that they understand the importance of research design and pilot work. The supervisor can quickly spot common pitfalls in research projects at an early stage and can advise students so that these are prevented.

Supervisor role

The supervisor's experience is beneficial at all stages of the research project. The initial discussions about dissertation ideas may take place before students enter the final year of their degree programme. During the initial discussions about the problem area, the supervisor will broadly consider interest in the area and the feasibility of the study. With respect to performance analysis in sport, the main feasibility issues are the availability of appropriate video, the possibility of filming matches and potential travel and time issues. The supervisor will also think ahead to the methods that might be used in the research and consider whether the volume of work will be appropriate for the dissertation module. Some initial ideas may involve too much work, whereas others might involve too little. In either case, the supervisor will explain the issues to the students and make suggestions as to how to ensure the research project involves the appropriate volume of work. Volume of work is not the only issue that needs to be considered in this respect. A research project could involve a considerable volume of data collection and analysis activity but lead to a simplistic results chapter if sufficient variables are not included. Given that the student intends to analyse performances, the supervisor will be keen to ensure that sufficient data are gathered from each performance to produce a large enough but concise results chapter. Some issues relating to variables might be discussed at a later time as the supervisor may be confident that the project will produce sufficient results if done well. The reason for deferring discussion of specific variables is that the supervisor will be keen that system design and development are part of the project rather than completed prior to the project.

Once students arrive at the final year of an undergraduate degree or complete the taught modules of a master's programme, they are ready to commence their research project. The project will have usually been discussed before this stage. The supervisor's main concern at the start of the research project is to make sure the student plans the project and gets started. An initial meeting is used to explain the supervisor's expectations of the student. The student will typically be advised how meetings work, how work should be done between meetings and how the student

4

should prepare for meetings (e.g., having a list of questions). The supervisor may also discuss the purpose of the study and the type of results that should be produced. It is useful to draw a grid of eight squares on a sheet of A4 paper and ask the student what types of results they are expecting to produce. The supervisor might express a need for six to eight 'nuggets' of information that could be produced, hence the use of eight squares. Of course the student will not be aware of the ultimate values that will appear in any tables, charts or pitch diagrams. However, the student, in discussion with the supervisor, should be able to identify the types of charts and tables that need to be produced to answer the research question. These are sketched into the squares that have been created on the sheet of A4 paper. Each result type should answer part of the research question. It may be about one subset of dependent variables of interest to the study. If there is a possibility of too many charts, it may be a good idea to use a single table instead of several charts. Once six to eight results types have been identified, the student will have a better understanding of the purpose of the study, where it is going and why the chosen input data are being collected. The intended results format acts as a goal post that the student is aiming for. One other thing that the supervisor really needs to make sure of at this early stage is that the student has proper ownership of the project. The initial discussion of the project and setting out the aims and intended results format can help in this respect.

A project plan should be produced to identify the main data collection, analysis and write-up activities, together with related deliverables. These should be scheduled over the project period to ensure the project is completed on time. The plan should recognise other coursework, exams and commitments the student has to ensure that neither dissertation work nor other work is compromised during the student's final year of study. The supervisor should discuss the plan with the student and give appropriate advice on research based on experience of supervising and doing research. The project plan acts as a useful mechanism for project planning, management and control. There is only one thing worse than falling behind schedule during a research project and that is falling behind and not being aware that you are behind. The project plan helps avoid this situation.

A job that needs to be completed early during the research project is gaining ethical approval. The supervisor has very important responsibilities here to check over students' ethics applications and, in the case of non-contentious research, may be able to approve these. Where

5

student research needs to be scrutinised by a research ethics committee, the supervisor needs to ensure that the student's ethics application is in a good enough state to be sent to the committee. Ethical issues and application for ethical approval for research projects will be discussed more fully in Chapter 6. A final point about ethics that will be made in the current chapter is that delays in gaining ethical approval delay the recruitment of participants for studies and delay the start of data collection.

November is an important month in the final year of undergraduate programmes within UK universities. Students will be completing end-of-term coursework for other modules in December, and so November is a critical month for the review of literature and commencing data collection. The supervisor will need to make sure that the student is progressing with project work during this period and should check progress against the project plan during this stage. Some supervisors may wish to see completed introduction and literature review chapters during the first term. These chapters will not necessarily be finalised, as the student will find further useful literature to include during the second term of their final year. However, getting these chapters drafted in the first term will take pressure off the student in the second term.

The supervisor should use the final meeting with the student before Christmas to check where the student is at with the dissertation and, if necessary, set priorities for the period before the student returns to university in January. The student should be encouraged to take a break over the Christmas period but also to use some of the time to continue progress on the dissertation.

The second term is a very busy period for final-year students as they approach the deadline for dissertation submission while still having to work on other modules that contribute towards their degree classification. Indeed some students are so busy that they begin to contact supervisors by email rather than through face-to-face meetings. Draft methods and results chapters are typically read by supervisors during this period, with feedback given to the student. The student and supervisor should consider the results found, the correlated variables, the unrelated variables and the similarities and differences found. Many universities require students to complete the discussion chapter without feedback from the supervisor. However, planning the discussion chapter is important. The argument to be made explaining the results, the use

6

of supporting literature and the structure of the discussion are worth talking about before embarking on this chapter.

The supervisor's role at the postgraduate level works very much in the same way as at the undergraduate level: being a 'sounding-board' for ideas, providing support and guidance, assisting with planning and providing academic discussion. At the authors' current university, the postgraduate dissertation is scheduled to take place in the period following the completion of the taught modules, starting from the summer period and finishing at the end of January. During this period, many students return home; therefore, supervision can be provided remotely via email, phone and Skype tutorials.

This section has discussed the supervisor role, but ultimately students need to complete their dissertations. Students should not be surprised when the supervisor insists that they find out how to undertake tasks rather than showing them how to do such tasks. The supervisor will not show students how to do analyses, but will expect students to revise things they have been taught in previous years and to look up analysis processes within relevant textbooks and other resources. Students working in this way will become more self-reliant, which will benefit them in their future careers.

Assessment of research projects

Some universities include a mark for the process of doing a research project as well as a mark for the final dissertation. However, most universities assess research projects solely based on the dissertation report. Therefore, students need to make sure that the dissertation report does justice to their research. This also means that it is essential that the project is the student's own work, as there is no process mark to reflect differing levels of assistance that students may have had from supervisors. The distribution of marks for an empirical research project at the authors' university are currently as follows:

- Title and abstract 5%
- Introduction and literature review 25%
- Methods 15%
- Results 15%
- Discussion and conclusions 30%
- Presentation 10%

The content of these chapters and guidance for writing them is covered in more detail in Chapter 9 of the current book. There are two points we wish to make here about the assessment of the dissertation. Firstly, the number of marks for a section is not necessarily correlated with the time students need to spend producing the given chapter. Consider the results and discussion chapters; it actually takes more time to produce a results chapter than a discussion chapter. This is because data have to be collected and analysed in order to produce the results chapter. Students may spend 100 effort hours of their dissertation just on data collection. The discussion, on the other hand, can be written over a shorter time period. So why are there so many marks for the discussion and conclusions? The answer is that the discussion is assessing students' knowledge and intellectual ability at the end of their whole degree programme. There have been examples of students who have received first-class marks for discussion chapters written in three days. This is fair because the students who are capable of producing excellent discussion chapters have developed relevant knowledge as they have progressed through their programme of study and undertaken the literature review of the project. The students' ability to form an argument explaining results by linking the findings of their study to existing theory will have developed through reading research papers over the course of their degree programme. Secondly, students do not need to achieve a pass mark for each chapter in order to pass the whole project. The reason for mentioning this is that some students worry unnecessarily that they may fail their dissertation if they are unable to produce inferential statistics. The most important statistics are the descriptive statistics, which show the means or medians as well as standard deviations or inter-quartile ranges for the dependent performance variables in the study. The inferential statistics may be more difficult to produce, but they are actually supplementary to the main descriptive statistics. Students will lose more marks if they produce inferential statistics without the all-important descriptive statistics than if they produce the descriptive statistics without the supporting inferential statistics. A student who may have been awarded 10 or 11 marks out of 15 for the results chapter, if they include inferential statistics, may well be awarded 6 or 7 marks if inferential statistics have not been included; 6 out of 15 is a pass mark for the section of 40 per cent. Even if the student were to be awarded 4 out of 15 for the results chapter, they only need 36 out of 85 (42.3%) for the remainder of the dissertation to pass. It is true that, without inferential statistics, a dissertation where quantitative methods have been used will lose some marks in the discussion and conclusions as well due to limitations in the analysis. There may also be some

8

marks lost in the methods section if the statistical procedures necessary to answer the research question have not been fully articulated. However, students can still pass their dissertation with a critical literature review and the remaining chapters being strong but with the limitation of not being supported by inferential statistics. There is another way of thinking about this for students who lack the practical and intellectual ability to produce inferential statistics. They may actually lose more marks in other sections than they would for a lack of inferential analysis if they spend too much time struggling to do inferential statistics at the expense of other chapters where there are a lot of marks at stake.

The distribution of marks for theoretical/philosophical research projects is different to that of empirical projects. This is because there is no original data reported on, meaning that the traditional methods and results chapters are not appropriate for theoretical/philosophical research. The distribution of marks for theoretical/philosophical research projects at the authors' university at the time of writing is as follows:

- Title and abstract 5%
- Extended introduction 20%
- Research methods 15%
- Critical review 35%
- Explicit summary 15%
- Presentation 10%

The extended introduction outlines the background context and justifies the research question. The research methods chapter justifies the use of secondary data and describes the systematic process used to identify secondary data, criteria for inclusion and exclusion and a justification for the approach taken. The critical review is the end product of a systematic process of reviewing secondary data. This is assessed based on conceptual understanding, discussion of theory, the argument made about the problem of interest and the position formed in relation to the research question. The explicit summary is a much more expanded conclusion than those presented in an empirical research report. This includes the position stated, limitations and directions for future research.

At postgraduate level, the assessment of research projects is in the main assessed by written reports of the research project(s) undertaken. Other assessments may also be coupled with the dissertation, such as an oral presentation of a research proposal, or indeed a written research proposal, or perhaps an oral examination of the final submission. Every university and programme will have their own matrix of assessment, which should be outlined in the programme or module specification.

Currently at the authors' university, the dissertation is assessed under the guise of two different modules. The Research Methods module houses the research proposal element of the dissertation, in which the students are required to complete an oral project proposal presentation that constitutes 40 per cent of the module mark. Prior to this, students have had the opportunity to informally discuss initial embryonic ideas with staff in order to develop the research study in preparation for the project proposal presentation. This presentation is then made individually towards a panel of staff members. The distribution of marks for the research proposal presentation is as follows:

- Background knowledge 30%
- Proposed research design 30%
- Presentation skills 20%
- Ability to answer questions posed 20%

The dissertation is then assessed within its own module by a further two assessment points of a written dissertation report and an oral examination (viva voce). At the authors' current university, MSc taught students have two potential formats for submission of the dissertation report: 'full thesis' or 'journal article' format. A 'full thesis' or traditional dissertation format affords the student greater scope to show the breadth and depth of knowledge and understanding of the research topic. The dissertation will normally include an abstract, introduction and literature review and method, results, discussion and conclusions chapters, with the full report not exceeding 12,000 words. The option of a 'journal article' format submission has been provided to promote vocational relevance, encourage potential publications of MSc dissertations, promote succinct writing and prepare students for further subsequent postgraduate research. This 'journal article' format is a shorter format that requires greater writing skills, and those taking this option may find that they cannot produce the depth that their work requires. The distribution of marks for either submission at the authors' current university are as follows:

- Statement of the problem – aims, limitations, relevance to the study of performance 10%

10

- Background reading and research – organisation, depth, relevance and critical analysis 20%
- Methods – study design, rationale for sample, data collection, analysis and overall integrity of the investigative process 15%
- Presentation of findings – logical, clear appropriateness of tables, figures and appendices; correct statistical applications 15%
- Interpretation and discussion of findings – logical relevance to the purpose and use of literature; critical analysis and interpretation 30%
- Written presentation – command of language; typescript; appropriate presentation of statistical analysis, figures, tables, and so on 10%

The step up – undergraduate to postgraduate research

It's a common misconception made by many students that the difference between an undergraduate and postgraduate research project is the amount of analysis conducted. Whilst there are an associated number of hours that are designated to the collection of data for a dissertation project, the volume of analysis is not a predetermining factor. The standard of work required to satisfy the criteria for award at either the master's or doctorate level are outlined by the Quality Assurance Agency (QAA) Framework for Higher Education Qualifications in Wales and Northern Ireland. This framework stipulates descriptors of work for all levels of study. Higher Education has five levels, three of which are undergraduate (Levels 4–6) and two postgraduate (Levels 7 and 8) (QAA, 2008). According to these descriptors, the main differential is that undergraduate students will have to show that they have an understanding of a complex body of knowledge within a subject area; be able to evaluate evidence and construct arguments and assumptions to reach sound judgment; and, in turn, be able to communicate those arguments and assumptions effectively. Postgraduates need to show originality in the application of their knowledge, demonstrate an ability to deal with complex issues both systematically and creatively, and show originality in tackling and solving problems. The main facets that distinguish postgraduate work from undergraduate work are the cognitive level of thinking, the complexities of the research undertaken and the methods used for data collection.

TYPES OF PROJECT

The majority of undergraduate dissertations in sports performance analysis are descriptive studies that compare samples of matches or report on correlations between performance variables. There are other types of sports performance analysis dissertation that are done at the undergraduate level. These include enterprise and development projects, which are covered in Chapter 4 of the current book. An enterprise project involves market research related to some business idea of interest rather than scientific research. Development projects involve developing and evaluating some product or process. A further type of project undertaken by some undergraduate students in sports performance analysis is a theoretical study that does not involve any collection of primary data. The section of the current chapter on the assessment of such projects has already covered the content of such projects and their use of secondary data. Some projects investigate attitudes towards performance analysis from the perspective of athletes, coaches or analysts themselves. These projects can use interviews, focus groups or questionnaires to survey opinions and beliefs of different types of participants.

As mentioned, many undergraduate research projects in sports performance analysis tend towards describing how technical, tactical or physical aspects are influenced by variables such as gender, playing location, age range, level of competition and playing positions. Whilst these are good ideas for undergraduate students, those students studying at the master's level would require a greater level of sophistication to satisfy the assessment criteria. Doing such descriptive studies, but with a larger volume of data, is often seen as adequate by some students studying at the master's level, but the additional volume of data gathering and analysis activity is simply not sufficient. In order to satisfy the marking criteria at the master's level, there needs to be an increase in the theoretical or methodological challenge that is not typically apparent within undergraduate student dissertations.

MSc taught programmes, such as the ones currently offered at Cardiff Metropolitan University in the areas of Sport Performance Analysis, require students to undertake an independent research project. The project affords students an opportunity to continue study in their chosen field through the completion of an original research project. It is expected that students will make use of the knowledge that they have

12

gained during the taught elements of their programme, as well as extending that knowledge.

Research-based degrees distinguish themselves from their taught programme counterparts by their sole-reliance on the research project to assess the students' level of knowledge in their chosen area. Students will engage with this via either Master's of Philosophy (MPhil), Doctor of Philosophy (PhD) or Professional Doctorate (DProf) routes and will be tasked with the completion of a thesis accordingly. An MPhil project will provide a critical evaluation and analysis of a body of knowledge or an original contribution to learning or knowledge, whereas a PhD will provide both elements.

SUMMARY

This introductory chapter has described the role of research projects within different types of degree programmes, the assessment of dissertations and the different types of research projects that can be done in sports performance analysis. Sports performance analysis projects can be classified by the type of work done as well as the level of work done. Enterprise projects, development projects, theoretical projects and empirical research projects are all possible in sports performance analysis. The main distinction between undergraduate and postgraduate research projects is in the "step up" in academic level, methodological sophistication and theoretical development involved rather than in the volume of data gathered and analysed in the project.

REFERENCE

QAA (2008) *The framework for higher education qualifications in England, Wales and Northern Ireland*. Mansfield, UK: QAA.

CHAPTER 2

SPORTS PERFORMANCE ANALYSIS RESEARCH

OVERVIEW

The first chapter of the current book discussed the role of independent research projects within academic degree programmes. These projects are done in areas of special interest to the students. Chapter 3 will discuss some of the emerging topics within sports performance analysis. The current chapter takes a more general look at research processes that are used during independent research projects in the area. Methodologies, data types and the ontological, epistemological and praxeology assumptions of alternative approaches are discussed. Sports performance analysis is a discipline of sport and exercise science concerned with actual sports performance. When investigating sports performance, we are investigating aspects of sports performance of interest. These aspects may be technical, tactical or physical. Therefore, there is an overlap between sports performance analysis and other disciplines of sport and exercise science. This chapter describes the nature of sports performance analysis research and outlines the types of investigation that fall within its scope. There are two broad types of research projects that are done in the area of sports performance analysis. Firstly, there are investigations of sports performance that involve sports performance analysis methods. These may be scientific investigations into factors influencing sports performance or reflective studies on the provision of sports performance analysis services. The second type of research project does not involve analysing sports performance. Instead these projects may be concerned with underlying theory explaining behaviour in sports performance, as well as perceptions or experiences of sports performance analysis.

14

The chapter commences by describing the wider discipline of sports performance analysis before focussing on research methods in the area. Traditional observational studies, qualitative research studies and intervention studies are all described in the next section before the chapter continues with a discussion of the underlying assumptions of different research processes.

THE SPORTS PERFORMANCE ANALYSIS DISCIPLINE

The scope of sports performance analysis research

Traditionally, notational analysis or performance analysis research projects have been observational and descriptive in nature. This type of research tends to use a reductive approach to discover behaviours that can be generalised within populations of sports performances. Studies may compare different sets of performances to discover factors that influence behaviours within sport. These factors include gender, level, positional role, period within matches, type of performance, quality of opposition and match state. O'Donoghue (2010: 2) described sports performance analysis as a discipline of sports science that primarily investigates actual sports performance but also recognised an expanding array of methods that could be used in sports performance research, including some laboratory experiments, physiological measurement and self-report. The rationale for including laboratory experiments is that there are details of important techniques that cannot feasibly be measured in sufficient biomechanical detail during actual sports performance. Lees (2008) classified skills as event skills, major skills and minor skills. Event skills include the high jump in athletics and the vault in gymnastics. The skill is the whole event that is being performed. Examples of major skills include hurdle clearance in the 100m / 110m hurdles and golf swing, which have a dominant role within the given sports. Minor skills, on the other hand, are important to the sport but not as dominant to the event as major skills would be. Examples of minor skills are the spike in volleyball and kicking the ball in soccer. There are occasions when performance of event skills, major skills and minor skills of sports need to be analysed in detail requiring controlled laboratory investigation and equipment that cannot be used during actual sport performance. The justification for such laboratory investigations coming within the scope of sports performance analysis is that these skills are normally performed during the sports of interest. Laboratory studies of technique may also gather and analyse EMG (electromyography) or EEG (electroencephalogram) data during the performance of relevant skills. These are measurements that could not feasibly be made during actual sports performance. The scope of sports performance analysis has also expanded to include self-report data that clearly relate to actual sports performance. There are thought processes, decision-making processes, anxieties and other mental processes that occur during actual sports performance that cannot be directly observed using traditional notation techniques, irrespective of whether manual or computerised methods are employed. Poizat et al. (2013) described self-confrontational interviews that occur while players watch videos of their performances. These allow players to recall and discuss thoughts that occurred during actual performance. Such qualitative data about the experience of sports performance are considered to be data derived from actual sports performance.

Investigations of sports performance often use literature from other disciplines to create a rationale for studies or to discuss findings. This does not, however, mean that such literature fits within the scope of performance analysis. The literature referred to is typically published within journals and other outlets that focus on those other disciplinary areas. There are occasions when investigations are needed to develop theory about sports performance that do not actually involve the direct observational methods typically used in performance analysis investigations. Such studies do fit within the scope of sports performance analysis because the theoretical development is primarily in relation to sports performance rather than some other discipline of sports science. Interview studies could be used to gain an understanding of why players use the tactics they use, how their performance may or may not see momentum shifts, how they deal with matches played at home versus away venues, or how they approach tournaments or campaigns as opposed to individual matches. There are many other examples of factors that influence the way players play and how well they perform where observational data do not provide sufficient insight to allow theory to be developed.

A further type of study that does not include observational data gathering techniques are surveys into sports performance analysis services. Interview studies can be used to gauge perceptions of athletes and coaches about performance analysis support (Sarmento, Pereira et al., 2013; Sarmento, Bradley, and Travassos, 2015). Questionnaires can also be

16

used for this purpose (Wright et al., 2013). The satisfaction and experience of consumers of infotainment and other media served by sports performance data can be investigated using survey techniques. These survey techniques can also be used with analysts to develop knowledge about their perceptions of their role within the coaching context. Experience reports by analysts involve reflection on the provision of performance analysis services within coaching contexts. The authors of these studies are working as performance analysts, but performance analysis is what is being studied within such investigations rather than being the research method that is used. Despite not using observational techniques, these survey studies and experience reports clearly develop knowledge about the sports performance analysis discipline in its applied setting. Thus such investigations fall within the scope of the area.

Research reviews are important in sports performance analysis just as they are in any other subject area. Review papers do not report on original data but instead review existing published research to sum up the state of the art in some area of interest. They cover areas of debate in the literature, recognising the evidence supporting different positions. The *Routledge Handbook of Sports Performance Analysis* (McGarry et al., 2013) contains review papers on performance analysis of various sports types as well as on methods used in performance analysis. There are examples of such review chapters on soccer (Tenga, 2013), rugby (Prim and van Rooyen, 2013), basketball (Sampaio et al., 2013), volleyball (Mesquita et al., 2013), handball (Volossovitch, 2013), cricket (Petersen and Dawson, 2013), racket sports (O'Donoghue and Mayes, 2013), combat sports (Witte, 2013), target sports (Heller and Baca, 2013), cyclic sports (Marinho et al., 2013), field athletics events (Campos, 2013) and rhythmic gymnastics (Hökelmann et al., 2013). There are also review papers on performance analysis in particular sports published in journals. Examples of these are a review of futsal research (Agras et al., 2016) and a review of field hockey research (Lidor and Ziv, 2015). Examples of review chapters and review papers on different methods used in sports performance analysis are Carling and Bloomfield's (2013) review of time-motion analysis techniques, Butterworth et al.'s (2013) review of profiling techniques and Arriaza and Zuniga's (2016) review of feedback technology. While such reviews are usually of papers contributing to existing theory, occasionally there are reviews that lead to new theoretical models. For example, Hibbs and O'Donoghue (2013) looked at practical text books on individual and team games that include the

17

words 'strategy' or 'tactics' in the title. The material covered supported a general model of factors influencing strategy and tactics that was proposed in the chapter.

Meta-analyses can also be done in sports performance analysis just like they can in many other disciplines. However, meta-analyses are rare in sports performance analysis. One reason for this is that other disciplines of sports science have standardised variables that are commonly used in many different studies. For example, there are standard laboratory tests and field tests used in exercise physiology and in strength and conditioning research. In sports performance analysis, many studies use unique variables that are devised and operationalised within the papers reporting on the research. There are some variables in sports performance analysis that have been used in a number of studies. For example, the distances covered using high-speed running (5.5 m.s^{-1} or faster) and sprinting (7 m.s^{-1} or faster) have been used in several studies of soccer player work-rate (Di Salvo et al., 2009; Gregson et al., 2010; O'Donoghue and Robinson, 2016a/b). However, while review studies have been done in sports performance analysis, there are not sufficient numbers of studies using common variables to warrant a meta-analysis.

Overlap with other disciplines

There is an overlap between sports performance analysis and other disciplines of sports and exercise science, because when we analyse actual sports performance, we analyse some aspect of sports performance that is grounded in some other discipline (O'Donoghue, 2010: 15). For example, when we undertake work-rate analysis in team games, the results need to be explained considering the physiology of intermittent high-intensity exercise. Laboratory-based studies of intermittent exercise have provided physiological results indicating the use of different energy systems and the buildup of fatigue-causing metabolites (Hughes et al., 2005). These published results, combined with the type of intermittent activity observed in a time-motion study of a sport, allow an argument to be made about the energy systems used. The durations of high-intensity bursts and of recovery periods are of particular interest when discussing the physiological demands of the sport.

Analysing techniques may use kinetic or kinematic analyses. Some such studies may be viewed as also being within the scope of the biomechanics

18

discipline. These studies would be a subset of biomechanics studies that specifically investigate the performance of relevant skills in sport. Other performance analysis investigations of sports techniques may fall short of achieving the criteria necessary to be considered biomechanics investigations.

Research into tactical aspects of play is related to coaching and practical knowledge of sports. Observational studies of sports performance can examine patterns of play in games, allowing inferences to be made about the tactics adopted. When a study concludes that particular tactics have been adopted, the explanation for this needs to be supported by practical literature about the sport of interest. There will be advantages and disadvantages of the tactics under discussion, as well as conditions under which they should and should not be used. The discussion of tactics in sports may also draw on wider, more general theory about tactics, strategy and decision making in sports.

There is also an overlap between sports psychology and performance analysis in studies of aggression, attentional focus, score-line effects and other situational factors during sports performance. A study of score-line effects on work-rate variables may find differences in work-rate between different score-line states. Researchers finding such results need to consider the mechanisms that explain such differences. Do players attribute the score-line to factors that are beyond their control? Do the events that led to the given score-line affect player confidence? Do such causal attributions, locus of control perceptions and changes in efficacy expectation lead to changes in player motivation? Do such changes in motivation lead to changes in observed work-rate of players when the score-line changes within games? The work-rate data on their own leave a "black box" between score-line and dependent work-rate variables. The researchers need to explain any score-line effect on observable variables by discussing potential responsible mechanisms and drawing on relevant supporting sports psychology literature.

There is an overlap between performance analysis and coaching science within investigations of the effectiveness of performance analysis support within coaching contexts. Such studies include intervention studies testing the effectiveness of different types of performance analysis feedback (Murray et al., 1998; Horne, 2013; McKenzie and Cushion, 2013) as well as surveys into professional practice in performance analysis (Reeves and Roberts, 2013; Wright et al., 2013, 2014; Palao and

Hernández-Hernández, 2014; Francis and Jones, 2014; Sarmento et al., 2015). These studies are grounded in the coaching context of performance analysis and consider theory about feedback and communication in coaching. Theories about timing of feedback (Maslovat and Franks, 2015), type of feedback (Maslovat and Franks, 2015) and volume of feedback (Hodges and Franks, 2008) for different sports contexts are all relevant to these studies.

In discussing the discipline that we currently refer to as sports performance analysis, it is worth considering whether it should be termed 'sports performance' or 'sports performance analysis'. The three main sports science disciplines of sports biomechanics, sports and exercise physiology and sports psychology do not include the word 'analysis' in the name of the discipline. This is because they are much more than a set of methods. These disciplines comprise subject matter and theory as well as methodology. Sharp (1997) described notational analysis (as performance analysis was then termed) as a research tool that could be used in both good and bad research into sports performance. The word 'analysis' does tend to suggest methods and tools. As the discipline gradually establishes theory in areas such as momentum in sports performance, opposition effect, tactics, strategy and creativity, there will be more of a case for dropping the word 'analysis' from the name of the discipline and simply referring to it as 'sports performance'. A sports performance discipline would encompass the subject matter of actual sports performance, relevant theory and methodology. The view of the authors of the current textbook is that the discipline is not in a position to do this at the time of writing, and so greater research efforts are encouraged to develop theory about sports performance.

SPORTS PERFORMANCE RESEARCH – WHAT, WHY, WHO, WHERE, WHEN, AND HOW?

Applied sports performance analysis

O'Donoghue (2010) included a section titled 'Performance Analysis of Sport: What? Why? Who? Where? When? How?' in the introductory chapter of his *Research Methods for Sports Performance Analysis* textbook. In considering what performance analysis of sport is, O'Donoghue described it as a discipline that typically investigates actual sports performance. The reason performance analysis support is provided in coaching is to provide more complete and accurate information to inform coaching decisions (Franks and Miller, 1991; Laird and Waters, 2008). The reasons for doing performance analysis also include the main purposes of performance (notational) analysis described by Hughes (1998): tactical analysis, technique analysis and analysis of movement. These main purposes of performance analysis research are discussed more fully in Chapter 3 of the current book, which covers current and emerging research topics. In considering the question of 'how?', O'Donoghue discussed who uses information produced by performance analysis and who gathers the data required. Sports performance analysis has applications within coaching (O'Donoghue and Mayes, 2013), high performance management (Wiltshire, 2013), the media (James, 2008; Kirkbride, 2013b), judging (Johns and Brouner, 2013; Kirkbride, 2013a) and academic research. So who gathers and analyses sports performance data? The simple answer is performance analysts, except some coaches may need to do this themselves (Wright et al., 2012), and students do performance analysis work on performance analysis modules and within dissertation projects in the area. O'Donoghue (2010) listed many locations where performance analysis activity is done, ranging from specialist performance analysis laboratories to match venues, team hotels, the match analyst's home, the team bus, airport lounges, and so on. When performance analysis is done depends on the purpose and when information is required. The main performance analysis activities are data gathering, data analysis and communication of information. These can be done in sequence, but there are some possibilities for activities being done in parallel. For example, during interactive use of commercial video analysis packages, analysis and communication of information to coaches and players could be done at the same time. This involves criteria for events of interest being specified to the system, summary statistics being provided by the system using a standard matrix of frequencies or a special-purpose output window and relevant video sequences being shown and discussed. Similarly, as data are gathered, some systems are able to process the data as they arrive, continually updating output information. Choi (2008) distinguished between live match analysis and lapse-time match analysis in considering when performance analysis activities are done. In considering the question of how performance analysis is done, O'Donoghue (2010) distinguished between manual and computerised performance analysis. In recent years, feedback technology has continued to take advantage of technological advances. Portable devices, wireless technology and player and ball tracking technology have all been applied in sports performance analysis.

The purpose of this chapter of the book is not merely to update O'Donoghue's (2010) description of the what, why, who, where, when and how of sports performance analysis but to ask these questions about sports performance analysis research rather than its practical context.

Why do we do sports performance analysis research?

O'Donoghue (2010: 51) considered the words 'where', 'why', 'what' and 'how' within a V-shaped model of the research process in that particular order (see Figure 2.1). The reason why any study is done is important; there needs to be a rationale for the study. Therefore, 'why' we do performance analysis research should be considered before answering the other questions. The broad reason for undertaking performance analysis research is to gain an understanding of what is involved in sports performance. This can be broken down into the main purposes of performance analysis of sport that were discussed by Hughes (1998): analysis of tactics, analysis of technique, analysis of movement, coach and player education and sports performance modelling. These main purposes are

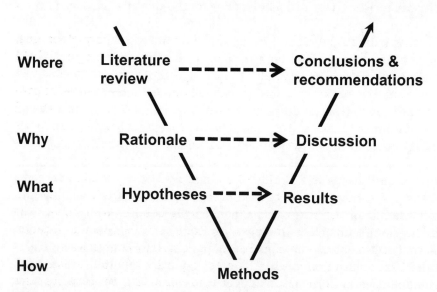

Figure 2.1 The V-shaped model of the research process

22

broken down further in Chapter 3 of the current book, which lists current and emerging research topics in sports performance.

Research into sports performance generates general knowledge about sports performance that informs practitioners. Research into tactics used in different sports identifies how frequently different tactical options are used in various situations. This research can also identify which tactical options are the most successful choices in different situations based on the outcomes of actions. In many game sports, the success of performers' tactics can depend on the tactical style of their opponents. Thus, there are many combinations of teams' (or individuals') tactical variables that can be combined within studies, making this a productive area of future research. The technique of performers of different abilities provides useful information that informs coaching. Work-rate analysis provides general knowledge about the physical demands of sports and how these demands are influenced by level, role, gender and age of players, as well as by situational variables. This knowledge informs the development of conditioning elements of players' training programmes. Large-scale studies can be undertaken exploring any of these types of variables to provide norms for performance indicators that can then be used to evaluate performance in practice.

What is sports performance analysis research?

Sports performance analysis research, like research in any other area, involves specifying a research question of interest, designing a study to answer that question with supporting evidence, conducting the study and communicating the research findings. The overall process of conducting a research project in sports performance analysis is illustrated by the V-shaped model shown in Figure 2.1. The objectives of sports performance research are different to those of performance analysis in its applied coaching context. Within coaching, performances are analysed in their own right to identify aspects that are positive and areas that require attention. Of course, coaches and analysts will also consider trends in performance by looking at sequences of matches. The information produced in the coaching context has a direct application to practical decision making. Sports performance analysis research is different because performances are not typically reported in isolation. A standard empirical observational study of sports performance uses a reductive approach whereby data from individual performances are analysed to produce results for an average performance that is reported with respect to the research question. Sports performance research produces general knowledge about sports performance that may be useful in practice. However, the information produced is not directly used by practitioners and is not specifically about particular players or teams. The way in which information is presented to audiences also differs between the coaching and academic contexts of performance analysis. Performance analysis support within coaching produces reports on performers as well as their opponents. However, much of the information produced is presented interactively in the form of basic performance statistics and related video sequences. Performance analysis research, on the other hand, is presented in a more scientific manner as a dissertation report, paper, poster or presentation. A key difference between performance analysis in its applied and academic contexts is the audience for the information produced. In applied coaching settings, the information is very sensitive and not for public consumption. It is used to help teams make tactical decisions to give them an advantage over competitors. Academic research is for a wider audience. The purpose is to make a contribution to knowledge about sports performance; this knowledge is communicated publicly, adding to the volume of research evidence that we have about the nature of sports performance. This book covers the reporting of research findings in more detail in Chapter 9.

The distinctions between coaching and academic contexts discussed in the previous paragraph hold for the standard observational research projects that are typically done in sports performance analysis. As has already been mentioned in this chapter, there are other types of research projects that fall under the umbrella of sports performance analysis research. There are experience reports that may involve action research where individual performances are reported on. The real findings of such investigations are about the effectiveness of performance analysis support and attitudes towards the service provided. Performance results are provided in a way that does not compromise the team's preparation but that does support the findings about the effectiveness of performance analysis in practice.

When is sports performance analysis done?

The first chapter of the current book covered the general timetable of activity involved in sports performance research. There is a great deal of background work that needs to be done before the researcher identifies a

24

research question to investigate. Undergraduate students will have been developing in relevant ways for many years prior to the research project formally commencing. They may have been involved in sports as a competitor, a coach and a spectator. This will develop interests in unanswered questions about sports performance or areas of debate about tactical or technical aspects of sports performance. Interest in how sports science can be applied to sport will develop during standard taught modules within programmes. Undergraduate students need to develop a research question of interest by the time they commence the final year of their degree programme.

The timing of data collection activity depends on when the data can be collected. For example, students wishing to analyse performances in a sport that is played in the summer months may need to collect the data or at least record the matches before returning for their final year. More typically, students collect data for their research projects during the final year of their degree programme. Whenever data are collected, it is vitally important that the study is designed to answer the research question before data collection commences. Students need to be sure that their study will generate results that will lead to an effective and optimally sized results chapter that answers the research question one way or another. Students should not commence data collection without knowing what they are doing, why they are doing it and where the project is going. We discuss research ethics in Chapter 6 of the current book. Data collection cannot commence until the project has received ethical clearance from the students' university.

The delivery of the final dissertation report is usually on a set deadline. However, the timing of individual chapter drafts needs to be scheduled to ensure feedback from supervisors can be provided and acted upon. Students may be very reluctant to complete any chapters too early as they may become aware of further literature they wish to review. However, they can be working on their literature review from the early stages of the project. Students should have an introduction drafted and agreed with the supervisor before data collection commences. The introduction sets out the research question, identifies the variables involved, defines the scope of the study and helps focus the students' remaining efforts within the project. They may have a research proposal which includes a background section that can act as a starting point for the literature review. The methods chapter can be drafted before data collection starts; indeed the methods for some investigations may have been specified in detail much earlier in order to apply for ethical approval. When projects are well planned and understood, the methods chapter describes what has to be done. If there are any issues with the methods, early consideration of this chapter by the supervisor and the student can improve the methods prior to data collection commencing. However, many students may see an early writing up of the methods chapter as something that can hold up data collection and analysis. One of the advantages of writing up the methods chapter after data collection has commenced is that students will be describing work tasks that they have engaged in. This makes the chapter much easier to write due to the greater familiarity with the methods used. Once the data have been collected and analysed, the student can complete the results, discussion and conclusion chapters.

Some student research projects can lead to publication or presentation at scientific conferences. For example, the British Association of Sport and Exercise Sciences (BASES) organises conferences that are specifically for student research. These conferences will have set deadlines for the submission of abstracts, and then any podium or poster presentation will need to be completed prior to the conference. There may be deadlines for papers being submitted to particular issues of research journals. However, there are future issues of the journal, meaning that researchers do not need to be too worried about such deadlines. They do need to consider the currency of their research if publishing in a journal. If they delay publication too long, the rules of the sport may change, rendering the study out of date. Other research may be published, which means the paper will not be as original as it would have been if submitted earlier. With respect to student research, the question is not so much when to publish but whether to publish. Students are at university to do their degree and to achieve as good a result as they can. Having a publication on their curriculum vitae (resumé) may be beneficial but may also be at the expense of effort made in modules the student is being assessed on. Students are best delaying publication of their research until after their programme of study is completed. The supervisor needs to assist in preparing the paper, especially if its publication will benefit the university as much as it will the student.

Where is performance analysis research done?

There are different locations where the various tasks within a research project take place. Many of these activities can be performed anywhere

26

that a laptop computer can be used. Research papers that are surveyed during background reading can be downloaded as PDF files from electronic journals that the student's university has subscribed to. Data can be pre-processed and analysed in Excel, and, even if specialist statistical analysis packages are being used, some universities have schemes allowing students to have temporary licenses to the software on their own computers. Writing up dissertation reports is done using word-processing packages and, thus, can be done anywhere that a laptop computer can be used. Some of the work can be done at the student's home or term-time residence, in the library, while having a coffee in a canteen, or on a train. Students typically balance their studies with other commitments and work they have, meaning that there is a wide variety of locations where research activity is done.

Research projects done within undergraduate and postgraduate programmes as well as at the PhD level involve supervision. Students can meet with supervisors in the supervisor's office, the university café or social learning places. In the experience of the authors of the current book, meetings with dissertation students can also take place in other locations. For example, a supervisor might accompany a student to the library to check recent texts and to recommend which sections of which books students need to read. They may also meet in the performance analysis computer laboratory in order for the supervisor to advise on aspects of system development, reliability studies or data collection tasks when students have practical queries or need assistance. At the PhD level, the researcher and supervisor may be attending a conference where they take the opportunity to discuss progress and plans while travelling to the conference or during free time within the conference programme.

Performances used in some research projects can be obtained from publicly available media channels that the university or the student are subscribed to. These can be downloaded onto external hard disks, allowing students to analyse the matches at times of their choosing. Other projects may require filming performances at sports venues where the matches are taking place. Sports performance research can involve the use of specialist software systems such as video-tagging systems that students may need to use within performance analysis computer laboratories when timetabled classes are not being delivered in those rooms. Some universities have arrangements with software providers for students enrolled in performance analysis modules or doing performance analysis dissertations to have licensed copies of the software on their own machines. This may not be the case for premium products, but there are freely available video-tagging packages that can be downloaded that are good enough for many research purposes. Having the package on the student's own machine gives much greater flexibility for data collection in terms of time and location. PhD students are more likely to have licensed copies of premium performance analysis software packages on their machines than undergraduate students are, giving them greater flexibility for data collection.

A final word on 'where' is, where should students keep backups of research data and writings they have produced? Backups should be done regularly, especially at the most productive periods during the project, when losing a week's work could be particularly stressful. Today there is no excuse for students not making regular backups of project work. Students can email files to themselves or use cloud storage to keep backup copies. This has a great advantage over external hard disks, which the students may keep in the same geographic location as their laptop computers. This is not to say that external hard disks are not useful; they certainly are, especially for day-to-day work with video and document files. However, for backup of project work, the student needs additional storage from which material can be retrieved in the event of computers and disks being damaged or stolen.

Who is involved in sports performance analysis research?

The people involved in a sports performance research project are the researcher(s), the supervisor(s) and the participants. Participants in standard observational studies are typically passive participants who are performing in their sport without having to perform any additional activity as a result of the performances being studied. When studies involve more invasive measurement, such as the use of GPS devices or heart rate monitors, the participants are active participants in the research rather than passive participants. The role of participants within studies and their rights as participants are discussed in detail in Chapter 6 of the current book.

Chapter 1 of the current book discussed the roles of students and supervisors within research projects. One additional point to make here is that some projects involve teams of students. For example, a group of six students may be doing different projects related to a sport using the same set of dependent variables. The first might be interested in venue effect, the second may be studying positional role, the third may be comparing performances at different levels of the game, the fourth may be comparing the first and second halves, the fifth may be comparing cup matches with league matches, and the sixth student may be examining score-line effect. If the supervisor has managed the students well, they could all be using the same system to collect the same variables, meaning that they each only have to collect one sixth of the data, but each student will be able to analyse all of the data for their own purpose. This also helps when it comes to reliability analysis for the system because each of the students is familiar with the system, allowing inter-operator agreement tests to be conducted without having to train additional users. The supervisor will need to ensure that all students on the team of six make a sufficient contribution to system development. It is possible that the students all have different systems as long as they produce the necessary output information for the agreed set of dependent variables.

How is sports performance analysis research done?

In considering the broad question of how any research should be done, the main things to say are that the research should be systematic, planned and well organised. The research project should be feasible and of interest to the student as well as of general interest and importance. The written report produced at the end of the research study should provide a rationale for the study, set out the purpose, describe what was done and what was found and discuss the results, explaining why the study found what it found. There are specific elements of performance analysis research projects, such as reliability studies, that are not included in many other projects. Chapter 9 discusses the process of writing up a sports performance analysis project.

A research project in the area of sports performance analysis involves a background literature survey, data analysis and writing up of the project the same way as any other research project does. There is nothing special about surveying literature in sports performance analysis that distinguishes it from any other discipline except there are fewer places where sports performance research is published. This means that it is often necessary to draw upon literature from other disciplines for sports performance analysis dissertations. The design of a sports performance analysis study often involves the development of a system to tag match videos with events of specific interest to the given study. Specific system development, data collection and analysis methods for sports performance analysis are covered in detail in Chapters 7 and 8 of the current book.

ASSUMPTIONS OF RESEARCH APPROACHES

Ontology

When we study sports performance, we are studying human sports performers. Therefore, the research methods used need to be suitable for studying human behaviour. There are different philosophical positions on human nature and behaviour that underpin social research methods (Cohen et al., 2011: 5–30). Ontology is concerned with the nature of existence, with research methods texts contrasting realism with nominalism. Realism assumes that reality is independent of individuals' views of it. Therefore, when assuming realism, events within a sports performance are considered to be matters of fact that are measurable. Nominalism, on the other hand, assumes that different people may have different views of the events. Most sports performance researchers understand that different commentators have different interpretations of incidents in sport with respect to the rules that apply. Indeed, when human subjective judgement is involved in classifying human movement, reliability studies are undertaken to report the limits of consistency of observational methods. Nonetheless, it is realism that underpins the quantitative approach used in traditional notational analysis; a rationale made for notational analysis is that there is a need for objective information (Franks, 2004; Maslovat and Franks, 2015).

Epistemology

Epistemology studies the nature of knowledge and how knowledge is justified given that there may be differences between truth and what is believed. The quantitative reductive approach that is used in traditional notational analysis represents knowledge as objective facts – things that can be classified and measured, counted and timed. This is an example of a more general approach referred to as positivism. The variables

30

and values used in traditional notation are a means of communicating about the sports performances being studied. Research investigations typically use samples and summarise data as sample averages with associated measures of dispersion. Anti-positivism, by contrast, assumes knowledge is more complex, with beliefs, attitudes and emotions being communicated through the use of words. There is a contrast between performance analysis within a coaching context and within scientific research. In the coaching context, performances are analysed in isolation, with important conclusions being drawn and acted upon from a single performance in its own right. The match statistics may be objective, but they focus attention on relevant video sequences, where more unrestricted, complex, richer, expert analysis is done. A further contrast between the positivist approach used in traditional notation research and performance analysis in its applied coaching context is that, in coaching, performance analysis is part of an action research cycle that is underpinned by critical theory (O'Donoghue, 2010: 36–37, 48–49). Researchers investigating attitudes towards or experiences of performance analysis support in coaching need to be aware of the underlying assumptions of the methods used to generate and use data in this context.

Praxeology

Praxeology is concerned with the purpose of human behaviour, choices made about behaviour and the ethical and economic reasons behind those choices. There is a range of behaviour from reflexive behaviour to habitual behaviour to behaviour initiated after more strategic thought. In assuming an average sports person, the quantitative reductive approaches used in traditional notational research also assume that behaviour is deterministic. Deterministic behaviour is usually past oriented in how behavioural choices are made. There are aspects of sports performance that are generalised in this way. Some situations in sport are associated with a limited number of optional choices for players, and other behaviours in sport are rehearsed in training prior to competition. There are also norms for both process and outcome indicators of sports performance that can be used to evaluate performance. The opposite of determinism is voluntarism, which is more suited to idiographic methods such as those used in qualitative research. Voluntarism may be a more appropriate assumption for creative and improvised play in sport. Voluntarism views behavioural choice as being more individual and future oriented; readers will be able to think of many sports persons who have individual performance characteristics in this respect. Averaging data from such unique individuals inappropriately imposes methods that assume determinism on the research.

Challenging the assumptions of realism, positivism and determinism

The problems presented to sports performance analysis by the assumption of realism are greater in research than they are in practical coaching applications. This is because the quantitative performance analysis done in coaching contexts guides the selection and use of video material in briefing and debriefing sessions. Rich, complex video data are used in discussions between players and coaches and in making decisions about forthcoming training and match-play. Much academic research in sports performance analysis uses a reductive quantitative approach that involves considerable information loss as performances are represented by a fingerprint of numerical variables, with individual performances being combined to determine sample averages.

Traditional notation findings have been presented in the form of charts and tables of summary statistics. Scatter plots showing event locations on playing surfaces are more pattern like and open to interpretation by readers. Other graphical displays of spatio-temporal data are becoming more common in research publications in the area. For example, Sarmento, Barbosa et al. (2013) did a temporal analysis of attacking play in soccer using T-patterns but presented the resulting patterns of play as pitch diagrams showing key movements of the ball and players. This approach is also used in soccer textbooks that are familiar to a practical coaching audience.

The human nature assumption of determinism that is associated with quantitative approaches is open to criticism by those studying sports performance. Elite athletes in game sports are known for individual strengths, inventive play, improvisation, genius and creativity. These characteristics are more reflective of a voluntaristic nature, with free will and responsibility being exhibited. This is a challenge to research into elite sports performance to utilise methods that are more appropriate to analysing high-profile individual cases.

32

SUMMARY

This chapter discussed the nature of sports performance analysis research and implications for research in the area given the expanding scope of sports performance analysis. There is an unavoidable and necessary overlap between sports performance analysis and other areas of sports science. Their normative, interpretive and critical theory paradigms (Cohen et al., 2011: 5–47) are all relevant to sports performance analysis research. Traditional notation is underpinned by the normative paradigm. However, there is a role for the interpretive paradigm in interview surveys about performance analysis in coaching as well as in considering the individual nature of sports performance at the elite level. Critical theory is the underlying paradigm of action research and is, therefore, suitable when considering performance analysis in its coaching context. However, given that research into performance analysis in applied coaching contexts is relevant and to be encouraged, critical theory is also relevant in some performance analysis research studies.

REFERENCES

Agras, H., Ferragut, C. and Abraldes, J.A. (2016) 'Match analysis in futsal: a systematic review', *International Journal of Performance Analysis in Sport*, 16: 652–686.

Arriaza, E.J. and Zuniga, M.D. (2016) 'Soccer as a study case for analytic trends in collective sports training: a survey', *International Journal of Performance Analysis in Sport*, 16(1): 171–190.

Butterworth, A.D., O'Donoghue, P. and Cropley, B. (2013) 'Performance profiling in sports coaching: a review', *International Journal of Performance Analysis in Sport*, 13: 572–593.

Campos, J. (2013) 'Field athletics', in T. McGarry, P.G. O'Donoghue and J. Sampaio (eds), *Routledge handbook of sports performance analysis* (pp. 464–474). London: Routledge.

Carling, C. and Bloomfield, J. (2013) 'Time-motion analysis', in T. McGarry, P.G. O'Donoghue and J. Sampaio (eds), *Routledge handbook of sports performance analysis* (pp. 283–296). London: Routledge.

Choi, H. (2008) Definitions of performance indicators within real-time and lapse time analysis systems in performance analysis of sport. Ph.D. thesis, University of Wales Institute, Cardiff, UK.

Cohen, L., Manion, L. and Morrison, K. (2011) *Research methods in education*, 7th edn. London: Routledge.

Di Salvo, V., Gregson, W., Atkinson, G., Tordoff, P. and Drust, B. (2009) 'Analysis of high intensity activity in Premier League soccer', *International Journal of Sports Medicine*, 30: 205–212.

33

Francis, J. and Jones, G. (2014) 'Elite rugby union players' perceptions of performance analysis', *International Journal of Performance Analysis in Sport*, 14: 188–207.

Franks, I.M. (2004) 'The need for feedback', in M. Hughes and I.M. Franks (eds), *Notational analysis of sport, 2nd edn: systems for better coaching and sports performance* (pp. 8–16). London: Routledge.

Franks, I.M. and Miller, G. (1991) 'Training coaches to observe and remember', *Journal of Sports Sciences*, 9: 285–297.

Gregson, W., Drust, B., Atkinson, G. and Di Salvo, V. (2010) 'Match-to-match variability of high-speed activities in Premier League Soccer', *International Journal of Sports Medicine*, 31: 237–242.

Heller, M. and Baca, A. (2013) 'Target sports', in T. McGarry, P.G. O'Donoghue and J. Sampaio (eds), *Routledge handbook of sports performance analysis* (pp. 425–435). London: Routledge.

Hibbs, A. and O'Donoghue, P.G. (2013) 'Strategy and tactics in sports performance', in T. McGarry, P.G. O'Donoghue and J. Sampaio (eds), *Routledge handbook of sports performance analysis* (pp. 248–258). London: Routledge.

Hodges, N.J. and Franks, I.M. (2008) 'The provision of information', in M. Hughes and I.M. Franks (eds), *The essentials of performance analysis: an introduction* (pp. 21–39). London: Routledge.

Horne, S (2013) 'The role of performance analysis in elite netball competition structures', in D. Peters and P.G. O'Donoghue (eds), *Performance analysis of sport IX* (pp. 3–9). London: Routledge.

Hökelmann, A., Liviotti, G. and Breitkreutz, T. (2013) 'Rhythmic gymnastics', in T. McGarry, P.G. O'Donoghue and J. Sampaio (eds), *Routledge handbook of sports performance analysis* (pp. 475–483). London: Routledge.

Hughes, M.D. (1998) 'The application of notational analysis to racket sports', in A. Lees, I. Maynard, M. Hughes and T. Reilly (eds), *Science and racket sports II* (pp. 211–220). London: E and FN Spon.

Hughes, M.G., Rose, G. and Amara, I. (2005) 'The influence of recovery duration on blood lactate accumulation in repeated sprint activity', *Journal of Sports Sciences*, 23: 130–131.

James, N. (2008) 'Performance analysis in the media', in M. Hughes and I.M. Franks (eds), *The essentials of performance analysis: an introduction* (pp. 243–263). London: Routledge.

Johns, P. and Brouner, J. (2013) 'The efficacy of judging within trampolining', in D. Peters and P.G. O'Donoghue (eds), *Performance analysis of sport IX* (pp. 214–221). London: Routledge.

Kirkbride, A. (2013a) 'Scoring/judging applications', in T. McGarry, P.G. O'Donoghue and J. Sampaio (eds), *Routledge handbook of sports performance analysis* (pp. 140–152). London: Routledge.

Kirkbride, A. (2013b) 'Media applications of performance analysis', in T. McGarry, P.G. O'Donoghue and J. Sampaio (eds), *Routledge handbook of sports performance Analysis* (pp. 187–209). London: Routledge.

Laird, P. and Waters, L. (2008) 'Eye-witness recollection of sports coaches', *International Journal of Performance Analysis in Sport*, 8: 76–84.

Lees, A. (2008) 'Qualitative biomechanical analysis of technique', in M. Hughes and I.M. Franks (eds), *The essentials of performance analysis: an introduction* (pp. 162–179). London: Routledge.

Lidor, R. and Ziv, G. (2015) 'On-field performances of female and male field hockey players – A review', *International Journal of Performance Analysis in Sport*, 15: 20–38.

Marinho, D.A., Barbosa, T.M., Neiva, H.P., Costa, M.J., Garrido, M.D. and Silva, A.J. (2013) 'Swimming, running, cycling and triathlon', in T. McGarry, P.G. O'Donoghue and J. Sampaio (eds), *Routledge handbook of sports performance analysis* (pp. 436–463). London: Routledge.

Maslovat, D. and Franks, I.M. (2015) 'The importance of feedback to performance', in M.D. Hughes and I.M. Franks (eds), *The essentials of performance analysis in sport, 2nd edn* (pp. 11–17). London: Routledge.

McGarry, T., O'Donoghue, P.G. and Sampaio, J. (2013) *Routledge handbook of sports performance analysis*. London: Routledge.

McKenzie, R. and Cushion, C. (2013) 'Performance analysis in professional soccer: player and coach perspectives', in D. Peters and P.G. O'Donoghue (eds), *Performance analysis of sport IX* (pp. 23–32). London: Routledge.

Mesquita, I., Palao, J.M., Marcelino, R. and Afonso, J. (2013) 'Indoor volleyball and beach volleyball', in T. McGarry, P.G. O'Donoghue and J. Sampaio (eds), *Routledge handbook of sports performance analysis* (pp. 367–379). London: Routledge.

Murray, S., Maylor, D. and Hughes, M. (1998) 'A preliminary investigation into the provision of computerised analysis feedback to elite squash players', in A. Lees, I. Maynard, M. Hughes and T. Reilly (eds), *Science and racket sports II* (pp. 235–240). London: E and FN Spon.

O'Donoghue, P.G. (2010) *Research methods for sports performance analysis*. London: Routledge.

O'Donoghue, P.G. and Mayes, A. (2013) 'Performance analysis, feedback and communication in coaching', in T. McGarry, P.G. O'Donoghue and J. Sampaio (eds), *Routledge handbook of sports performance analysis* (pp. 155–164). London: Routledge.

O'Donoghue, P.G. and Robinson, G. (2016a) 'The effect of dismissals on work-rate in English FA Premier League soccer', *International Journal of Performance Analysis in Sport*, 16: 898–909.

O'Donoghue, P.G. and Robinson, G. (2016b) 'Score-line effect on work-rate in English FA Premier League soccer', *International Journal of Performance Analysis in Sport*, 16: 910–923.

Palao, J.M. and Hernández-Hernández, E. (2014) 'Game statistical system and criteria used by Spanish volleyball coaches', *International Journal of Performance Analysis in Sport*, 14: 564–573.

Petersen, C. and Dawson, B. (2013) 'Cricket', in T. McGarry, P.G. O'Donoghue and J. Sampaio (eds), *Routledge handbook of sports performance analysis* (pp. 393–443). London: Routledge.

Poizat, G., Sève, C. and Saury, J. (2013) 'Qualitative aspects in performance analysis', in T. McGarry, P.G. O'Donoghue and J. Sampaio (eds), *Routledge handbook of sports performance analysis* (pp. 309–320). London: Routledge.

Prim, S. and van Rooyen, M. (2013) 'Rugby', in T. McGarry, P.G. O'Donoghue and J. Sampaio (eds), *Routledge handbook of sports performance analysis* (pp. 338–356). London: Routledge.

Reeves, M.J. and Roberts, S.J. (2013) 'Perceptions of performance analysis in elite youth football', *International Journal of Performance Analysis in Sport*, 13: 200–211.

Sampaio, J., Ibáñez, S. and Lorenzo, A. (2013) 'Basketball', in T. McGarry, P.G. O'Donoghue and J. Sampaio (eds), *Routledge handbook of sports performance analysis* (pp. 357–366). London: Routledge.

Sarmento, H., Barbosa, A., Anguera, M.T., Campaniço, J. and Leitão, J. (2013) 'Regular patterns of play in the counter-attacks of the FC Barcelona and Manchester United football teams', in D. Peters and P. O'Donoghue (eds), *Performance analysis of sport IX* (pp. 57–64). London: Routledge.

Sarmento, H., Bradley, P. and Travassos, B. (2015) 'The transition from match analysis to intervention: optimising the coaching process in elite futsal', *International Journal of Performance Analysis in Sport*, 15: 471–488.

Sarmento, H., Pereira, A., Campaniço, J., Anguera, M.T. and Leitão, J. (2013) 'Soccer match analysis: a qualitative study of Portuguese First League coaches', in D. Peters and P.G. O'Donoghue (eds), *Performance analysis of sport IX* (pp. 10–16). London: Routeldge.

Sharp, B. (1997) 'Notational analysis: it's so simple', *BASES Newsletter*, 7(8): 4.

Tenga, A. (2013) 'Soccer', in T. McGarry, P.G. O'Donoghue and J. Sampaio (eds), *Routledge handbook of sports performance analysis* (pp. 323–337). London: Routledge.

Volossovitch, A. (2013) 'Handball', in T. McGarry, P.G. O'Donoghue and J. Sampaio (eds), *Routledge handbook of sports performance analysis* (pp. 380–392). London: Routledge.

Wiltshire, H. (2013) 'Sports performance analysis for high performance managers', in T. McGarry, P.G. O'Donoghue and J. Sampaio (eds), *Routledge handbook of sports performance analysis* (pp. 176–186). London: Routledge.

Witte, K. (2013) 'Combat sports', in T. McGarry, P.G. O'Donoghue and J. Sampaio (eds), *Routledge handbook of sports performance analysis* (pp. 415–424). London: Routledge.

Wright, C., Atkins, S. and Jones, B. (2012) 'An analysis of elite coaches' engagement with performance analysis services (match, notational analysis and technique analysis)', *International Journal of Performance Analysis in Sport*, 12: 436–451.

Wright, C., Atkins, S., Jones, B. and Todd, J. (2013) 'The role of performance analysts within the coaching process: Performance Analysts Survey "The role of performance analysts in elite football club settings"', *International Journal of Performance Analysis in Sport*, 13: 240–261.

Wright, C., Carling, C. and Collins, D. (2014) 'The wider context of performance analysis and its application in the football coaching process', *International Journal of Performance Analysis in Sport*, 14: 709–733.

CHAPTER 3

SPORTS PERFORMANCE ANALYSIS RESEARCH TOPICS

OVERVIEW

The current chapter reviews research topic areas in sports performance analysis. A previous book on research methods in sport performance analysis (O'Donoghue, 2010: 19–27) covered research topics under the following subheadings:

- Critical incidents and perturbations
- Analysis of coach behaviour
- Performance indicators in different sports
- Work-rate analysis and evaluation of injury risk
- Reliability of methods
- Analysis of technique
- Technical effectiveness
- Tactical patterns of play
- Performance profiling
- Effectiveness of performance analysis support
- Analysis of referees and officials

There have been further review chapters on different topics and research in different sports in the *Routledge Handbook of Sports Performance Analysis* (McGarry et al., 2013). In writing the current chapter, the authors used O'Donoghue's (2010: 19–27) chapter on research topics and the *Routledge Handbook of Sports Performance Analysis* as a starting point and then reviewed original research papers in sports performance analysis written from the beginning of 2013 to the end of 2016. The sample included papers from the *International Journal of Performance Analysis in Sport* and key performance analysis papers published in other journals.

The papers surveyed are grouped into the topic areas identified by the subheadings used in this chapter. Some areas are not entirely independent as some research projects may use independent variables from one of the topic areas and dependent variables from another topic area. In discussing the areas, the authors have not undertaken an exhaustive review of the literature and have not summed up the state of the art with respect to research findings, theoretical developments or methodological advances. Therefore, students are advised not to use this chapter as a model for their own literature reviews. The current chapter is simply looking at what the emerging topics of interest are and how students can identify dissertation ideas related to these topics for their own sports.

OUTCOME INDICATORS

Performance analysis has typically involved analysing the process of performance, whether analysing work-rate, tactical aspects, technique or the effectiveness with which skills are performed (Hughes, 1998). Indeed Olsen and Larsen (1997) have stated that match analysis needs to go beyond the result of matches to understand performance. However, the performance indicators used to assess sports performance do include outcome indicators as well as process indicators (Hughes and Bartlett, 2002). Sports performance can be viewed at various levels of abstraction; at each level, performance can be considered, leaving lower-level detail as a black box. It is possible to look at factors influencing participation in different levels of sport without even analysing performances. The fact that given athletes will have reached particular levels of competition is evidence of successful performance. For example, Tirp et al. (2014) found that a greater proportion of left dominant stance judo players competed at Olympic Games than in German national or German university championships. Similar research has found that left-handed players enjoy similar advantages in tennis (Loffing et al., 2010) and boxing (Gursoy, 2009). There has been some research into relative age effect on broad participation level published in the *International Journal of Performance Analysis in Sport* over the years (Fleming and Fleming, 2012). There has also been research on age of peak performance in track and field athletics (Radek, 2014). However, in recent years such studies would need to use very large data sets or have some element of novelty to the methods in order to be published in the journal.

Entire careers can be analysed in terms of results, or large sections of athletes' careers during age groups of interest might be studied. For example, Dormehl and Williams (2016) examined the stability of athletes' swimming performances over a period of seven years. Long-term studies could also look at broad trends in sports performance using different athletes' or teams' performances to characterise the sport in particular seasons. For example, van Rooyen (2016) found a decrease in the points scored by winning teams in international rugby sevens matches over a sixteen-season period. Similarly, there have been studies of long-term trends in Spanish-league basketball (Puente et al., 2015), home advantage in European rugby union (García et al., 2013) and handball goalkeeping performances (Espina-Agulló et al., 2016).

Some research on broad performance outcomes has used shorter term data. For example, Goossens et al. (2015) showed that winning early round matches in straight sets improves the chances of winning Grand Slam tennis tournaments. Studies of momentum in tennis have considered outcomes of sets (O'Donoghue, 2013), games (Moss and O'Donoghue, 2015) and points (O'Donoghue and Brown, 2009; Moss and O'Donoghue, 2015). The study of momentum in sports performance has found that some performances exhibit sequences of events supporting the existence of momentum while other performances do not contain such sequences (Mortimer and Burt, 2014). This leads to a fundamental question about how concepts such as momentum should be studied. Some aspects of tactical performance can be investigated by analysing high-level events. For example, O'Donoghue (2016) discussed risk taking in one-day international cricket based solely on a study of wicket losses. Other broad events within performances that can be analysed without looking at every player action include possessions and set plays in team games. For example, Clay and Clay (2014) investigated the effectiveness of substitutions in NCAA (National Collegiate Athletic Association) Division 1 men's basketball using points per possession to evaluate offensive play and opposition points per possession as a measure of defensive success.

Other broad analysis techniques can consider injury occurrence during sport. Such studies might not include any detail of technique that may have caused injury but the audit data are nonetheless useful to identify broad injury risk within sports. An example was a study of 647 class 1 steeplechase horse races over a twelve-year period that found that speed, number of runners, race distance and soft surface conditions all resulted in more falls occurring (Williams et al., 2014). Other studies have assessed injury risk using subjective assessment of technique (Lage et al., 2016) or contact situations (Rahnama et al., 2002).

COACH DECISIONS WITHIN MATCHES

Decision making is a mental process that cannot be directly observed. However, there are observable behaviours that allow inferences to be made about tactical decisions that have been taken. This applies not only to tactical decisions of players that can be inferred from observable patterns of play but also to the decisions of coaches during matches. The use of time-outs is an example of coach decision making that has been investigated in handball (Gomes et al., 2014; Gutiérrez-Aguilar et al., 2016). Studies of time-outs look at such factors as match status, scoring patterns prior to time-outs being called, game period and venue. The impact of time-outs can also be analysed by looking at scoring patterns after play resumes. Another aspect of coach decision making that can be analysed is the use of substitutions. Smyth and Hughes (2016) looked at the use of substitutions within the 2015 rugby world cup. Rey et al. (2015) used decision tree analysis to study the association between substitutions in Union des Associations Européennes de Football (UEFA) Champions League soccer and situational variables such as match status, venue, match period, positional roles involved and stage of the tournament. Lythe and Kilding (2013) studied the effect of substitutions using experimental matches rather than real competitive matches. They used six field hockey games where the same pair of teams played each other but different substitution strategies were applied in the different games. This allowed the effect of different substitution strategies on distance covered by players in different speed ranges to be compared.

SITUATIONAL VARIABLES

Readers are encouraged to read Chapter 21 of the *Routledge Handbook of Sports Performance Analysis* (Gómez et al., 2013), which is specifically about situational variables that influence sports performance at a behavioural level. The situational variables covered in the chapter include game location, match status, quality of opposition, game period, type of competition and combinations of these (interaction effects). The current chapter builds on the work of Gómez et al. by reviewing research into situational variable effects on sports performance that has been published since the beginning of 2013.

Venue

Home advantage in sport is now so well understood that research needs to go beyond merely investigating whether home advantage exists or not and analyse why home advantage occurs (Courneya and Carron, 1992). Recent research has introduced details of distances travelled and time zones crossed into the study of home advantage (Goumas, 2014). Other research has gone beyond the results of matches with respect to home and away teams by analysing scoring trends within matches. One such study looked at game dynamics of close basketball games within the fourth quarter considering venue effects (Gomez et al., 2016). Lago-Peñas et al. (2013) investigated home advantage in the Spanish professional handball league, finding that indicators are effected by home advantage in different ways depending on the quality of the away team.

Opposition

Opposition quality is considered to be the largest source of variability in sports performance (McGarry and Franks, 1994). Tactical, technical and work-rate variables can all be hypothesised to be influenced by the quality of the opposition in individual and team games. Carroll (2013) classified Gaelic football teams as being top or bottom teams based on league division. This allowed the effect of playing top- and bottom-level opposition to be described using quartile norms. An alternative approach to analysing upper- and lower-half soccer teams in matches against upper- and lower-ranked opposition used 90 per cent confidence intervals and related effect sizes (Mao et al., 2016). Castellano et al. (2013) analysed the effect of opposition quality on tactical positioning in Spanish first-league soccer using player movement data captured by the Amisco system (Amisco, Nice, France). The quality of opposition can be characterised by ranking or level of competition they participate in. However, the opposition is not only characterised by its overall quality, but also in terms of style of play. A simple categorical factor such as handedness (Gursoy, 2009; Loffing et al., 2010) can distinguish between different opposition situations with respect to location of events and other tactical variables. There are direct and elaborate styles of attacking in field games that may be independent of team quality; they are just different ways of playing. Similarly tennis players may be characterised by how often they approach the net. Again, this may be unrelated to world ranking, with both baseline players and serve-volley exponents residing in the upper and lower areas of the world rankings. One investigation examined the effect of opposition defensive pressure on basketball shooting performance (Csataljay et al., 2013). The percentage of all shot types that were scored was lower when maximal defensive pressure was applied as opposed to minimum or half pressure.

Match status

The effect of match status can also be assessed for a full range of different classes of dependent variable. Paixão et al. (2015) studied match status effects on the passing sequences of top European soccer teams, finding that possessions had longer durations and contained more passes when teams were winning than when they were drawing or losing.

Playing surface

Surface effect has been studied in tennis (O'Donoghue and Ingram, 2001) when different Grand Slam tournaments are played on different court surfaces. The introduction of artificial surfaces in field games has necessitated research into the effects of playing surface on technical, tactical and physical aspects of performance. Surface effect on player movement has been analysed in junior tennis, finding that hard courts involve more high-intensity efforts and a greater distance covered accelerating than clay courts (Galé-Ansodi et al., 2016). Garcia et al. (2015) compared soccer performances during three variants of small-sided game played on three different surfaces (soil (dirt), grass and artificial turf). They found that there were more attacks and more touches of the ball on artificial turf than on the other surfaces.

42

Numerical superiority

Numerical superiority is a factor of interest to sports practitioners. There have been occasions when outnumbered teams have performed relatively successfully, and other occasions when dismissals or exclusions have had negative impacts on performance. However, recent research has revealed that technical soccer performance improves for the advantaged team after a dismissal and decreases for the disadvantaged team (Lago-Peñas et al., 2016). Therefore, research is needed into how teams play when they perform relatively successfully and not-so-successfully when they have numerical superiority and when they are outnumbered (O'Donoghue and Robinson, 2016a). The effect of exclusions has been investigated in basketball (Prieto et al., 2015), while experimental games have been used to study tactical play when one team has numerical superiority in small-sided soccer games (Travassos et al., 2014).

Combined situational variables

More ambitious studies have looked at more than one situational variable, allowing the individual and combined effects of independent variables on aspects of performance to be studied. These studies typically require more data as the number of performances needed increases as we increase the number of factors and as the number of levels of those factors increases. What we mean by number of levels is the number of values of an independent variable (factor). For example, match status might be measured at three levels (winning, drawing and losing), while venue might be measured at two (home and away). Such studies include venue and opposition effect on the results of Brazilian League futsal matches (Campos et al., 2015); the effect of quarter score, quality of opposition and match status on waterpolo performance (Gómez et al., 2014); and venue, opposition quality and first goal effect on match outcome in UEFA Champions League soccer (García-Rubio et al., 2015). García et al. (2014) undertook a study of factors associated with success in basketball. They distinguished among balanced (score difference of 1 to 12 points), unbalanced (score difference of 13 to 28 points) and blowout games (score difference above 28 points). The factors that distinguished winning and losing teams in these different types of game were examined, considering venue effects as well. The effect of scoreline, venue and quality of teams on work-rate has been examined in soccer (O'Donoghue and Robinson, 2016b); this study was done using automatic player data.

PERFORMER EFFECTS

Positional role

Performer effects are different than situational variables in that they are characteristics of teams and players, such as demographic factors, regional factors, level of performer and positional role. Positional role effect has been studied in many sports with respect to work-rate and the skills required by players. Recent research has looked at the effect of positional role on technical event involvement in elite women's beach volleyball (Palao et al., 2015) and work-rate in Europa League soccer (Andrzejewski et al., 2014).

Age group

Knowledge about sports performance at different age groups is important to athletes moving into older age groups as well as to their coaches. Therefore, age group can be used as an independent variable within sports performance analysis research projects. Recent research in male volleyball has shown that older age groups play at a higher tempo than younger age groups do (García-de-Alcaraz et al., 2015). The actions performed by junior Malaysian taekwondo athletes are more diverse than those of their senior counterparts (Tan and Krasilshchikov, 2015). However, Tan and Krasilshchikov (2015) also found that senior taekwondo athletes performed actions more effectively than juniors. Relative age and broad sports participation was mentioned earlier in this chapter. There is, however, very little research on relative age effects on playing style and technical effectiveness. One study on tennis has found a relative age effect on the percentage of points when players go to the net in men's singles at Grand Slam tournaments (O'Donoghue, 2014).

Gender

There are many sports in which women and men play separately but under the same rules. Despite this, there are often differences between

44

play in women's and men's performances, and we cannot simply assume that the same styles of play or frequencies of technical actions will appear in both games. Therefore, there is a need to investigate both women's and men's versions of games, as well as doing studies that directly compare women's and men's games using the same variables. Movement patterns in soccer have been compared between women's and men's Spanish league matches (Tenga et al., 2015). Rally times and stroke techniques used have been compared between male and female elite paddle tennis (Torres-Luque et al., 2015). Another recent study found that female judo players had a greater tendency to use the opposite grip to opponents than male players did in national championship matches (Kajmovic and Radjo, 2014) and that the female players apply the opposite grip more effectively than their male counterparts do.

Level of competition

There is a distinction between a level effect and an opposition quality effect. Opposition quality is a factor that is assumed to influence sports performance for the same teams. For example, the performance of the top five soccer teams in a league may differ between matches in which they are playing top five, middle-ranked and bottom five opposition. Level effects are different because we are comparing the performances of different teams based on the level they play at. For example, we might wish to compare performances in first- and second-division league matches for a given team sport. Examples of studies into level effects on sports performance are a comparison of World Cup and domestic futsal matches (Mohammed et al., 2014), differences in the depth and width of defences between first- and second-division Spanish soccer (Castellano and Casamichana, 2015) and speed zones of movement and heart rate response of international and club-level Italian field hockey players (Buglione et al., 2013). These examples use completely independent performances from different levels of performance. However, there are some other studies examining performances of different levels within the same competitions but without looking at opposition effect. For example, Adams et al. (2013) found distinctions between top four and bottom four English FA Premier League teams for defender passing success and midfielder passing success in the opposition half. Liu et al. (2015) used a similar approach, comparing high-, medium- and low-strength teams during UEFA Champions League soccer when they were winning, drawing and losing at home and away. Team strength was classified using UEFA's season club coefficients. The performances of teams in the top and bottom halves of the Turkish professional basketball league have been compared in an attempt to identify performance indicators associated with success (Doğan et al., 2016).

Geographical region

Pulling and Stenning (2015) compared the use of offloads between Northern Hemisphere and Southern Hemisphere international rugby union teams, finding that Southern Hemisphere teams used offloads more effectively as an attacking strategy. Although Southern Hemisphere teams have been more successful than their Northern Hemisphere counterparts in rugby World Cup tournaments, the difference between Northern and Southern Hemisphere teams is not a level effect. Both types of team compete in the rugby World Cup. Therefore, such comparisons are best considered to be between different regions when examining tactical style of play and effectiveness of performance. Similarly, Abián et al. (2014) compared men's singles badminton matches performances between two successive Olympic Games. This was not a study of rule changes, and the level is the same, so the study should be viewed as a short-term trend study to see whether there were any changes in the standard or style of play at Olympic level. A further type of study that should not be looked upon as a level effect study is where individual teams of interest are being compared. For example, Sarmento et al. (2014) compared temporal behaviour during attacks of three of Europe's leading soccer teams (Inter Milan, Barcelona and Manchester United). A useful development of this research was that the findings from temporal analysis of attacks were presented as pitch diagrams highlighting typical player and ball movement during different classes of attack identified. This helps communicate the research findings in a form understandable at the practical coaching level.

Combined performer effects

Studies including enough performance data can evaluate the influence of more than one of these performer effects, as well as their interactions, on different aspects of performance. For example, Hogarth et al. (2014) studied the effect of gender, positional role and level on movement patterns in tag football using GPS data.

46

CRITICAL INCIDENTS

There is a great deal of complex data that could be collected and analysed from sports performances, and some of this work may be unproductive in scientific and practical terms. This has motivated the analysis of "critical incidents" that have a large influence on the outcomes of matches. Students considering studying critical incidents should not consider this to be a shortcut to completing a research project. They will still need to demonstrate that there is sufficient data collection activity, analysis of data and theoretical development within the project to justify the hours required by the given dissertation module. Critical incidents are clearly important in sports performance. However, a conclusion to a project that states that performers need to manage critical incidents to avoid conceding scores and to create critical incidents enabling scoring opportunities is too obvious. We need to know how to create critical incidents, what factors are associated with critical incidents and what the consequences are of different types of critical incidents. A further issue is defining critical incidents so that research findings can be properly understood. There may be critical incident types defined in previous research that can be referred to by students (Hughes et al., 1997; 1998; 2001). The advantage of using these is that they allow students to compare and discuss their findings in relation to previous research in which the same variables have been used. Classifying critical incidents is not a straightforward task. One study required interviews with seventeen expert coaches in order to define a conceptual framework and a set of observable variables for analysing critical incidents in basketball (Ferreira et al., 2014). Such studies provide a set of valid variables related to critical incidents, but individual research projects still need to demonstrate that these variables can be measured reliably by the specific researchers.

Once critical incident types have been identified within the literature or defined by students undertaking projects, there are a number of ways critical incidents can be studied within research projects. Descriptive studies can determine the frequency and timing of different types of critical incident and can also compare these factors between different types of match and levels of sports. The independent variables and situational variables that might influence critical incidents are the same as those that could be investigated in relation to any other hypothesised dependent variables. The likelihood of scoring opportunities from different types of critical incident can be investigated. For example, Roddy et al. (2014) used logistic regression to model the chance of winning a rally in the Australian Open squash championships in terms of different types of critical incidents.

TACTICAL ANALYSIS

There is a distinction between tactics and strategy, in that strategy is considered to be planned before competition commences, whereas tactics are moment-to-moment decisions made during the competitive performance (Fuller and Alderson, 1990). In each case, the decision-making processes are not directly observable, and so inferences about tactics and strategy are made using patterns of play. It is, therefore, important to choose dependent variables that indicate types of tactics and strategies being adopted. For example, Hewitt et al. (2016) discussed game style in soccer and how it can be quantified. Hewitt et al.'s paper is a good example of how broad and relevant principles of play can be identified from available academic and professional literature. Once this has been done, operational variables need to be defined to represent tactical aspects. This applies to individual players, collective behaviour, set play and open play in team games. It is possible to create variables related to decision making (Lorains et al., 2013) and use these within performance analysis research. This does require conceptual development for many sports and expert observation; these challenges make it more likely that projects on decision making are undertaken at the master's level or above, rather than within undergraduate projects.

Students rarely do projects that describe tactical patterns of play in a sport as a whole. Typically, students look at how some independent variable of interest influences tactics. We have already discussed such independent variables (situational variables and performer qualities) earlier in the chapter. However, there is a more common comparison of tactics that is made by students that does need to be discussed here: the different tactics used by successful and unsuccessful performers. Success is often viewed as an outcome of performance, whether it is represented by match outcome or final tournament placing. Thus, there has been recent research using logistic regression techniques (Harrop and Nevill, 2014; Casal et al., 2014) to model success in terms of tactical variables. However, in comparing successful and unsuccessful performers

48

in terms of tactics, we need to consider that tactics may be associated with pre-planned strategies and different philosophies of play used by performers. Thus the success of teams may be to some extent determined by their preparation rather than being purely an outcome of the performance. This justifies researchers considering success level to be an independent variable when comparing tactical variables within different sets of performances. There are alternative ways of distinguishing successful and unsuccessful performers that have relative advantages and disadvantages over each other. Winning and losing teams within matches can be compared, tactical variables can be correlated with margin of victory, or teams reaching different stages of tournaments or finishing in high or low league positions can be compared. A variation on comparing winning and losing teams within matches is to make such comparisons separately for close games and more one-sided games. The disadvantage of considering individual match outcomes is that very successful teams can play each other during competitions, and one of the teams might be deemed unsuccessful for losing the match. Similarly, there are fixtures between teams at the bottom of leagues when one team might be deemed to be a successful team. Thus, distinguishing teams as successful or unsuccessful based on league position overcomes this. However, we might be interested in the performance indicators that make the difference between winning and losing in matches between top-of-the-table teams or during finals and semi-finals of tournaments. There are other issues that need to be considered when comparing the tactics of successful or unsuccessful performers. One such issue is how often individual performers are included within the study. Imagine a knockout tournament of seven rounds including 128 performers with a total of 127 matches. The two finalists will be involved in seven matches, whereas the 64 players eliminated during round 1 will be represented by one performance each within the data set. It could be argued that the data are distorted by the performances of finalists and semi-finalists (26 out of 254 performances). Alternatively, it could be argued that the finalists and semi-finalists should have all of their matches included within studies because their styles of play are more representative of what players will encounter within tournaments than is the style of a player eliminated in the first round.

There are many recent examples of research comparing the tactics of winning and losing performers within matches. In these studies the matches, rather than individual performances, are the units of analysis allowing paired comparisons of winning and losing performances within matches. This is important because the performances of winning and losing performers are related by direct opposition effect; the winning and losing performances within matches should not be treated as independent samples during statistical analysis. Winning and losing performances have been compared within high-level judo (Miarka, Fukuda et al., 2016), European cadet championship Greco-Roman wrestling (Kajmovic et al., 2014), world championship kick-boxing (Ouergui et al., 2013), women's volleyball (Valladares et al., 2016), wheelchair tennis (Sanchez-Pay et al., 2015) and World Cup rugby union (Bishop and Barnes, 2013; Villarejo et al., 2015).

There are some variants to this general approach of comparing winning and losing performances. Harrop and Nevill (2014) analysed performance indicators associated with success for a Tier 3 English League team, comparing won games with games that were drawn or lost. These were not paired samples, and logistic regression was used to identify variables that distinguish winning performances from other two outcomes. Bremner et al. (2013) compared the winning and losing performances of a single rugby union team. Najdan et al. (2014) investigated English domestic Twenty20 cricket comparing winning and losing performances, although there were thirty losing innings and twenty-nine winning innings, so this was not a paired samples design. Effect sizes were used to compare wicket variables, scoring rates, partnership scores, proportion of different shot types and bowling types. Saavedra et al. (2016) compared game statistics in waterpolo between winning and losing teams in close (1 to 3 goal-winning margin), unbalanced (4 to 11 goal-winning margin) and very unbalanced matches (more than an 11 goal-winning margin). Ordóñez et al. (2015) studied indicators in waterpolo that distinguish between matches won by three or more goals and lost by three or more goals, as well as balanced matches where the difference between the teams was less than three goals.

Finishing position within tournaments has been used to classify successful and unsuccessful performers, allowing their tactics to be compared within performance analysis studies. Technical effectiveness and tactical variables have been used to model ranking of seven teams in the International Rugby Board (IRB) World Series (Higham et al., 2014). Tactics in devil-elimination international cycling races have been evaluated using pacing variables, correlating these with finishing position (Gill et al., 2014). Similarly, Woods (2016) has described performance indicators for Australian rules football teams finishing in different ladder positions. Broad grouping of successful and unsuccessful performers could simply be made based on where they finished in a league table (Perez et al., 2016). A variation on this general approach was a comparison of tactics of A and B finalists using pacing variables in international sprint kayak (Borges et al., 2013). Students need to be careful in considering pacing variables as indicators of strategy because they may be related to fatigue rather than being intentional pacing strategies. Similarly, observed patterns of play in invasion games might reflect chosen tactics of performers or might be dictated by opposing players. This is a concept students need to consider in designing studies on tactics as well as in discussing the results of such studies. It is also possible to combine the two approaches of comparing winning and losing performances within matches and distinguishing performances of teams achieving different tournament rankings; this has been done in a study of men's volleyball tactics (Stutzig et al., 2015).

Sometimes events do not occur frequently enough within single matches to allow meaningful frequency and percentage conversion variables to be calculated for individual performances. In such cases, when the event types represent valid and relevant aspects of play, students can justify using the event as the unit of analysis rather than using summary statistics from whole performances. This often leads to categorical variables being used to represent timings, locations, players involved, optional choices and success. It can lead to chi-square tests being used for data that are not entirely independent, and so such an approach is not recommended if the data could be analysed at a whole performance level rather than at the event level. There are several recent examples of event-level tactical analysis in sport. Pulling et al. (2016) compared the success of centre passes in English Superleague netball when the centre pass was played to four different team mates. Possessions in US Major League soccer have been analysed to identify associations between pass types, opposition defence style, situational variables and possessions that led to scoring opportunities or not (Gonzalez-Rodenas et al., 2015). Casal et al. (2014) analysed free kicks in World Cup and Champions League soccer at an event level. Defensive style and situational variables have also been analysed with respect to the success of corner kicks in soccer (Casal et al., 2015). Pulling et al. (2013) analysed corners using an event-level approach but did so from the point of view of defending against corners rather than taking them. Serve returns in tennis have been analysed using spatial analysis to represent tactics (Hizan et al., 2014). Stance and grip type in judo have been analysed at a throw level to compare success of different tactics in terms of scoring points and winning bouts (Courel et al., 2014).

TECHNIQUE

There are many methods used to analyse technique, ranging from completely unrestricted qualitative analysis by expert observers to very sophisticated biomechanical measurement and analysis. Qualitative methods for analysing performances include inspection of photographs, viewing of videos of performances, self-confrontational interviews while watching videos of performances and qualitative movement diagnosis (O'Donoghue, 2015: 27–36). Detailed analysis of technique can be done using kinematic and/or kinetic analyses during laboratory or field-based experiments. While the techniques being analysed might not be being performed during real competitive sport, there is a case for including such research within the scope of sports performance analysis. The detail required cannot be feasibly gathered during real sports performance. However, important techniques performed during competition can be performed by participants during laboratory studies, allowing valuable findings about technique to be produced. Lees (2008: 162–163) classified skills in sport as event skills, major skills and minor skills. An example of an event skill is the long jump, because the skill is the event. An example of a major skill is the golf swing in golf, whereas an example of a minor skill is different ways of kicking a ball in soccer. Once students have decided on a technique to study within their chosen sport, they need to ensure that they have framed the research project well and have identified a clear purpose for the study. Some examples of sports technique research that have been published recently in the *International Journal of Performance Analysis in Sport* are covered in the following three paragraphs.

The way in which different aspects of a technique contribute to overall performance can be analysed using correlation or regression techniques. For example, the distance achieved using a long jump technique could be modelled by breaking the overall technique down into a hierarchy of components, identifying different phases of the technique (Hay and Reid, 1988). Similarly, research into Yurchenko layout vaults has developed

52

a conceptual hierarchical model of the technique consisting of six levels and four broad phases. Correlation techniques were used to relate detailed variables to higher order variables within the hierarchical model right up to the overall performance score (Penitente, 2014). A similar approach has been used to identify biomechanical parameters that correlate with score in pistol shooting (Hawkins and Bertrand, 2015). Further biomechanics work that has related technique to broader performance parameters includes studies of biomechanical variables associated with club head velocity in golf (Sinclair, Currigan et al., 2014) and ball release velocity in place kicking in rugby union (Sinclair, Taylor et al., 2014).

Some students may decide to compare alternative techniques to provide evidence about which is more effective. For example, Callaghan et al. (2015) compared static and rolling starts when Australian first-grade regional cricket players attempted to bat looking for a single run. Fletcher et al. (2015) compared the Rosenberg and Pose rowing techniques, while Fronczek–Wojciechowska et al. (2016) compared balance in ballet dances when tasks were performed with eyes opened and closed. Rouissi et al. (2015) compared side stepping and bypassing techniques used by elite youth soccer players to change direction. Štirn et al. (2016) examined how overall reaction time of basketball players was effected by different types of stance technique. Lockie et al. (2014) compared planned and unplanned 45-degree cutting movements performed by basketball players to the side of the dominant and non-dominant leg using electromyography (EMG) data and Y agility test times. An experimental study of rugby union spin passing examined technique when passes were performed at a range of movement speeds and the ball was passed over different distances (Worsfold and Page, 2014). This showed that the percentage of spin passes that included a 'body drop' phase increased with pass distance and that including a 'body drop' phase resulted in higher ball velocities and accuracy of passing. The different techniques being compared in a study could actually be the same technique but performed at different times. For example, Hampson and Randle (2015) analysed the biomechanical technique of Canadian dressage horse-rider pairs to evaluate the effect of an eight-week core fitness programme. This was done by comparing biomechanical values pre- and post-intervention.

Another broad purpose of analysing technique is to compare the techniques of performers of different levels. For example, Zhang et al. (2016) compared the mechanics of table tennis shots performed by experienced and novice players. Sharp et al. (2014) compared EMG and kinetic data during the engagement phase of rugby scrummaging between professional, amateur and junior players. Morland et al. (2013) did an experiment to compare ten female school/club field hockey players' and ten regional hockey players' change of direction speed when pre-planned, reacting to hockey-specific and light stimuli. A further example of technique analysis comparing different groups is the study of kinetic and kinematic variables for lower extremities during lunges performed by female and male fencers (Sinclair and Bottoms, 2013).

TECHNICAL DEMANDS OF A SPORT

The demands of a sport can be estimated based on the frequency with which techniques are performed and knowledge of the mechanical energy demands of the different techniques. This type of approach can also help identify injury risk involved in different sporting activities. There are recent examples of performance analysis studies that have counted the number of times different techniques are performed in a number of sports. Miller et al. (2015) counted the throw types performed by junior and senior men and women in the British Judo Championships, finding that women did more Ashi throws than men. The number of punches of different types that are made during amateur boxing competition has been compared between different weight divisions and ability levels (Thomson and Lamb, 2016). The number of different serve types and striking techniques performed in volleyball has been examined when serving to different zones and in different directions (Fernandez-Echeverria et al., 2015). Foot strike patterns have been compared between female and male distance runners using observation of filmed running strides during races (Latorre-Román et al., 2015). Contributions to knowledge about the physical demands of rugby union have been made by studies of tackles and collisions (Schoeman et al., 2015; Cummins and Orr, 2015). Fox et al. (2013) counted the landing techniques used by Australian international netball players to provide information about the agility requirements of the sport.

TECHNICAL EFFECTIVENESS

Counting the number of occurrences of different techniques performed in sport and looking at kinematic and kinetic detail of the techniques are two ways of studying technique within sport. Technical effectiveness studies count not only the number of times different techniques are performed, but also the success with which the techniques are performed. This has a role in tactical analysis where some techniques are found to be clearly more productive than others. Evans and O'Donoghue (2013) classified the outcomes of chop and other tackles performed by club and international rugby players as unsuccessful, successful, or successful and leading to a turnover. They found that the chop tackle was a high-risk tackle with a higher chance of resulting in a turnover of possession than other tackles, but it also had a higher chance of being unsuccessful. Palao and Ortega (2015) examined the effectiveness with which different techniques were performed in beach volleyball competition, using point to error ratios.

WORK-RATE

Observational methods

Observational techniques have been used to give indirect estimations of physical demands of different sports since the pioneering study of English League football undertaken by Reilly and Thomas (1976). Technology has improved over the decades and now the movements of players have been automatically tracked by GPS devices and image-processing technology. Further research has recorded heart rate response, lactate buildup and perceived exertion during real and synthesised competition. This section will commence with a review of recent time-motion analysis research, followed by reviews of research using player-tracking technology and physiological measurements.

Time-motion analysis has been applied to martial arts, with recent studies describing the intensity of standing and ground action in mixed martial arts (Miarka, Coswig et al., 2015) and the broad types of attacking and defending activity in international judo (Miarka, Del Vecchio et al., 2016). Time-motion analysis has also allowed the volume of low-, moderate- and high-intensity activity to be compared among three different types of fencing bout (Wylde et al., 2013). Rally and rest durations have been used to reflect the demands of singles and doubles badminton (Gawin et al., 2015), wheelchair tennis (Sánchez-Pay et al., 2015) and men's volleyball (Sánchez-Pay et al., 2015). Team sports can be analysed by classifying movements and determining the distribution of match time spent performing movements of different intensities. An example of such a study was a comparison of the activity performed in different match quarters by Spanish female basketball players (Del-extrat et al., 2015). Another form of observational analysis that can be applied to team games is manually keying in the locations of movements recorded on videos of player performances. This has been done in Chinese national league field hockey, allowing the distribution of movement among different speed zones to be compared between players of different positions (Liu, Zhao et al., 2013). A further time-motion study in field hockey concentrated on substitutes finding a "first-minute rush" in their performances (Linke and Lames, 2016). Time-motion analysis has also been used to compare the behaviours of male and female climbers using the Sport Climbing Observational Tool (SCOT) (Arbulu et al., 2015). While automated techniques are being used in many time-motion studies, there are many movements and events that need to be classified by human observation. Semi-automatic digitisation of player locations shown on two camera views has been combined with direct linear transformation (DLT) to analyse movements in beach volleyball competition (Hank et al., 2016).

GPS devices

One of the major difficulties of observational time-motion analysis methods is that individual players needed to be analysed when they are involved in on-the-ball activity as well as during their off-ball movement. This has typically meant that only one player's activity could be recorded per match (O'Donoghue, 1998), or multiple cameras were needed to record the activity of more than one player. GPS devices allow the activity of multiple players to be recorded simultaneously during matches. There are still measurement issues that need to be acknowledged within studies using GPS devices, but the technology does overcome the errors associated with the subjective classification of movement by human observers. The availability of GPS devices has stimulated a great deal of movement analysis work within practical coaching contexts for tactical and work-rate analysis purposes. This can lead to large data sets being accumulated over time, which is advantageous to research. However, there is also an issue that studies may be poorly designed if the data collection has been done first and the selection of a research topic to utilise the data is done afterwards. It is very easy, for example, for practitioners to write up trend studies or compare different small-sided games using

56

data collected from their own players. If the data all come from the same squad, then the data will be viewed as a convenience sample that is not generalizable to performance the given sport. There are, nonetheless, examples of good time-motion studies using GPS data that have been published. Sparks et al. (2016a) used GPS devices to look at high-intensity running performed in semi-professional soccer, comparing successive five-minute periods of matches. Barbero et al. (2014) used GPS data and heart rate responses to compare the demands of different positional roles at different game stages in professional handball. There have also been two recent studies of work-rate in Australian rules football that have used GPS data. GPS and heart rate data were also combined in a study of elite African badminton player movements (Bisschoff et al., 2016). Bauer et al. (2015) derived movement variables from GPS data and determined the correlations among these, player rankings and coach ratings of players. Gronow et al. (2014) used GPS data to determine the percentage of time that soccer players spent moving faster than 14 km.h^{-1}, 19 km.h^{-1} and 24 km.h^{-1} with and without the ball. Other player-tracking technologies have been used to analyse work-rate in soccer. One study compared activity performed in the first half, second half and extra time by ninety-nine players in 2014 FIFA World Cup matches that went to extra time (Lago-Peñas et al., 2015). Morgans et al. (2014) used player-tracking variables to investigate player work-rate over an English FA Premier League season, finding evidence of fatigue in mid to late season based on measures of high-intensity running distance.

Physiological data

Heart rate measures can be taken during actual or simulated competition depending on the nature of the sport. Examples of heart rate response data taken during competition are a study of pre-shot routines of Lithuanian national youth golfers (Zienius et al., 2015) and match play in South African A-League soccer (Sparks et al., 2016b). Gavrlilovic et al. (2016) compared heart rate responses between different training and sparring activities performed by kickboxers. Other research into the demands of kickboxing has used heart rate data, lactate response and perceived exertion during three-round laboratory-based bouts (Salci, 2015). Heart rate response and perceived exertion data have also been used to describe the training loads of gymnasts (Fernandez-Villarino et al., 2015). Rosario et al. (2015) combined heart rate data with lactate measures and the distribution of observed locomotive movements of beach soccer players. Blood lactate accumulation and clearance has been evaluated using blood samples taken immediately after and ten minutes after Brazilian Jiu Jitsu bouts (Diaz-Lara et al., 2015). This study also used countermovement jump test and hand-grip strength data to estimate fatigue caused by the bouts. Kirk et al. (2015) used a combination of lactate measures and time-motion data during an investigation of the demands of mixed martial arts performance. The lactate measurements were taken at rest, after the warm up, after each of the three rounds and five minutes post bout. The time-motion data used a detailed movement classification of twenty-one state and event variables. An example of a state variable is being in dominant position, while an example of an event is making a takedown attempt. Heart rate, blood lactate, triglycerides measures, glucose measures and perceived exertion were combined in a study of simulated judo competition (Stavrinou et al., 2016). Simulated female basketball competition has also been investigated using heart rate measures (Abad et al., 2016). A further example of physiological measurement is Shaw et al.'s (2015) study of the physiological demands of a CrossFit bout that used a variety of cardiopulmonary and metabolic responses.

RULE CHANGES

Students interested in undertaking projects on the effect of rule changes are encouraged to read the book chapter by Williams (2008) which discusses various reasons for rule changes as well as the role of notational analysis in studying the effect of rule changes. Rules can be changed to make sports more fair, to increase entertainment value or to improve safety. Performance can be influenced by the development of better equipment that necessitates rule changes to maintain fairness and safety. Over time, the physical characteristics of players in some sports have changed, giving rise to greater injury risk when players have become bigger and faster. Rule changes may be introduced to reduce injury risk and injury occurrence in such cases.

In sport, players and teams try to succeed within the constraints of the rules of the games they play. Playing styles evolve, often seeing players and teams 'testing the boundary of a rule' (Williams, 2008). Hibbs and O'Donoghue (2013) argued that breaking rules was not cheating when there are sanctions in place for rule breaking. They used the simple example of a

58

ball being played out for a throw in during a soccer match and the opposition being awarded a throw in; these rules are broken as part of the game. Indeed, there are often tactical decisions that need to be made about breaking rules and risking breaking rules depending on the consequences of doing so or not.

Most studies into the effects of rule changes compare performances within the same competitions before and after rule changes are made. The research uses dependent performance variables that can be reasonably hypothesised to be influenced by the rule change. The selection of dependent variables can be made considering the aspects of play the rule changes were intended to address. This approach has been used in research into rule changes in rugby union (Stean et al., 2015; Vahed et al., 2014) and judo (Franchini et al., 2013). It is also possible to compare games played under two different sets of rules where no rule change has taken place but there are different sets of rules applied in different types of matches. For example, Scanlan et al. (2016) compared performances in forty- and forty-eight-minute basketball games.

PROFESSIONAL PRACTICE

Attitude and perceptions

So far this chapter has covered scientific studies that have found general knowledge about sports performance. Performance analysis is also used in a practical coaching context to provide feedback to athletes to help them improve. Hayes (1997: 5) highlighted the need for more evidence about the effectiveness of using performance analysis within coaching contexts: 'show me the results of notational analysis, not the notational analysis results'. At the end of a literature review paper, Wright et al. (2014) also called for more intervention studies to look at the effectiveness of performance analysis in coaching practice. There are two broad types of study into performance analysis in its practical context. The first type is surveys that can be done using interviews and/or questionnaires. These can study the attitudes and beliefs of coaches and athletes about performance analysis support, or they can describe performance analysis support from the performance analyst's perspective in terms of methods used, volumes and types of work done, and technology involved. The second type of study is an intervention study where a performance analysis service is provided to coaches and athletes, allowing effects on performance to be monitored. These studies can also involve reflections of practitioners on the experience of working in the practical context.

Over the years, there have been papers discussing performance analysis technology (Liebermann et al., 2002; Liebermann and Franks, 2008; Arriaza and Zuniga, 2016). Butterworth et al. (2013) undertook a review of methods that could be used within performance profiling in sport. As technology continues to advance, performance analysis systems exploit new storage technology, communications technologies and portable devices. Therefore, there is a need for further research as further technological advances take place. Players' perceptions of performance analysis have been investigated using interview studies (Reeves and Roberts, 2013) and online questionnaires (Wright et al., 2016). Interviews have also been used in a study of coach perceptions of performance analysis, leading to a coaching model for soccer being proposed (Sarmento et al., 2013). A further interview study has been done on futsal coach perceptions of performance analysis support (Sarmento et al., 2015). Soccer analysts have provided an insight into their role at different levels of the game through an online questionnaire survey (Wright et al., 2013). Palao and Hernández-Hernández (2014) used a questionnaire survey with twenty-two Spanish volleyball coaches, finding that coaches individualise the way they analyse technical and tactical data within their own coaching processes. Francis and Jones (2014) used a combination of four interviews and a questionnaire survey of seventy-three respondents to gauge elite rugby players' perceptions of performance analysis. The players indicated that video information was more useful than the quantitative information available, that iPads allowed productive use of breaks in physical training and that information about opponents was beneficial.

Experience reports

The second type of study into professional practice includes intervention studies and experience reports. These are not controlled experiments, and there are many uncontrollable factors within such studies. This has meant that researchers have avoided doing such studies, instead opting to do more scientific studies. However, since 2010 there has been an increase in the number of professional practice studies that have been

60

published. Early studies into the effectiveness of performance analysis looked at winner and error statistics of squash players who were given different types of feedback (Brown and Hughes, 1995; Murray et al., 1998). The nature of tournaments and time between matches has been found to influence the approach to performance analysis and the types of feedback given in netball (Horne, 2013). Cultural factors have also been found to influence the way in which performance analysis support is utilised within a professional soccer case study (McKenzie and Cushion, 2013). These studies provide scholars of performance analysis with valuable insights into the real world of performance analysis in a sports coaching context and are valuable reference material for work experience modules. Students who are more vocationally oriented performance analysts, rather than interested in pursuing scientific studies, should consider undertaking reflective practice dissertations. These studies are needed to add to the balance of evidence about the effectiveness of performance analysis in coaching. The ethical issues involved in such studies and the role of storytelling approaches to address some ethical issues are discussed in Chapter 6.

VALIDITY AND RELIABILITY OF SYSTEMS

Performance analysis studies often use variables that are specific to the given study, meaning that there is no pre-existing evidence about the reliability and validity of such variables. It is therefore necessary for such studies to justify the relevance of the variables used and to include a reliability study within the methods section. Where a performance analysis system or method could be used in many studies, the reliability and validity of that system or method can be published as a paper in its own right and then be referred to by subsequent studies in which the system or method is used. GPS devices are used in multiple performance analysis studies, and so there is a need for up-to-date evidence about the validity and reliability of GPS devices as the technology improves over time. One such study validated GPS distance measures against known distances for a team sport simulation circuit done by the participants (Johnston et al., 2013). The study found that error increased as movement speed of players increased. Opta (Opta Sports, London, UK) match statistics are used commercially in soccer as well as within scientific studies of the sport. Therefore, Liu, Hopkins et al. (2013) have done a reliability study of Opta match statistics by duplicating the complete data collection and analysis process using independent, trained operators to analyse the same match. This showed a good level of inter-operator agreement for event data. The validity and reliability of other potentially useful methods have also been investigated recently. Larkin et al. (2016) have done a reliability study of the Movement Awareness and Technical Skills (MATS) instrument. Thomas (2015) has developed a method to allow shot locations in tennis to be entered onto the elevated view of a tennis court provided during broadcast coverage so that the court location can be determined on a bird's-eye view image using two-dimensional direct linear transformation. This was demonstrated to be more reliable than when an operator attempted to enter shot locations directly onto a bird's-eye-view image of the court after having watched television coverage showing an elevated view. A further method that is promising in performance analysis research is automatic jump detection from inertial sensor data (Gageler et al., 2015). This method has detected 95 per cent of jumps performed in volleyball, with 4 per cent additional false positive jump detections to add to the 5 per cent of false negative detections. This study also validated the method against force plate data, finding that it under-estimated flight time by 0.015s ±0.058s.

UMPIRE AND REFEREE PERFORMANCE

The performance of referees and umpires can be investigated for practical, media or research purposes. The recent research into the performance of match officials can be grouped into studies looking at the accuracy of their decisions and studies about the work-rate required to referee matches. The accuracy of the amount of additional time played at the end of professional soccer matches has received recent research attention (Siegle and Prüßner, 2013; Prüßner and Siegle, 2015). Coleclough (2013) compiled a video of 106 contact incidents to compare the correctness of assessments made by coaches and referees about the decisions taken and the decisions that should have been taken by the actual referees in the matches. A further study of decision accuracy examined the correctness of calls made by umpires and line judges when the challenge system was used in Grand Slam tennis (Carboch et al., 2016). The study found that errors were made on 27 per cent of occasions when the challenge system was used. This is an over-estimation of errors because the study only analysed points where the review system was used.

Recent studies into the work-rate of referees include Hogarth et al.'s (2015) description of the demands of tag football refereeing using GPS and heart rate data. Elsworthy et al.'s (2014) study related decision making of officials in elite Australian rules football matches with movement data. Elsworthy et al. (2014) found that the distance of the official from the incident being assessed did not influence the accuracy of decisions but movement speed during the five seconds prior to the decision did have an influence, with higher speeds associated with more errors.

EMERGING METHODS IN PERFORMANCE ANALYSIS

The study of sports performance has seen an expansion in methods and variables used in recent years. Some students have been able to study data from actual sports performance, while others have used experimental conditions to study performance of sport-specific actions. Tracking data from GPS or other systems can be processed to provide variables about tactical movement, work-rate and individual and collective behaviour. Recent studies have used new approaches to processing player movement data, including Voronoi diagrams to study the interaction between opposing teams (Fonseca et al., 2013) and player coverage variables when a team is in possession of the ball (Clemente et al., 2014). Network analysis has been used to analyse passing patterns and the success of passing between different pairs of players in team games (Gama et al., 2014; Clemente, Martins, Wong et al., 2015; Clemente, Martins, Kalamaras et al., 2015). These studies are presenting this information in graphical form but also testing exploratory variables to reflect aspects of collective behaviour in team games.

Stöckl and Morgan (2013) have used contour maps to visualise activity areas in field hockey attacks. Temporal analysis is another approach to analysing data from actual sports performances. Rather than presenting total frequencies, durations and percentage of match time for different events, temporal analysis represents sequences of events that are concealed by traditional analysis techniques. Judo has been analysed by looking at temporal patterns of behaviours leading to errors (Lage et al., 2014) and Markov chains (Miarka, Branco et al., 2015). Temporal analysis has also been applied in children's basketball, with recurring sequences of behaviours being pictorially reconstructed and presented on court diagrams understandable at the practical level (Lapresa et al.,

2013). Another new type of variable that has been analysed using observational techniques is deceptive behaviour. DeFreitas (2015) compared deceptive behaviours between elite and sub-elite academy soccer players' performances. Examples of deceptive variables analysed were uncompleted movements, atypical techniques, passes made at atypical angles and step-overs.

Mental aspects of sports performance cannot be directly observed using traditional observational techniques. Self-confrontational interviews have been proposed as a technique to capture the thought processes of athletes during competition (Poizat et al., 2013). These involve athletes watching their performances on video and recalling thoughts they had at different points during the performances. A recent study using this approach was Martinent and Ferrand's (2015) study of thirty self-confrontational interviews with national-level table tennis players. This study also used a quantitative approach to compare facilitative and debilitative joy, serenity, hope, anger, discouragement disgust, anxiety, pride and relief between winning and losing sets.

Other studies have had to synthesise aspects of performance of interest within laboratory situations in order to record the variables of interest. Examples of such studies use of eye-fixation recordings during complex, game-like volleyball tasks (Afonso and Mesquita, 2013) and reaction time to on-screen stimuli of karate kumite competitors (Mudric et al., 2015).

SUMMARY

The current chapter has reviewed sports performance analysis research done between the start of 2013 and the end of 2016. There is a wide variety of studies, ranging from investigations of behaviours of players and referees to studies of the effectiveness of performance analysis of sport in coaching contexts. The most common studies involve analysing the effect of some independent factor on some dependent performance variables. The independent variables could be situational variables or performer qualities. The dependent performance variables could be tactical, technical or work-rate variables. There are still many original ideas to be investigated by students wishing to undertake sports performance analysis research projects because previous research has not investigated the effects of all potential independent variables on all aspects of performance

64

in every sport. There remain unanswered questions in all sports, which gives dissertation students plenty of potential topics to choose from.

REFERENCES

Abad, C.C.C., Pereira, L.A., Kobal, R., Kitamura, K., Cruz, I.F., Loturco, I.F. and Nakamura, F.Y. (2016) 'Heart rate and heart rate variability of Yo-Yo IR1 and simulated match in young female basketball athletes: A comparative study', *International Journal of Performance Analysis in Sport*, 16: 776–791.

Abián, P., Castanedo, A., Feng, X.O., Sampedro, J. and Abian-Vicen, J. (2014) 'Notational comparison of men's singles badminton matches between Olympic Games in Beijing and London', *International Journal of Performance Analysis in Sport*, 14: 42–53.

Adams, D., Morgans, R., Sacramento, J., Morgan, S. and Williams, M.D. (2013) 'Successful short passing frequency of defenders differentiates between top and bottom four English Premier League teams', *International Journal of Performance Analysis in Sport*, 13: 653–668.

Afonso, J. and Mesquita, I. (2013) 'Skill-based differences in visual search behaviours and verbal reports in a representative film-based task in volleyball', *International Journal of Performance Analysis in Sport*, 13: 669–677.

Andrzejewski, M., Chmura, J. and Pluta, B. (2014) 'Analysis of motor and technical activities of professional soccer players of the UEFA Europa League', *International Journal of Performance Analysis in Sport*, 14(2): 504–523.

Arbulu, A., Usabiaga, O. and Castellano, J. (2015) 'A time motion analysis of lead climbing in the 2012 men's and women's world championship finals', *International Journal of Performance Analysis in Sport*, 15: 924–934.

Arriaza, E.J. and Zuniga, M.D. (2016) 'Soccer as a study case for analytic trends in collective sports training: a survey', *International Journal of Performance Analysis in Sport*, 16(1): 171–190.

Barbero, J.C., Granda-Vera, J., Calleja-González, J. and Del Coso, J. (2014) 'Physical and physiological demands of elite team handball players', *International Journal of Performance Analysis in Sport*, 14: 921–933.

Bauer, A.M., Young, W., Fahrner, B. and Harvey, J. (2015) 'GPS variables most related to match performance in an elite Australian football team', *International Journal of Performance Analysis in Sport*, 15: 187–202.

Bisschoff, C.A., Coetzee, B. and Esco, M.R. (2016) 'Relationship between heart rate, heart rate variability, heart rate recovery and global positioning system determined match characteristics of male, elite, African badminton players', *International Journal of Performance Analysis in Sport*, 16: 881–897.

Bishop, L. and Barnes, A. (2013) 'Performance indicators that discriminate winning and losing in the knockout stages of the 2011 Rugby World Cup', *International Journal of Performance Analysis in Sport*, 13: 149–159.

Borges, T.O., Bullock, N. and Coutts, A.J. (2013) 'Pacing characteristics of international Sprint Kayak athletes', *International Journal of Performance Analysis in Sport*, 13: 353–362.

Bremner, S., Robinson, G. and Williams, M.D. (2013) 'A retrospective evaluation of team performance indicators in rugby union', *International Journal of Performance Analysis in Sport*, 13: 461–473.

Brown, D. and Hughes, M. (1995) 'The effectiveness of quantitative and qualitative feedback on performance in squash', in T. Reilly, M. Hughes and A. Lees (eds), *Science and racket sports* (pp. 232–236). London: E and FN Spon.

Buglione, A., Ruscello, B., Milia, R., Migliaccio, G.M., Granatelli, G. and D'Ottavio, S. (2013) 'Physical and physiological demands of elite and sub-elite Field Hockey players', *International Journal of Performance Analysis in Sport*, 13: 872–884.

Butterworth, A.D., O'Donoghue, P. and Cropley, B. (2013) 'Performance profiling in sports coaching: a review', *International Journal of Performance Analysis in Sport*, 13: 572–593.

Callaghan, S.J., Jeffries, M.D., Mackie, S.L., Jalilvand, F. and Lockie, R.G. (2015) 'The impact of a rolling start on the sprint velocity and acceleration kinematics of a quick single in regional first grade cricketers', *International Journal of Performance Analysis in Sport*, 15: 794–808.

Campos, F.A.D., Pellegrinotti, Í.L., Pasquarelli, B.N., Rabelo, F.N., SantaCruz, R.A.R. and Gómez, M-Á. (2015) 'Effects of game-location and quality of opposition in futsal league', *International Journal of Performance Analysis in Sport*, 15: 598–607.

Carboch, J., Vejvodova, K. and Suss, V. (2016) 'Analysis of errors made by line umpires on ATP tournaments', *International Journal of Performance Analysis in Sport*, 16: 264–275.

Carroll, R. (2013) 'Team performance indicators in Gaelic Football and opposition effects', *International Journal of Performance Analysis in Sport*, 13: 703–715.

Casal, C.A., Maneiro, R., Ardá, T., Losada, J.L. and Rial, A. (2014) 'Effectiveness of indirect free kicks in elite soccer', *International Journal of Performance Analysis in Sport*, 14: 744–760.

Casal, C.A., Maneiro, R., Ardá, T., Losada, J.L. and Rial, A. (2015) 'Analysis of corner kick success in elite football', *International Journal of Performance Analysis in Sport*, 15: 430–451.

Castellano, J., Álvarez, D., Figueira, B., Coutinho, D. and Sampaio, J. (2013) 'Identifying the effects from the quality of opposition in a Football team positioning strategy', *International Journal of Performance Analysis in Sport*, 13: 822–832.

Castellano, J. and Casamichana, D. (2015) 'What are the differences between first and second divisions of Spanish football teams?', *International Journal of Performance Analysis in Sport*, 15: 135–146.

Clay, D.C. and Clay, K.E. (2014) 'Player rotation, on-court performance and game outcomes in NCAA men's basketball', *International Journal of Performance Analysis in Sport*, 14: 606–619.

Clemente, F.M., Martins, F.M.L., Couceiro, M.S., Mendes, R.S. and Figueiredo, A.J. (2014) 'Inspecting teammates' coverage during attacking plays in a football game: a case study', *International Journal of Performance Analysis in Sport*, 14: 384–400.

Clemente, F.M., Martins, F.M.L., Kalamaras, D., Wong, D.P. and Mendes, R.S. (2015) 'General network analysis of national soccer teams in FIFA World Cup 2014', *International Journal of Performance Analysis in Sport*, 15: 80–96.

Clemente, F.M., Martins, F.M.L., Wong, D.P., Kalamaras, D. and Mendes, R.S. (2015) 'Midfielder as the prominent participant in the building attack: A network analysis of national teams in FIFA World Cup 2014', *International Journal of Performance Analysis in Sport*, 15: 704–722.

Coleclough, J. (2013) 'Soccer coaches' and referees' perceptions of tackle incidents with respect to the laws of the game', *International Journal of Performance Analysis in Sport*, 13: 553–566.

Courel, J., Franchini, E., Femia, P., Stankovic, N. and Escobar-Molina, R. (2014) 'Effects of *kumi-kata* grip laterality and throwing side on attack effectiveness and combat result in elite judo athletes', *International Journal of Performance Analysis in Sport*, 14: 138–147.

Courneya, K.S. and Carron, A.V. (1992) 'The home advantage in sports competitions: a literature review', *Journal of Sport and Exercise Psychology*, 14: 13–27.

Csataljay, G., James, N., Hughes, M. and Dancs, H. (2013) 'Effects of defensive pressure on basketball shooting performance', *International Journal of Performance Analysis in Sport*, 13: 594–601.

Cummins, C. and Orr, R. (2015) 'Collision characteristics of shoulder charge tackles in elite rugby league', *International Journal of Performance Analysis in Sport*, 15: 1090–1101.

DeFreitas, R. (2015) 'Do deceptive and disguised movement behaviours exist in actual soccer match play and does their use indicate elite performance?', *International Journal of Performance Analysis in Sport*, 15: 1047–1064.

Delextrat, A., Badiella, A., Saavedra, V., Matthew, D., Schelling, X. and Torres-Ronda, L. (2015) 'Match activity demands of elite Spanish female basketball players by playing position', *International Journal of Performance Analysis in Sport*, 15: 687–703.

Diaz-Lara, F.J., del Coso, J., García, J.M. and Abián-Vicén, J. (2015) 'Analysis of physiological determinants during an international Brazilian Jiu-jitsu competition', *International Journal of Performance Analysis in Sport*, 15: 489–500.

Doğan, I., Işik, Ö. and Ersöz, Y. (2016) 'Examining the Turkish men's professional basketball team's success according to game-related statistics with discriminant analysis', *International Journal of Performance Analysis in Sport*, 16: 829–836.

Dormehl, S.J. and Williams, C.A. (2016) 'Stability of within-sport specialisation in competitive adolescent sub-elite swimmers', *International Journal of Performance Analysis in Sport*, 16: 12–29.

Elsworthy, N., Burke, D. and Dascombe, B.J. (2014) 'Factors relating to the decision-making performance of Australian football officials', *International Journal of Performance Analysis in Sport*, 14: 401–410.

Espina-Agulló, J.J., Pérez-Turpin, J.A., Jiménez-Olmedo, J.M., Penichet-Tomás, A. and Pueo, B. (2016) 'Effectiveness of male handball goalkeepers: a historical overview 1982–2012', *International Journal of Performance Analysis in Sport*, 16: 143–156.

Evans, L. and O'Donoghue, P. (2013) 'The effectiveness of the chop tackle in elite and semi-professional rugby union', *International Journal of Performance Analysis in Sport*, 13: 602–611.

Fernandez-Echeverria, C., Gil, A., Moreno, A., Claver, F. and Moreno, M.P. (2015) 'Analysis of the variables that predict serve efficacy in young volleyball players', *International Journal of Performance Analysis in Sport*, 15: 172–186.

Fernandez-Villarino, M.A., Sierra-Palmeiro, E., Bobo-Arce, M. and Lago-Peñas, C. (2015) 'Analysis of the training load during the competitive period in individual rhythmic gymnastics', *International Journal of Performance Analysis in Sport*, 15: 2, 660–667.

Ferreira, A.P., Volossovitch, A. and Sampaio, J. (2014) 'Towards the game critical moments in basketball: a grounded theory approach', *International Journal of Performance Analysis in Sport*, 14: 428–442.

Fleming, J. and Fleming, S. (2012) 'Relative age effect amongst footballers in the English Premier League and English Football League, 2010–2011', *International Journal of Performance Analysis in Sport*, 12: 361–372.

Fletcher, G., Bartlett, R., Docksteadder, A. and Romanov, N. (2015) 'Determining key biomechanical performance parameters in novice female rowers using the Rosenberg and Pose techniques during a 1 km ergometer time trial', *International Journal of Performance Analysis in Sport*, 15: 723–748.

Fonseca, S., Milho, J., Travassos, B., Araújo, D. and Lopes, A. (2013) 'Measuring spatial interaction behavior in team sports using superimposed Voronoi diagrams', *International Journal of Performance Analysis in Sport*, 13: 179–189.

Fox, A.S., Spittle, M., Otago, L. and Saunders, N. (2013) 'Descriptive analysis of landings during international netball competition: enhancing ecological validity of laboratory testing environments', *International Journal of Performance Analysis in Sport*, 13: 690–702.

Franchini, E., Takito, M.Y. and Calmet, M. (2013) 'European judo championships: impact of the new rule changes on points and penalties', *International Journal of Performance Analysis in Sport*, 13: 474–479.

Francis, J. and Jones, G. (2014) 'Elite rugby union players' perceptions of performance analysis', *International Journal of Performance Analysis in Sport*, 14: 188–207.

Fronczek–Wojciechowska, M., Padula, G., Kowalska, J., Galli, M., Livatino, S. and Kopacz, K. (2016) 'Static balance and dynamic balance related to rotational movement in ballet dance students', *International Journal of Performance Analysis in Sport*, 16: 801–816.

Fuller, N. and Alderson, G.J.K. (1990) 'The development of match analysis in game sports', in G.J.K. Alderson, N. Fuller and P. Treadwell (eds), *Match analysis in sport: a state of the art review*. Leeds: SportTech Recreation Consultancy, National Coaching Foundation.

Gageler, W.H., Wearing, S. and James, D.A. (2015) 'Automatic jump detection method for athlete monitoring and performance in volleyball', *International Journal of Performance Analysis in Sport*, 15: 284–296.

Galé-Ansodi, C., Castellano, J. and Usabiaga, O. (2016) 'Effects of different surfaces in time-motion characteristics in youth elite tennis players', *International Journal of Performance Analysis in Sport*, 16: 860–870.

Gama, J., Passos, P., Davids, K., Relvas, H., Ribeiro, J., Vaz, V. and Dias, G. (2014) 'Network analysis and intra-team activity in attacking phases of professional football', *International Journal of Performance Analysis in Sport*, 14: 692–708.

García, M.S., Aguilar, Ó.G., Lazo, J.C.V., Marques, P.S. and Romero, J.J.F. (2013) 'Home advantage in Home Nations, Five Nations and Six Nations rugby tournaments (1883–2011)', *International Journal of Performance Analysis in Sport*, 13: 51–63.

García, J., Ibáñez, S.J., Gómez, M.A. and Sampaio, J. (2014) 'Basketball game-related statistics discriminating ACB league teams according to game location, game outcome and final score differences', *International Journal of Performance Analysis in Sport*, 14: 443–452.

García-de-Alcaraz, A., Ortega, E. and Palao, J.M. (2015) 'Effect of age group on male volleyball players' technical-tactical performance profile for the spike', *International Journal of Performance Analysis in Sport*, 15: 668–686.

García-Rubio, J., Gómez, M-Á., Lago-Peñas, C. and Ibáñez, S.J. (2015) 'Effect of match venue, scoring first and quality of opposition on match outcome in the UEFA Champions League', *International Journal of Performance Analysis in Sport*, 15: 527–539.

Gavrlilovic, D., Petrovic, A., Dopsaj, M., Kasum, G., Pajic, Z. and Koprivica, V. (2016) 'Work and rest peak heart rate variability response during the different technical and tactical situations of elite kickboxers', *International Journal of Performance Analysis in Sport*, 16: 96–110.

Gawin, W., Beyer, C. and Seidler, M. (2015) 'A competition analysis of the single and double disciplines in world-class badminton', *International Journal of Performance Analysis in Sport*, 15: 997–1006.

Gill, K.S., White, C. and Worsfold, P.R. (2014) 'Track cycling: an analysis of the pacing strategies employed during the devil elimination race', *International Journal of Performance Analysis in Sport*, 14: 330–344.

Gomes, F., Volossovitch, A. and Ferreira, A.P. (2014) 'Team timeout calling in handball', *International Journal of Performance Analysis in Sport*, 14: 98–110.

Gomez, M-Á., Gasperi, L. and Lupo, C. (2016) 'Performance analysis of game dynamics during the 4th game quarter of NBA close games', *International Journal of Performance Analysis in Sport*, 16: 249–263.

Gómez, M.Á., Lagos-Peñas, C. and Pollard, R. (2013) 'Situational variables', in T. McGarry, P.G. O'Donoghue and J. Sampaio (eds), *Routledge handbook of sports performance analysis* (pp. 259–269). London: Routledge.

Gonzalez-Rodenas, J., Lopez-Bondia, I., Calabuig, F., Pérez-Turpin, J.A. and Aranda, R. (2015) 'The effects of playing tactics on creating scoring opportunities in random matches from US Major League Soccer', *International Journal of Performance Analysis in Sport*, 15: 851–872.

Goossens, D.R., Kempeneers, J., Koning, R.H. and Spieksma, F.C.R. (2015) 'Winning in straight sets helps in Grand Slam tennis', *International Journal of Performance Analysis in Sport*, 15: 1007–1021.

Goumas, C. (2014) 'Tyranny of distance: Home advantage and travel in international club football', *International Journal of Performance Analysis in Sport*, 14: 1–13.

Gronow, D., Dawson, B., Heasman, J., Rogalski, B. and Peeling, P. (2014) 'Team movement patterns with and without ball possession in Australian Football

League players', *International Journal of Performance Analysis in Sport*, 14: 635–651.

Gursoy, R. (2009) 'Effects of left- or right-hand preference on the success of boxers in Turkey', *British Journal of Sports Medicine*, 43: 142–144.

Gutiérrez-Aguilar, Ó., Montoya-Fernández, M., Fernández-Romero, J.J. and Saavedra-García, M.A. (2016) 'Analysis of time-out use in handball and its influence on the game performance', *International Journal of Performance Analysis in Sport*, 16: 1–11.

Hampson, A. and Randle, H. (2015) 'The influence of an 8-week rider core fitness program on the equine back at sitting trot', *International Journal of Performance Analysis in Sport*, 15: 1145–1159.

Hank, M., Malý, T., Zahálka, F., Dragijský, M. and Bujnovský, D. (2016) 'Evaluation of the horizontal movement distance of elite female beach volleyball players during an official match', *International Journal of Performance Analysis in Sport*, 16: 1087–1101.

Harrop, K. and Nevill, A. (2014) 'Performance indicators that predict success in an English professional League One soccer team', *International Journal of Performance Analysis in Sport*, 14: 907–920.

Hawkins, R. and Bertrand, P. (2015) 'Relationship between twelve mechanic measures and score for national-level pistol shooters', *International Journal of Performance Analysis in Sport*, 15: 332–342.

Hay, J.G. and Reid, J.G. (1988) *Anatomy, mechanics and human motion.* Englewood Cliffs, NJ: Prentice Hall.

Hayes, M. (1997) 'Notational analysis – the right of reply', *BASES Newsletter*, 7(8): 4–5.

Hewitt, A., Greenham, G. and Norton, K. (2016) 'Game style in soccer: what is it and can we quantify it?', *International Journal of Performance Analysis in Sport*, 16: 355–372.

Hibbs, A. and O'Donoghue, P.G. (2013) 'Strategy and tactics in sports performance', in T. McGarry, P.G. O'Donoghue and J. Sampaio (eds), *Routledge handbook of sports performance analysis* (pp. 248–258). London: Routledge.

Higham, D.G., Hopkins, W.G., Pyne, D.B. and Anson, J.M. (2014) 'Patterns of play associated with success in international rugby sevens', *International Journal of Performance Analysis in Sport*, 14: 111–122.

Hizan, H., Whipp, P., Reid, M. and Wheat, J. (2014) 'A comparative analysis of the spatial distributions of the serve return', *International Journal of Performance Analysis in Sport*, 14: 884–893.

Hogarth, L.W., Burkett, B.J. and McKean, M.R. (2014) 'Movement patterns in tag football: Influence of playing position, representative selection and fatigue', *International Journal of Performance Analysis in Sport*, 14: 367–383.

Hogarth, L.W., Burkett, B.J. and McKean, M.R. (2015) 'Activity profiles and physiological responses of tag football referees: a case study', *International Journal of Performance Analysis in Sport*, 15: 203–216.

Horne, S (2013) 'The role of performance analysis in elite netball competition structures', in D. Peters and P.G. O'Donoghue (eds), *Performance analysis of sport IX* (pp. 3–9). London: Routledge.

70

Hughes, M.D. (1998) 'The application of notational analysis to racket sports', in A. Lees, I. Maynard, M. Hughes and T. Reilly (eds), *Science and racket sports II* (pp. 211–220). London: E and FN Spon.

Hughes, M.D. and Bartlett, R.M. (2002) 'The use of performance indicators in performance analysis', *Journal of Sports Sciences*, 20: 739–754.

Hughes, M.D., David, R. and Dawkins, N. (2001) 'Critical incidents leading to shooting in soccer', in M. Hughes (ed), *Notational analysis of sport III* (pp. 10–21). Cardiff, UK: CPA Press, UWIC.

Hughes, M., Dawkins, N., David, R. and Mills, J. (1997) 'The perturbation effect and goal opportunities in soccer', *Journal of Sports Sciences*, 16: 20.

Hughes, M., Dawkins, N., David, R. and Mills, J. (1998) 'The perturbation effect and goal opportunities in soccer', *Journal of Sports Sciences*, 16: 20.

Johnston, R.J., Watsford, M.L., Pine, M.J., Spurrs, R.W. and Sporri, D. (2013) 'Assessment of 5 Hz and 10 Hz GPS units for measuring athlete movement demands', *International Journal of Performance Analysis in Sport*, 13: 262–274.

Kajmovic, H., Kapur, A., Radjo, I. and Mekic, A. (2014) 'Differences in performance between winners and defeated wrestlers in the European championships for cadets', *International Journal of Performance Analysis in Sport*, 14: 252–261.

Kajmovic, H. and Radjo, I. (2014) 'A comparison of gripping configuration and throwing techniques efficiency index in judo between male and female judoka during Bosnia and Herzegovina senior state championships', *International Journal of Performance Analysis in Sport*, 14: 620–634.

Kirk, C., Hurst, H.T. and Atkins, S. (2015) 'Measuring the workload of mixed martial arts using accelerometry, time motion analysis and lactate', *International Journal of Performance Analysis in Sport*, 15: 359–370.

Lage, I.P., Gutiérrez-Santiago, A., Curran, T.P. and Lage, M.Á.P. (2016) 'Injury assessment of common nage-waza judo techniques for amateur judokas', *International Journal of Performance Analysis in Sport*, 16: 961–982.

Lage, I.P., Guttiérrez-Santiago, A. and Lage, M-Á.P. (2014) 'The teaching-learning process of judo techniques improved using knowledge of errors in Tai-otoshi as a case study', *International Journal of Performance Analysis in Sport*, 14: 841–851.

Lago-Peñas, C., Dellal, A., Owen, A.L., Gómez-Ruano, M-Á. (2015) 'The influence of the extra-time period on physical performance in elite soccer', *International Journal of Performance Analysis in Sport*, 15: 830–839.

Lago-Peñas, C. Gómez-Ruano, M., Sampaio, J. and Owen, A.L. (2016) 'The effects of a player dismissal on competitive technical match performance', *International Journal of Performance Analysis in Sport*, 16: 792–800.

Lago-Peñas, C., Gómez-Ruano, M-Á., Viaño, J., González-García, I. and Fernández-Villarino, M.d.L.Á. (2013) 'Home advantage in elite handball: the impact of the quality of opposition on team performance', *International Journal of Performance Analysis in Sport*, 13: 724–733.

Lapresa, D., Anguera, M.T., Alsasua, R., Arana, J. and Garzón, B. (2013) 'Comparative analysis of T-patterns using real time data and simulated data by assignment of conventional durations: the construction of efficacy in children's basketball', *International Journal of Performance Analysis in Sport*, 13: 321–339.

Larkin, P., O'Connor, D. and Williams, A.M. (2016) 'Establishing validity and reliability of a movement awareness and technical skill (MATS) analysis instrument in soccer', *International Journal of Performance Analysis in Sport*, 16: 191–202.

Latorre-Román, P.Á., Jiménez, M.M., Hermoso, V.M.S., Sánchez, J.S., Molina, A.M., Fuentes, A.R. and García-Pinillos, F. (2015) 'Acute effect of a long-distance road competition on foot strike patterns, inversion and kinematics parameters in endurance runners', *International Journal of Performance Analysis in Sport*, 15: 588–597.

Lees, A. (2008) 'Qualitative biomechanical analysis of technique', in M. Hughes and I.M. Franks (eds), *The essentials of performance analysis: an introduction* (pp. 162–179). London: Routledge.

Liebermann, D.G. and Franks, I.M. (2008) 'Video feedback and information technologies', in M. Hughes and I.M. Franks (eds), *The essentials of performance analysis: an introduction* (pp. 40–50). London: Routledge.

Liebermann, D.G., Katz, L., Hughes, M.D. and Franks, I.M. (2002) 'Advances in the application of information technology to sport performance', *Journal of Sports Sciences*, 20: 755–769.

Linke, D. and Lames, M. (2016) 'Substitutions in elite male field hockey – a case study', *International Journal of Performance Analysis in Sport*, 16: 924–934.

Liu, H., Hopkins, W., Gómez, M-Á. and Molinuevo, J.S. (2013) 'Inter-operator reliability of live football match statistics from OPTA Sportsdata', *International Journal of Performance Analysis in Sport*, 13: 803–821.

Liu, H., Yi, Q., Giménez, J-V., Gómez, M-Á. and Lago-Peñas, C. (2015) 'Performance profiles of football teams in the UEFA Champions League considering situational efficiency', *International Journal of Performance Analysis in Sport*, 15: 371–390.

Liu, H., Zhao, G., Gómez, M-Á., Molinuevo, J.S., Giménez, J.V. and Kang, H. (2013) 'Time-motion analysis on Chinese male field hockey players', *International Journal of Performance Analysis in Sport*, 13: 340–352.

Lockie, R.G., Jeffriess, M.D., McGann, T.S. and Callaghan, S.J. (2014) 'Ankle muscle function during preferred and non-preferred 45° directional cutting in semi-professional basketball players', *International Journal of Performance Analysis in Sport*, 14: 574–593.

Loffing, F., Hagemann, N. and Strauss, B. (2010) 'Automated processes in tennis: do left-handed players benefit from the tactical preferences of their opponents?', *Journal of Sports Sciences*, 28: 435–443.

Lorains, M., Ball, K. and MacMahon, C. (2013) 'Performance analysis for decision making in team sports', *International Journal of Performance Analysis in Sport*, 13: 110–119.

Lythe, J. and Kilding, A.E. (2013) 'The effect of substitution frequency on the physical and technical outputs of strikers during field hockey match play', *International Journal of Performance Analysis in Sport*, 13: 848–859.

72

Mao, L., Peng, Z., Liu, H. and Gómez, M-Á. (2016) 'Identifying keys to win in the Chinese professional soccer league', *International Journal of Performance Analysis in Sport*, 16: 935–947.

Martinent, G. and Ferrand, C. (2015) 'Are facilitating emotions really facilitative? A field study of the relationships between discrete emotions and objective performance during competition', *International Journal of Performance Analysis in Sport*, 15: 501–512.

McGarry, T. and Franks, I.M. (1994) 'Stochastic approaches to predicting competition squash match play', *Journal of Sports Sciences*, 12: 573–884.

McGarry, T., O'Donoghue, P.G. and Sampaio, J. (2013) *Routledge handbook of sports performance analysis*. London: Routledge.

McKenzie, R. and Cushion, C. (2013) 'Performance analysis in professional soccer: player and coach perspectives', in D. Peters and P.G. O'Donoghue (eds), *Performance analysis of sport IX* (pp. 23–32). London: Routeldge.

Miarka, B., Branco, B.H.M., Del Vecchio, F.B., Camey, S. and Franchini, E. (2015) 'Development and validation of a time-motion judo combat model based on the Markovian Processes', *International Journal of Performance Analysis in Sport*, 15: 315–331.

Miarka, B., Coswig, V.S., Del Vecchio, F.B., Brito, C.J. and Amtman, J. (2015) 'Comparisons of time-motion analysis of mixed martial arts rounds by weight divisions', *International Journal of Performance Analysis in Sport*, 15: 1189–1201.

Miarka, B., Del Vecchio, F.B., Julianetti, R., Cury, R., Camey, S. and Franchini, E. (2016) 'Time-motion and tactical analysis of Olympic judo fighters', *International Journal of Performance Analysis in Sport*, 16: 133–142.

Miarka, B., Fukuda, D.H., Del Vecchio, F.B. and Franchini, E. (2016) 'Discriminant analysis of technical-tactical actions in high-level judo athletes', *International Journal of Performance Analysis in Sport*, 16: 30–39.

Miller, G.A., Collins, N.A., Stewart, M.J. and Challis, D.G. (2015) 'Throwing technique and efficiency in the 2013 British judo championships', *International Journal of Performance Analysis in Sport*, 15: 53–68.

Mohammed, A., Shafizadeh, M. and Platt, G.K. (2014) 'Effects of the level of expertise on the physical and technical demands in futsal', *International Journal of Performance Analysis in Sport*, 14: 473–481.

Morgans, R., Adams, D., Mullen, R. and Williams, M.D. (2014) 'Changes in physical performance variables in an English Championship League team across the competitive season: the effect of possession', *International Journal of Performance Analysis in Sport*, 14: 493–503.

Morland, B., Bottoms, L., Sinclair, J. and Bourne, N. (2013) 'Can change of direction speed and reactive agility differentiate female hockey players?', *International Journal of Performance Analysis in Sport*, 13: 510–521.

Mortimer, P. and Burt, E.W. (2014) 'Does momentum exist in elite handball?', *International Journal of Performance Analysis in Sport*, 14: 788–800.

Moss, B. and O'Donoghue, P.G. (2015) 'Momentum in US Open men's singles tennis', *International Journal of Performance Analysis in Sport*, 15: 884–896.

Mudric, M., Cuk, I., Nedeljkovic, A., Jovanovic, S. and Jaric, S. (2015) 'Evaluation of video-based method for the measurement of reaction time in specific sport situation', *International Journal of Performance Analysis in Sport*, 15: 1077–1089.

Murray, S., Maylor, D. and Hughes, M. (1998) 'A preliminary investigation into the provision of computerised analysis feedback to elite squash players', in A. Lees, I. Maynard, M. Hughes and T. Reilly (eds), *Science and racket sports II* (pp. 235–240). London: E and FN Spon.

Najdan, M.J., Robins, M.T. and Glazier, P.S. (2014) 'Determinants of success in English domestic Twenty20 cricket', *International Journal of Performance Analysis in Sport*, 14: 276–295.

O'Donoghue, P.G. (1998) 'Time-motion analysis of work-rate in elite soccer', in M. Hughes and F. Tavares (eds), *Notational analysis of sport 4* (pp. 65–70). Porto, Portugal: University of Porto.

O'Donoghue, P.G. (2010) *Research methods for sports performance analysis*. London: Routledge.

O'Donoghue, P.G. (2013) 'Momentum in tennis matches in Grand Slam tournaments', in D. Peters and P.G. O'Donoghue (eds), *Performance analysis of sport IX* (pp. 174–179). London: Routeldge.

O'Donoghue, P.G. (2014) 'Relative age effect on elite tennis strategy for players born before and after 1st January 1985', *International Journal of Performance Analysis in Sport*, 14: 453–462.

O'Donoghue, P.G. (2015) *An introduction to performance analysis of sport*. London: Routledge.

O'Donoghue, P.G. (2016) 'Wicket loss and risk taking during the 2011 and 2015 Cricket World Cups', *International Journal of Performance Analysis in Sport*, 16: 80–95.

O'Donoghue, P.G. and Brown, E.J. (2009) 'Sequences of service points and the misperception of momentum in elite tennis', *International Journal of Performance Analysis in Sport*, 9: 113–127.

O'Donoghue, P.G. and Ingram, B. (2001) 'A notational analysis of elite tennis strategy', *Journal of Sports Sciences*, 19: 107–115.

O'Donoghue, P.G. and Robinson, G. (2016a) 'The effect of dismissals on work-rate in English FA Premier League soccer', *International Journal of Performance Analysis in Sport*, 16: 898–909.

O'Donoghue, P.G. and Robinson, G. (2016b) 'Score-line effect on work-rate in English FA Premier League soccer', *International Journal of Performance Analysis in Sport*, 16: 910–923.

Olsen, E. and Larsen, O. (1997) 'Use of match analysis by coaches', in T. Reilly, J. Bangsbo and M. Hughes (eds), *Science and football III* (pp. 209–220). London: E and FN Spon.

Ordóñez, E.G., Gonzalez, C.T. and Pérez, M.d.C.I. (2015) 'Offensive performance indicators in a regular season of water-polo', *International Journal of Performance Analysis in Sport*, 15: 1114–1123.

Ouergui, I., Hssin, N., Franchini, E., Gmada, N., Bouhlel, E. (2013) 'Technical and tactical analysis of high level kickboxing matches', *International Journal of Performance Analysis in Sport*, 13: 294–309.

Paixão, P., Sampaio, J., Almeida, C.H. and Duarte, R. (2015) 'How does match status affects the passing sequences of top-level European soccer teams?', *International Journal of Performance Analysis in Sport*, 15: 229–240.

Palao, J.M. and Hernández-Hernández, E. (2014) 'Game statistical system and criteria used by Spanish volleyball coaches', *International Journal of Performance Analysis in Sport*, 14: 564–573.

Palao, J.M. and Ortega, E. (2015) 'Skill efficacy in men's beach volleyball', *International Journal of Performance Analysis in Sport*, 15: 125–134.

Palao, J.M., López-Martínez, A.B., Valadés, D. and Ortega, E. (2015) 'Physical actions and work-rest time in women's beach volleyball', *International Journal of Performance Analysis in Sport*, 15: 424–429.

Penitente, G. (2014) 'Performance analysis of the female Yurchenko layout on the table vault', *International Journal of Performance Analysis in Sport*, 14: 84–97.

Pérez, M.d.C.I., Ordóñez, E.G. and Gonzalez, C.T. (2016) 'Keys to success in high level Water Polo teams', *International Journal of Performance Analysis in Sport*, 16: 995–1006.

Poizat, G., Sève, C. and Saury, J. (2013) 'Qualitative aspects in performance analysis', in T. McGarry, P.G. O'Donoghue and J. Sampaio (eds), *Routledge handbook of sports performance analysis* (pp. 309–320). London: Routledge.

Prieto, J., Gómez, M-Á. and Sampaio, J. (2015) 'Players' exclusions effects on elite handball teams' scoring performance during close games', *International Journal of Performance Analysis in Sport*, 15: 983–996.

Prüßner, R. and Siegle, M. (2015) 'Additional time in soccer – influence of league and referee', *International Journal of Performance Analysis in Sport*, 15: 551–559.

Puente, C., Del Coso, J., Salinero, J.J. and Abián-Vicén, J. (2015) 'Basketball performance indicators during the ACB regular season from 2003 to 2013', *International Journal of Performance Analysis in Sport*, 15: 935–948.

Pulling, C., Eldridge, D. and Lomax, J. (2016) 'Centre passes in the UK Netball Super League', *International Journal of Performance Analysis in Sport*, 16: 389–400.

Pulling, C., Robins, M. and Rixon, T. (2013) 'Defending corner kicks: analysis from the English Premier League', *International Journal of Performance Analysis in Sport*, 13: 135–148.

Pulling, C. and Stenning, M. (2015) 'Offloads in rugby union: Northern and Southern Hemisphere international teams', *International Journal of Performance Analysis in Sport*, 15: 217–228.

Radek, V. (2014) 'Identification of peak performance age in track and field athletics', *International Journal of Performance Analysis in Sport*, 14: 238–251.

Rahnama, N., Reilly, T. and Lees, A. (2002) 'Injury risk associated with playing actions during competitive soccer', *British Journal of Sports Medicine*, 36: 354–359.

Reeves, M.J. and Roberts, S.J. (2013) 'Perceptions of performance analysis in elite youth football', *International Journal of Performance Analysis in Sport*, 13: 200–211.

Reilly, T. and Thomas, V. (1976) 'A motion analysis of work rate in different positional roles in professional football match play', *Journal of Human Movement Studies*, 2: 87–97.

Rey, E., Lago-Ballesteros, J. and Padrón-Cabo, A. (2015) 'Timing and tactical analysis of player substitutions in the UEFA Champions League', *International Journal of Performance Analysis in Sport*, 15: 840–850.

Roddy, R., Lamb, K. and Worsfold, P. (2014) 'The importance of perturbations in elite squash: An analysis of their ability to successfully predict rally outcome', *International Journal of Performance Analysis in Sport*, 14: 652–679.

Rosario, S., Antonio, T., Carlo, M., Laura, C. and Antonio, A. (2015) 'Match analysis heart-rate and CMJ of beach soccer players during amateur competition', *International Journal of Performance Analysis in Sport*, 15: 241–253.

Rouissi, M., Chtara, M., Owen, A., Chaalali, A, Chaouachi, A., Gabbett, T. and Chamri, K. (2015) ' "Side-stepping manoeuvre": not the more efficient technique to change direction amongst young elite soccer players', *International Journal of Performance Analysis in Sport*, 15: 749–763.

Saavedra, J.M., Escalante, Y., Mansilla, M., Tella, V., Madera, J. and García-Hermoso, A. (2016) 'Water polo game-related statistics in women's international championships as a function of final score differences', *International Journal of Performance Analysis in Sport*, 16: 276–289.

Salci, Y. (2015) 'The metabolic demands and ability to sustain work outputs during kickboxing competitions', *International Journal of Performance Analysis in Sport*, 15: 39–52.

Sanchez-Pay, A., Torres-Luque, G., Cabello-Manrique, D., Sanz-Rivas, D. and Palao, J.M. (2015) 'Match analysis of women's wheelchair tennis matches for the Paralympic Games', *International Journal of Performance Analysis in Sport*, 15: 69–79.

Sarmento, H., Anguera, M.T., Pereira, A., Marques, A., Campaniço, J. and Leitão, J. (2014) 'Patterns of play in the counterattack of elite football teams – a mixed method approach', *International Journal of Performance Analysis in Sport*, 14: 411–427.

Sarmento, H., Barbosa, A., Anguera, M.T., Campaniço, J. and Leitão, J. (2013) 'Regular patterns of play in the counter-attacks of the FC Barcelona and Manchester United football teams', in D. Peters and P. O'Donoghue (eds), *Performance analysis of sport IX* (pp. 57–64). London: Routledge.

Sarmento, H., Bradley, P. and Travassos, B. (2015) 'The transition from match analysis to intervention: optimising the coaching process in elite futsal', *International Journal of Performance Analysis in Sport*, 15: 471–488.

Scanlan, A.T., Teramoto, M., Delforce, M. and Dalbo, V.J. (2016) 'Do better things come in smaller packages? Reducing game duration slows game pace and alters statistics associated with winning in basketball', *International Journal of Performance Analysis in Sport*, 16: 157–170.

Schoeman, R., Coetzee, D. and Schall, R. (2015) 'Positional tackle and collision rates in Super Rugby', *International Journal of Performance Analysis in Sport*, 15: 1022–1036.

Sharp, T., Halaki, M., Greene, A. and Vanwanseele, B. (2014) 'An EMG assessment of front row rugby union scrummaging', *International Journal of Performance Analysis in Sport*, 14: 225–237.

Shaw, B.S., Dullabh, M., Forbes, G., Brandkamp, J-L. and Shaw, I. (2015) 'Analysis of physiological determinants during a single bout of crossfit', *International Journal of Performance Analysis in Sport*, 15: 809–815.

Siegle, M. and Prüßner, R. (2013) 'Additional time in soccer', *International Journal of Performance Analysis in Sport*, 13: 716–723.

76

Sinclair, J. and Bottoms, L. (2013) 'Gender differences in the kinetics and lower extremity kinematics of the fencing lunge', *International Journal of Performance Analysis in Sport*, 13: 440–451.

Sinclair, J., Currigan, G., Fewtrell, D.J. and Taylor, P.J. (2014) 'Biomechanical correlates of club-head velocity during the golf swing', *International Journal of Performance Analysis in Sport*, 14: 54–63.

Sinclair, J., Taylor, P.J., Atkins, S., Bullen, J., Smith, A. and Hobbs, S.J. (2014) 'The influence of lower extremity kinematics on ball release velocity during in-step place kicking in rugby union', *International Journal of Performance Analysis in Sport*, 14: 64–72.

Smyth, G. and Hughes, M.D. (2016) 'Efficacy of half-back play in rugby and the impact of substitutions', ISPAS International Workshop, Carlow, Ireland, 22nd–23rd March 2016.

Sparks, M., Coetzee, B. and Gabbett, T. (2016a) 'Variations in high-intensity running and fatigue during semi-professional soccer matches', *International Journal of Performance Analysis in Sport*, 16: 122–132.

Sparks, M., Coetzee, B. and Gabbett, T.J. (2016b) 'Yo-Yo intermittent recovery test thresholds to determine positional internal match loads of semi-professional soccer players', *International Journal of Performance Analysis in Sport*, 16: 1065–1075.

Stavrinou, P.S., Argyrou, M. and Hadjicharalambous, M. (2016) 'Physiological and metabolic responses during a simulated judo competition among cadet athletes', *International Journal of Performance Analysis in Sport*, 16: 848–859.

Stean, D., Barnes, A. and Churchill, S.M. (2015) 'Effect of the "Crouch, Bind, Set" engagement routine on scrum performance in English Premiership Rugby', *International Journal of Performance Analysis in Sport*, 15: 1202–1212.

Štirn, I., Dolinar, R. and Erčulj, F. (2016) 'Influence of different heights and widths of basic athletic stance on the response time in basketball', *International Journal of Performance Analysis in Sport*, 16: 53–63.

Stöckl, M. and Morgan, S. (2013) 'Visualization and analysis of spatial characteristics of attacks in field hockey', *International Journal of Performance Analysis in Sport*, 13: 160–178.

Stutzig, N., Zimmermann, B., Büsch, D. and Siebert, T. (2015) 'Analysis of game variables to predict scoring and performance levels in elite men's volleyball', *International Journal of Performance Analysis in Sport*, 15: 816–829.

Tan, Y.L. and Krasilshchikov, O. (2015) 'Diversity of attacking actions in Malaysian junior and senior taekwondo players', *International Journal of Performance Analysis in Sport*, 15: 913–923.

Tenga, A., Zubillaga, A., Caro, O. and Fradua, F. (2015) 'Explorative study on patterns of game structure in male and female matches from elite Spanish soccer', *International Journal of Performance Analysis in Sport*, 15: 411–423.

Thomas, D.G.D. (2015) 'A comparison of positional measurement methods in tennis', *International Journal of Performance Analysis in Sport*, 15: 1227–1234.

Thomson, E. and Lamb, K. (2016) 'The technical demands of amateur boxing: Effect of contest outcome, weight and ability', *International Journal of Performance Analysis in Sport*, 16: 203–215.

Tirp, J.J., Baker, J., Weigelt, M. and Schorer, J. (2014) 'Combat stance in judo – laterality differences between and within competition levels', *International Journal of Performance Analysis in Sport*, 14: 217–224.

Torres-Luque, G., Ramirez, A., Cabello-Manrique, D., Nikolaidis, P.T. and Ramón Alvero-Cruz, J. (2015) 'Match analysis of elite players during paddle tennis competition', *International Journal of Performance Analysis in Sport*, 15: 1135–1144.

Travassos, B., Vilar, L., Araújo, D. and McGarry, T. (2014) 'Tactical performance changes with equal vs unequal numbers of players in small-sided football games', *International Journal of Performance Analysis in Sport*, 14: 594–605.

Vahed, Y., Kraak, W. and Venter, R. (2014) 'The effect of the law changes on time variables of the South African Currie Cup Tournament during 2007 and 2013', *International Journal of Performance Analysis in Sport*, 14: 866–883.

Valladares, N., García-Tormo, J.V. and João, P.V. (2016) 'Analysis of variables affecting performance in senior female volleyball World Championship 2014', *International Journal of Performance Analysis in Sport*, 16: 401–411.

van Rooyen, M.K. (2016) 'Seasonal variations in the winning scores of matches in the Sevens World Series', *International Journal of Performance Analysis in Sport*, 16: 290–304.

Villarejo, D., Palao, J.M., Ortega, E., Gomez-Ruano, M-Á. and Kraak, W. (2015) 'Match-related statistics discriminating between playing positions during the men's 2011 Rugby World Cup', *International Journal of Performance Analysis in Sport*, 15: 97–111.

Williams, J.J. (2008) 'Rule changes in sport and the role of notation', in M. Hughes and I.M. Franks (eds), *The essentials of performance analysis: an introduction* (pp. 226–242). London: Routledge.

Williams, J.J., Smith, K. and DaMata, F. (2014) 'Risk factors associated with horse-falls in UK Class 1 Steeplechases: 1999–2011', *International Journal of Performance Analysis in Sport*, 14: 148–152.

Woods, C.T. (2016) 'The use of team performance indicator characteristics to explain ladder position at the conclusion of the Australian Football League home and away season', *International Journal of Performance Analysis in Sport*, 16: 837–847.

Worsfold, P.R. and Page, M. (2014) 'The influences of rugby spin pass technique on movement time, ball velocity and passing accuracy', *International Journal of Performance Analysis in Sport*, 14: 296–306.

Wright, C., Atkins, S., Jones, B. and Todd, J. (2013) 'The role of performance analysts within the coaching process: Performance Analysts Survey "The role of performance analysts in elite football club settings"', *International Journal of Performance Analysis in Sport*, 13: 240–261.

Wright, C., Carling, C. and Collins, D. (2014) 'The wider context of performance analysis and it application in the football coaching process', *International Journal of Performance Analysis in Sport*, 14: 709–733.

Wright, C., Carling, C., Lawlor, C. and Collins, D. (2016) 'Elite football player engagement with performance analysis', *International Journal of Performance Analysis in Sport*, 16: 1007–1032.

Wylde, M.J., Tan, F.H.Y. and O'Donoghue, P.G. (2013) 'A time-motion analysis of elite women's foil fencing', *International Journal of Performance Analysis in Sport*, 13: 365–376.

Zhang, Z., Halkon, B., Chou, S.M. and Qu, X. (2016) 'A novel phase-aligned analysis on motion patterns of table tennis strokes', *International Journal of Performance Analysis in Sport*, 16: 305–316.

Zienius, M., Skarbalius, A., Zuoza, A. and Pukenas, K. (2015) 'Total time taken and heart rate changes of youth golfers during pre-shot routines in on-course conditions', *International Journal of Performance Analysis in Sport*, 15: 560–571.

CHAPTER 4

ENTERPRISE AND DEVELOPMENT PROJECTS

OVERVIEW

The previous chapters of this book have already mentioned enterprise and development projects. These projects are different than traditional scientific research projects done in sports performance analysis, and so the current chapter is included to describe them. Traditional scientific research projects generate general knowledge about sports performance in answering some question about the effect of some factor on sports performance or the relationship between performance variables of interest. Enterprise and development projects do not seek to produce general knowledge about the nature of sports performance or the factors that are associated with success. These projects are no less academic than scientific research projects, but the research conducted is of a much more applied nature. Enterprise projects involve market research about a business idea to develop a product or service. For example, a student may wish to provide a performance analysis support service for athletes and coaches, develop a system to be used within this service and provide the service in order to undertake market research about it. Alternatively the enterprise project could be to undertake market research about a product idea the student has. The market research done within enterprise projects is used as the basis of a business plan which is discussed by the student. Development projects differ from enterprise projects in that they evaluate the effectiveness of some product or service rather than making the business case for it. For example, a performance analysis service could be evaluated in terms of its effectiveness within the coaching process where it is used. This may include a combination of reflective analysis and performance trend monitoring. Coaches and/or players may be interviewed about their experiences of support services, any benefits from the services and areas for further enhancement. The chapter contains two broad sections; one on enterprise projects and one on development projects. Either project type could be undertaken for a product development task or a service provision. In this chapter, we will use an example of service provision in the discussion of enterprise projects and an example of software development to discuss development projects.

ENTERPRISE PROJECTS

Entrepreneurship

There has been an increase in small to medium enterprises and in the number of people they employ nationally in the United States (Barrow et al., 2005: 1 and 9), the UK (Williams, 2013: 4) and other countries (Burns, 2016: 16–18). Small businesses are important to the economy and are a breeding ground for new industries (Bolton, 1971). Enterprise is important to government in terms of employment, economic growth, regeneration and social inclusion (Bridge and O'Neill, 2013: 301–302). Government encourages enterprise; government policy on enterprise can involve early intervention to increase the number of start-up businesses or late intervention to increase the proportion of start-up businesses able to exploit opportunities (Burns, 2016: 45–48). Government support includes training, mentorship schemes and forums where problems can be discussed with other entrepreneurs (Williams, 2013: 27–36). Other support includes internet resources, media, books, exhibitions and forums.

Entrepreneurship and sports marketing are major academic areas in their own right, with major textbooks now being in their third editions or higher (Bridge and O'Neill, 2013; Burns, 2016; Williams, 2013). Entrepreneurship has been described as an applied science (Bygrave, 1989), with modules and whole programmes being delivered on entrepreneurship within universities (Bridge and O'Neil, 2013: 2). Students undertaking enterprise projects are strongly encouraged to read texts on enterprise development, business planning and marketing as well as material in the domain area of interest to their project. Some books on enterprise development describe real-world case studies (Barrow et al., 2005; Burns, 2016), some of which may be in areas or involving challenges that are similar to those encountered in the projects that students are planning to undertake.

Enterprise projects, in their widest sense, include real-world projects in which entrepreneurs develop business ideas, start businesses, and grow and maintain the businesses until they are mature. An enterprise project typically commences with the development of a business idea which is worked into a business concept. Market research may then be done to inform business planning. The business plan includes short-term and long-term forecasts of costs, income and growth as well as marketing strategies. The business plan is used when making decisions about whether or not to launch the business, product or service. There are two 'go/no-go' decision points described by Burns (2016: 139–140). The first is when the initial idea is being considered as a concept; the entrepreneur(s) may decide at that point that the idea is clearly not viable and there is little point in undertaking market research related to the proposed enterprise. The second 'go/no-go' point is when the concept has been considered and market research has been undertaken. A product specification will exist, and the entrepreneur(s) will have gathered useful market information through activities such as prototyping and market testing. A business model will have been formulated, allowing the prospects for a successful enterprise to be considered. A reasonably well-informed decision can be taken at this point to launch the product or not. Once launched, a successful enterprise can grow and mature. Over time, there may be innovations made to maintain the enterprise and stimulate further growth.

Enterprise projects undertaken within university degrees are done in a restricted time frame during students' final years of study. Therefore, these projects do not cover the full lifecycle of an enterprise through to maturity. The student's enterprise idea is more likely to be suited to sole trading, rather than partnership, limited partnership or co-operative arrangements. Once a student's degree programme has completed, they may decide to take the idea further and launch the given product or service. However, the current chapter will focus on those stages of enterprise projects likely to be done within a degree project. Growth and maintenance of the business, monitoring of market and technology changes, environmental scanning, growth strategies, succession planning and selling of businesses are outside the scope of the chapter. Issues such as legal obligations, taxation, accounting, auditing and the rights and responsibilities of employers are also outside the scope of the current chapter, and students interested in these areas are encouraged to consult specialist textbooks on entrepreneurship. Background history is also outside the scope of the current book, but an excellent history of entrepreneurship and government policy is provided within Bridge and O'Neill's (2013) textbook.

As has already been mentioned, entrepreneurship is an academic area, and enterprise projects involve academic study and writing as well as the practical and intellectual enterprise activities within the projects. An enterprise project is written up as a dissertation report, with some universities also having a 'Dragon's Den'–type presentation as part of the assessment of the enterprise project module. The write-up includes a literature review, methods, results and discussion, which is a similar format to a traditional scientific research project. Further detail of the written report is included in Chapter 9 of the current book. The purpose of this current section is to briefly discuss enterprise dissertation projects in general with specific coverage of enterprise projects in sports performance analysis. Enterprise projects will be discussed using an example of a performance analysis support service in a coaching context. In the example, the performance analysis service is tested in the coaching context in order to obtain market feedback.

Type of student

The type of student who undertakes an enterprise project in sports performance analysis is typically a student with a strong vocational focus who has aspirations to take the enterprise idea forward after the degree programme is completed. The enterprise idea could be to develop a sports performance analysis product or service. Students within joint honours programmes with relevant technology and/or engineering content may develop a physical product. Students who have completed software development modules within their programme of study may develop a software product within their enterprise product. Students with a strong vocational interest in sports performance analysis are well suited to enterprise projects in which they provide a sports performance analysis service. They have typically taken work experience modules in addition to performance analysis modules where their interest in practical performance analysis has developed.

As well as being aspiring performance analysts, students undertaking enterprise projects may have ambitions to run sports performance analysis businesses; therefore, they also need to be interested in entrepreneurship. Students who are interested in developing into sports performance analysis entrepreneurs should be encouraged to do so. They should not be put off by misperceptions of the characteristics of entrepreneurs. Drucker's (1999) research found that there are entrepreneurs with a full range of physiques and personalities. Indeed general perceptions of entrepreneurs have changed over the last 200 years (Burns, 2016: 9). Burns (2016: 61) discussed common myths about entrepreneurs who are stereotypically perceived as being different than other people: full of ideas, willing to take risks, having money and very good at forecasting. Burns states that these misperceptions are actually psychological barriers to entrepreneurship. While there may be individuals with natural entrepreneurial flair, entrepreneurship can be nurtured through training and support (Bridge and O'Neill, 2013: 76–80). In dispelling the myths about entrepreneurs, Burns (2016: 64) characterised entrepreneurs as people who are optimally ambitious, make decisions quickly (often based on incomplete information), manage risk and are able to set challenging but attainable goals in relation to their capabilities. New entrepreneurs come from a variety of backgrounds and may have planned to go into business or may have gone into business as a result of redundancy, to make up for cut hours or because of a reduced current income (Williams, 2013: 3–4). There are some characteristics that entrepreneurs should have, such as achievement motives, desire for independence, determination, creativity, initiative and self-confidence (Bridge and O'Neill, 2013: 66–68). They are also motivated by wealth creation and the given type of work (Williams, 2013: 4), and they are innovative (Barrow et al., 2015: 26).

Enterprise ideas

There are many sources of business ideas (Barrow et al., 2005: 16–18), including previous experience in business and personal interests and skills. Experience in business could be as an employee where skills such as customer care and selling may have been developed. Experience as a customer helps aspiring entrepreneurs identify gaps in the market for new products and services. Skills that have been developed in the given domain area may be marketable together with more general business skills. Entrepreneurs can use brainstorming to develop mind maps to

84

portray ideas under discussion (Burns, 2016: 103–107). A further way of identifying ideas is exploring existing products to identify gaps in features provided that can be addressed by the student's enterprise project (Burns, 2016: 107–110).

Burns (2016: 91–94) described how skills for discovering business ideas can be developed. These skills are association, questioning, observing, experimenting and networking. Associating and connecting apparently unrelated things can lead to business ideas, such as applying performance analysis technology within the training of firefighters. Simple questions such as 'why not' and 'what if' help entrepreneurs explore possible developments that others don't identify. Observing behaviour helps identify improvements in practice or leads to ideas for streamlining processes. Experimenting and prototyping not only tests products and services but also generates further ideas to solve emerging problems. Networking allows entrepreneurs to test ideas with individuals representing relevant market sectors.

As with any other type of dissertation, students may have a selection of ideas they are considering and need to make a decision about which one to follow for their project. In deciding on a single idea for their enterprise project, students can consider their own interests and aspirations as well as which idea is best suited to the given market.

Example: a performance analysis support service

The example used to illustrate an enterprise project is a student providing a performance analysis service for volleyball. The student develops a prototype system using a generic commercial video analysis package. In developing the system, the student has considered standard volleyball-specific packages such as Data Volley (www.dataproject.com, accessed 15 February 2017), listed their strengths and weaknesses, identified gaps in the information these systems provide and proposed some unique features in the new system that are not provided by competitors. The performance analysis service uses the commercial package within a wider system where event lists and data matrices are exported to spreadsheet packages, allowing volleyball-specific reports to be produced. Video sequences are provided online so that players can access these through a password-protected coaching support environment. All software and hardware used for performance analysis support belong to the university. This means that the student does not need to invest in equipment and software during the enterprise project, but if the idea is taken further, once the student completes their programme of study, then they will need to purchase the necessary resources. The system is developed by the student and undergoes several amendments as it is presented to coaches and players in order to gather further requirements and implement these. This gives the players and coaches a sense of ownership of the system, making acceptance of the system more likely. The performance analysis service is provided by the student over a ten-week period in which the team plays ten matches. During this ten-week period, the student makes reflective notes on their experience in providing the specific service, records usage statistics for the online coaching support environment, sits in on briefing and debriefing meetings of the squad and interviews coaches and key players about the system.

Market research

The main research activity of an enterprise project is market research. As has already been mentioned, the student in our example uses a variety of data gathering techniques during market research: interviews, reflective notes, usage statistics for the online coaching support environment as well as team performance statistics over the ten matches played during the ten-week period when the performance analysis service is provided. The main purpose of market research is to understand the market and identify potential consumers for the product or service being developed. Understanding the market involves understanding its characteristics, structure, size and growth potential (Williams, 2013: 13). The student needs to understand the attitudes and behaviour of people in different market sectors who could benefit from the given product or service. Market trends need to be recognised, especially in areas like sports performance analysis where technology is developing rapidly and coach and player expectations are become more demanding. In the example of the student providing a sports performance analysis service, the culture of a volleyball squad is important to understand. What are their training patterns during different times of the season? What aspects of play are emphasised in training? What areas of play are discussed during squad briefings and debriefings? How do coaches and players use information during matches, during training and between matches and training sessions? How are decisions made? What previous experience do they have

86

of sports performance analysis support? Do their competitors use sports performance analysis services? Ultimately, the student wants to understand the way the squad works and integrate the proposed service into their work pattern to enhance their use of information and the quality of decision making.

Providing the service gives the student first-hand experience of the challenges of providing performance analysis support to a competitive volleyball squad. The service can be experimented with as the student learns more about the coaching environment. The time required for the analyst to perform the range of tasks required by the squad can be recorded together with details of elements of the service that work well and elements the squad give the highest priority to. The student is trying to determine how much of a demand there is for the service, potential customers' reasons for investing in the service and how often they will use it, as well as the volume and quality of work involved. Ultimately, market research is about gathering and analysing data to determine whether there is a need for the product or service the entrepreneur (or student) has in mind (Barrow et al., 2005: 37–46). A comprehensive market research exercise helps to satisfy entrepreneurs and potential investors about the need and potential demand for the proposed enterprise idea.

Market research can use desk- and field-based methods (Burns, 2016: 125–129). Desk-based methods involve accessing publicly available pattern and trend information, usually on the internet, while field-based research involves gathering and analysing primary data from the potential market. Desk-based methods are cheap and quick, and they can provide good basic information. Field research, on the other hand, takes longer, is more comprehensive and specific to the enterprise idea and allows for greater quality control. One of the disadvantages of field research is that it increases the chances of competitors discovering what you are planning.

Field research methods include face-to-face interviews, postal questionnaires and online questionnaires (Williams, 2013: 24–26). A combination of methods can be used within a triangulation approach to improve the validity of the findings of market research (Barrow et al., 2005: 45). Competitor analysis can verify that there is a need for the product or service. For example, in our example the student will have reviewed volleyball analysis as provided using standard methods and software such as Data Volley. Direct access to competitors' products and services is a valuable source of market information, but in the absence of such information, advertising material of competitors can still be reviewed. The strengths and weaknesses of what the competition offers can be examined to help determine that the proposed service gives a volleyball squad a competitive edge and that the idea can withstand market pressures (Barrow et al., 2005: 46–48).

Business planning

The business plan must be done by the entrepreneur because they need to have an understanding of the sales levels and cost controls needed to bring the business to profitability. There is training and assistance for business planning, but ultimately it is not something that the entrepreneur should delegate. The student will be in a much better position to produce a business plan once market research has been completed. The business plan needs to forecast sales, estimate costs, set prices and assess the amount of start-up funding that is needed to launch the potential enterprise. The costs include start-up costs, running costs and costs associated with sales. The start-up costs include capital items such as software, computer equipment and camera purchases in the case of the student providing the performance analysis service in volleyball. There may also be initial costs in setting up websites to promote the enterprise, accountancy fees and registration fees. The running costs may include rental licenses for software packages such as video analysis software and online coaching support environments, insurance premiums, phone bills, travel costs, bank loan repayments including interest, and costs associated with services such as internet site maintenance.

Price setting is related to sales forecasts, assuming that fewer customers will pay for an overpriced service. The entrepreneur may have an upper capacity on the number of clients they are able to take on given the time demands of working with each client. The entrepreneur needs to control demand for their services by ensuring that the price is sufficiently high enough for them to earn a living from the enterprise if they will not have time to earn money through other work. The business plan can include expansion and taking on staff to assist with work in the future. However, the entrepreneur would want to become established and be certain they could attract the volume of additional business to justify expanding the staff base of their business. Market research will

88

have identified different types of customer with varying need for the proposed product or service and differing abilities to pay for it. Therefore, the entrepreneur should specify different packages of their product or service that are priced accordingly. The business may attract a blend of different customer types, some wanting a premium service and others being satisfied with a more basic provision. In considering sales, the entrepreneur also needs to consider the size of the potential market. For example, the student providing the volleyball analysis service needs to consider how many volleyball squads have the means to invest in the service. Are there potential conflicts of interest in working for different squads competing in the same tournaments? Do restrictions on performance analysts relating to conflicts of interest justify higher costs for exclusive services? Are there different age group squads within clubs or national governing bodies that could use different levels of the service?

Loan repayments and interest payments have already been mentioned. Loans may be necessitated by the need for start-up funds. The entrepreneur needs to consider the amount of money they can borrow in order to launch the business. Borrowing a large amount of money gives greater opportunity to provide the level of service and grow the business. However, borrowing heavily runs the risk of becoming a bad debtor if the business fails to attract the volume of sales needed to reach a break-even point and move into profit. Borrowing a lower amount of start-up funds reduces interest payments needed and the amount of time needed to pay back the loan. It will also lead to tighter budgets, and the entrepreneur will need to be careful in purchasing assets and using services in the early stages after the business is launched. This means they should avoid any unnecessary extravagances and concentrate on the most necessary purchases needed to launch the business and help it grow.

The development of the business is done after the student has completed their degree programme. Therefore, much of the activity described in the business plan is not done during the enterprise project, indeed it may never be done at all if the project concludes that the business plan is not viable.

Marketing strategy

Entrepreneurs offer different product and service levels at different prices. These different packages are attractive to different consumer types; therefore, they need to be marketed accordingly. The entrepreneur needs to consider whether the product or service can be sold to customers directly or whether intermediaries, such as agents, brokers, wholesalers and retailers, are required. The advent of the internet has made it much easier for enterprises to reach their customers directly. The website for an enterprise should be easy to enter and use, provide clear information and allow visitors to learn what they need to without having their time wasted (Williams, 2013: 146–148). In the case of the student providing the volleyball analysis service, there may be volleyball forums and performance analysis websites where they can advertise. Some of these sites and forums may permit banners for different businesses' websites to be included on a links page. Working with an initial client club can develop an analyst's reputation, and they become known within the given sport, leading to further opportunities for work.

Irrespective of whether the entrepreneur uses the internet, press releases, forums, leaflets or social media for marketing, the message of any marketing material should explain the product or service, including its features, benefits and evidence of these claims (Williams, 2013: 144–166). The marketing information should also be accurate to avoid mis-selling and violating consumer laws. Contact information is essential to include on any marketing material to allow potential customers to present any queries they have. Presentation is very important; the name of the business and the logo should be considered carefully, and marketing material should be effectively laid out, using effective main headlines and photographs, as well as language that potential customers will understand.

Attending exhibitions and conferences can also expose the product to potential customers; however, attending these may be costly and does involve travel and accommodation having to be paid for. Therefore any exhibitions and conferences attended must be worthwhile, with a high concentration of potential customers.

Success and failure

The enterprise project is a learning process within a student's degree programme. Most ideas proposed within enterprise projects are not launched during the student's time at university. Indeed some may never be launched. The success of the student's enterprise project does

90

not depend on whether the product or service is actually launched. At the authors' current university, the handbook (2015–2016) for the enterprise project is very clear about this: 'It is possible to get a first class mark with a business plan that shows the business would not be viable'. In such situations, students will have demonstrated that they are capable of undertaking market research and producing a business plan that informs a good 'no-go' decision and avoids potential business failure. Students should not feel they need to make the case for an enterprise to be launched in order to achieve a good mark for their enterprise project. Concluding that a business venture is viable when the evidence of the student's own market research suggests otherwise could result in marks being lost.

Success in enterprise requires a realistic assessment of strengths and weaknesses, good financial planning, experience of the market, a good idea and a market for the idea that has the potential to grow (Williams, 2013: 7). By completing the enterprise project, students will have gained valuable experience of a market, developed market research and business planning skills and have a much better understanding of their own strengths and weaknesses. With respect to the students' ideas, they will have also been able to "test the water" (Williams, 2013: 78–82) without needing to commit to launching an enterprise. The enterprise may eventually be launched, but even if it isn't, testing the water is something that many experienced and successful entrepreneurs do; they continue their current business ventures while looking for other opportunities, investing time in exploring new ideas and occasionally finding ideas that they do take through to launch.

Considering the example of the student developing the volleyball analysis service, there are additional areas of success to those of gaining experience and skills that have already been mentioned. In undertaking initial desk-based market research, the student will be more familiar with the performance analysis business community, such as where they communicate and advertise. The market research exercise will have been an intensive experience with a single client group: the volleyball squad. This is a limited experience of the market. However, developing knowledge of the sport, sports science support in the sport and squad cultures and their use of performance analysis is important. Some of the knowledge developed may be generic to team sports, and so the student may diversify the service to other sports during their career after university, rather than restricting their market to volleyball.

DEVELOPMENT PROJECTS

Software development within sports programmes

We will discuss development projects using a software development project as an example. The specific example is to develop a system to automatically recognise a tactical aspect of soccer using event and player movement data. The stages of requirements analysis, specification, design, implementation and testing apply to the development of other product types, but we have chosen to use a software development example due to the relevance of the software industry to sports performance analysis and the feasibility of undertaking such projects.

There are now specialist programmes in sports analytics and sports engineering in which students may do independent projects that develop and evaluate software. There are established joint honours programmes in sport and computing in which students may develop and evaluate software packages within independent projects. The software development project must be substantive enough to qualify as an independent project within the given degree programme. This means that the software development activity must require a sufficient number of effort hours and that the project can be demonstrated to be at the appropriate academic level for the given independent project module. Some activities that might not be sufficient to qualify as an independent project include

- Developing a code window using an existing timeline-based generic video analysis package
- Using existing software packages, such as Tableau (www.tableau.com, accessed 15 February 2017), to present data
- Developing data entry interfaces for performance analysis in standard commercial packages such as Microsoft Excel (Microsoft Inc., Redmond, Wa) and Microsoft Access (Microsoft Inc., Redmond, Wa)

These activities could form part of a project but would not qualify as an independent project in their own right.

Software development processes

The system development process used in a software development project typically covers the stages of the software lifecycle (Sommerville,

1992: 5–10) up to system delivery and evaluation but not long-term system operation and maintenance. The stages covered during a software development project are as follows:

- Requirements Analysis
- System Specification
- System Design
- Implementation
- Testing
- System Evaluation

The dissertation to be submitted at the end of the project tends to include chapters on these stages as well as an introductory chapter on the application area. However, these stages are not always done in sequence. Some prototyping approaches involve iterating a cycle of requirements gathering, analysis and implementation rather than producing an agreed specification before any design and implementation commences. In such situations, the written report still tends to document requirements, design and implementation within separate chapters.

Automatic tactical analysis

The example of a tactical analysis system used to illustrate development projects is concerned with challenging in soccer. The system is automatic because it identifies challenges based on player movement data and existing match event data without any additional human input. Bangsbo and Peitersen (2004: 31–33) described challenging as a player A (in Figure 4.1) dribbling the ball towards an opponent C, forcing C to defend the space they are in or to move towards the player A to prevent player A from shooting or dribbling further towards the goal. This, in turn, creates space for player A's teammate B so that player A can pass to player B. Bangsbo and Peitersen's (2004) book is aimed at a coaching and player practitioner audience rather than providing objective definitions of tactical events that could immediately be implemented as computerised algorithms to recognise such tactics. For example, they describe a situation where a challenge could be performed as when the opposing defence is badly organised and the nearest opposing defender is moving forward. The term 'badly organised' is vague, as are other terms in their description of challenging. We wish to stress that this is not a criticism

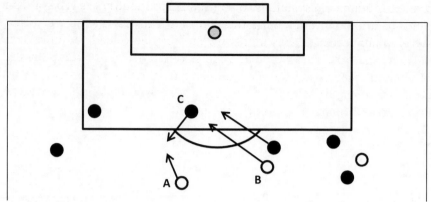

Figure 4.1 Challenging in soccer

of Bangsbo and Peitersen's (2004) book; it is very effective for its target audience, who would find the more formal specification of requirements needed for software development to be tedious if not impenetrable.

A more rigorous definition of when a challenge is being performed needs to be specified in order for a computerised system to recognise challenges. In the dissertation, this type of information about challenging in soccer would appear in an introductory chapter on the background to the application area.

Requirements analysis

Requirements need to be gathered before they can be analysed. Gathering requirements is a critically important stage of software development. If we fail to understand what user groups want from the software, we could end up developing an inappropriate product that will ultimately be rejected by the users. An error made during the requirements stage might not be detected until the system is developed, making the cost of correcting such errors particularly high (Jones, 1985). The methods for eliciting requirements depend on the nature of potential user groups. Where a system is required by a specific customer, whether an individual or an organisation, there will be opportunities to discuss requirements with the actual customer. This can be done through brainstorming meetings, discussion of mock-up interfaces or other prototypes, and discussion of the type of work the system is to be used for. Considering

94

scenarios where the system is to be used helps identify the type of data put into it and the output information that it needs to produce. Other systems are more general in nature and are produced for unknown customer groups. These products are developed where a need for the product is recognised by the developer rather than being identified by potential customers. Focus groups and trade shows are effective ways of eliciting requirements for such systems.

Once requirements are captured, they need to be analysed to ensure that they are complete, consistent and feasible. Viewpoint analysis allows system requirements to be considered from multiple perspectives (Finklestein and Fuks, 1989). These perspectives can be represented by different stakeholders and lead to a more complete set of system requirements than if a single source were consulted. There may, however, be conflicting requirements expressed by stakeholders representing viewpoints. These conflicts need to be resolved, which involves viewpoints being structured into a hierarchy so that there is a mechanism for conflicts from lower-level viewpoints to be resolved by arbitration. The main viewpoints from which requirements for the challenge identification system were drawn were the following:

- Soccer tactics
- Coaching and feedback
- Software and hardware constraints
- Software engineering

The different types of requirements of a software system are broadly classified into functional and non-functional requirements (Pyle et al., 1991: 32–43). Functional requirements include the inputs and outputs of the system, any data repositories to be maintained by the system, the system processing that transforms input data into outputs, and how data are created, used or updated within data repositories. Non-functional qualities include performance, dependability and interface requirements. System performance is concerned with system response time, throughput of transactions and resource utilisation (Jain, 1991). Dependability is concerned with system availability, mean time between failure and rate of failure occurrence (Dyer, 1985). Dependability and performance are not only influenced by the software but also by the hardware that it is implemented on. Other non-functional qualities include power consumption and system portability.

The development of the challenge identification system was motivated by a need for more ambitious use of player movement data that are now widely available in sport. These data have been largely used to produce distance, speed and acceleration measures (Di Salvo et al., 2009; Gregson et al., 2010), as well as abstract mathematical forms that may not be understandable to coaches and players (Fonseca et al., 2013). Bangsbo and Peitersen's (2004: 31–33) book was used to gather requirements from the soccer tactics viewpoint. The viewpoint of coaching and feedback considered how the system might be used by performance analysts, coaches and players. The requirements derived from this viewpoint include a way to identify players involved in challenge events, an ability to display graphical portrayals of challenging and a means of identifying video sequences of challenges. An example of a constraint could be that player movement and match event data files may be in a pre-existing format dictated by the technology that created them. From a software engineering perspective, reusability could be an important requirement to support the development of further systems for a variety of different tactical events. Future work of this type could be much more efficient if useful system components of common benefit to multiple analyses were separated from challenge-specific components of the system.

The student has the opportunity to discuss any special aspects of the requirements analysis process for the given application area. These are requirements capture and analysis activities that are so specific to the application area that they are not mentioned within software engineering textbooks. For example, the definition of what a challenge is may not have been tested before. Therefore, the system needs to be developed in an explorative way, allowing the definition to be tested and refined rather than insisting on a signed-off and completed system specification before system design and implementation commences.

System specification

Once requirements have been gathered and analysed, the system specification can be produced. The system specification explains what the system does, leaving algorithmic detail as a black box. Considering the example of the challenge analysis system, Figure 4.2 summarises the system in terms of the data files that it uses and the main outputs it produces. The student should describe the structure of the data files, the

96

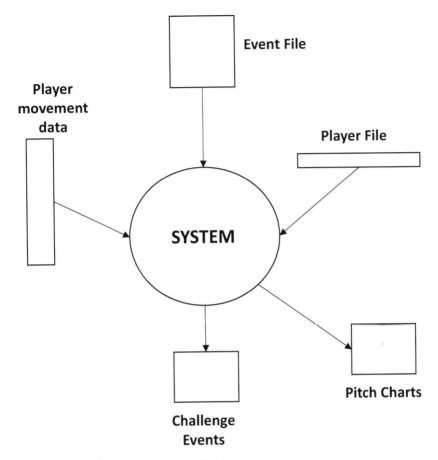

Figure 4.2 Challenge system specification

number of records they contain, the fields within each record and the data types of those fields. This level of detail is also needed for the input and outputs of the system.

Central to the specification of the challenge system are the criteria for identifying a challenge event. The event happens over a period of time, with three particular times being of interest. The time the dribbling player receives the ball (t_1), the time at which they make the pass (t_2) and the time at which their teammate receives the ball (t_3) are all important to the graphical output produced for each challenge. The path travelled by the challenging player and the challenged player from t_1 to t_2 will be shown on a pitch diagram. The paths travelled by all remaining players will be shown from t_1 to t_3. An arrow is drawn showing the pass from the challenging player to the teammate the ball is passed to in order to make clear who these players are on the diagram.

The challenge system is a good example of the detail needed in a system specification. The following criteria must all hold for a sequence of three events to be identified as a successful challenge:

1   The first event must be a player receiving the ball. The second event must be a pass performed by the same player. The third event must be a pass receive event, instantaneous pass, touch or shot event performed by a different player on the same team as the dribbling player.
2   The dribbling player is in the opponent's half.
3   The dribbling player moves forward.
4   The closest opponent (the challenged player) is goal-side of the dribbling player.
5   The closest opponent (challenged player) is closer to the dribbling player at the end of dribble than at the start of the dribble.
6   The teammate receiving the ball after the dribble has more space than at the start of the dribble. This means that the distance between the receiving player and their nearest opponent must be longer after the dribble than it was before.
7   The closest opponent to the dribbling player (the challenged player) was closer to the space eventually passed to by the dribbling player at the start of the dribble than at the end of the dribble. That is, the distance between the closest opponent and the receiving player has increased after the dribble.

There are occasions when a specification needs to be revisited, especially in an exploratory area such as tactical analysis algorithms. In our example, let us imagine that the eventual evaluation revealed a need for including unsuccessful challenges as well as successful ones. This means that Criterion 1 needs to be altered so that it is not necessary for a pass to be received by a teammate or even made. A second change could be to Criterion 5, which has failed to include a situation specified by Bangsbo and Peitersen (2004) where the challenging player actually "beats" the opponent, dribbling the ball past the opponent. This means the distance between the challenging player and the challenged opponent could actually increase by the end of the challenge event. Thus

98

Criterion 5 needs to be referred to as Criterion 5a with Criterion 5b being added to represent where the challenging player has beaten the opponent. Consider Criteria 6 and 7, which are about the space created by the teammate being passed to. For example, the receiving player may have moved into a more advanced penalty area. The fact that opposing defenders may have closed the space down could give the receiving player the opportunity to turn and beat the opponent or even draw a foul and be awarded a penalty. Students should not fear discussing such changes that are made after the system is specified. The student is essentially on a journey which gives many opportunities to discuss software development issues within the thesis. The alternative ways of applying Criteria 6 and 7 (neither, one or both of them) also gives an opportunity to evaluate the system when different sets of criteria are applied. It could be an important feature of the system that different coaches can apply different sets of criteria for recognising challenges.

System design

Having specified what the system will do, its inputs, outputs, data repositories and any non-functional qualities, the student can design the system. This involves moving from what the system is required to do to how the system will do what is required. Architectural design expresses the system in terms of main components, internal data structures and the process through which the system produces outputs using input data and internally stored data. These processes are lower-level subsystems that may be expressed as a flat network or pipeline of processes or as a hierarchy of processes depending on the size and complexity of the system. Ultimately, the lowest level processes of any hierarchy of processes should perform tasks that are appropriate to the program without further decomposition. Detailed design can then be used to outline internal data variables where intermediate data are produced and used during the process of producing system outputs. Detailed design is also used to introduce algorithmic detail to processes, devising methods of processing data. This is a 'data-oriented' approach in which the student (software developer) is primarily focussed on data and then on the subsystems required to process those data. There are alternative 'object-oriented approaches in which data and the functions that are applied to them are encapsulated into objects rather than being separated within the system design. The amount of system design activity that occurs between system specification and implementation depends on the size and nature of the system. Systems that take many man-years to develop by software engineering teams will require considerable design effort before the implementation of subsystems commences. This is to ensure that all involved have a full understanding of the system design and how the subsystems they are developing are integrated with other subsystems. Systems being produced within independent projects of university degrees are done on a smaller scale and being developed by a single person; therefore, they do not require the same level of design detail before implementation can commence. Considering the challenge example, a broad architectural design is sufficient without a detailed design stage. This is because once the architectural design of the system is understood, the subroutines can be programmed. The student should describe the main purpose of each subroutine and its role within the system.

Some useful reusable functions are used by various subroutines within the system. The 'Distance' function uses the Pythagorean theorem to determine the distance between any two locations on the pitch. This could be used for establishing the distance between teammates or the distance between a player and an opponent. A subroutine to draw the soccer pitch is separated from the rest of the graphical output function so that it can be reused in further tactical analysis systems.

Implementation and testing strategy

Once a system is designed, it can be implemented using a top-down or bottom-up approach. A top-down approach commences by implementing the main system before the subsystems that it invokes have been developed. This may mean that empty subroutines may have to exist initially or that 'stubs' are developed to synthesise the activity of given subsystems in order to allow testing of the main system. Bottom-up approaches involve developing low-level subroutines before the higher level processes that invoke them. In order to test that these low-level subroutines work, data that they use need to exist even if the subroutines producing such data have not been implemented yet. This can involve programming a temporary 'test harness' to replicate the normal conditions under which the subroutine is called and executes. These might provide synthetic rather than actual data in order to test a full range of conditions. A common characteristic of the top-down and bottom-up

100

approaches is that they test components of the system as they are developed rather than commencing testing when the entire system has been implemented. This is advised because systems of any complexity rarely work the first time, and debugging is much more challenging for large complex systems than for smaller subroutines.

Debugging

Syntax errors are where the programming language has been used incorrectly and instructions cannot be understood by the computer trying to execute them. Sematic errors are where the programming code follows the syntax of the programming language correctly but there may be mismatching data types between variables and/or expressions within assignment statements or conditions being tested. Syntax and semantic errors are highlighted by the program development environment when the student attempts to compile or run the program. The error messages related to syntax and semantic errors show exactly which line of the program code the error occurred at and the type of error that has been made. Many program development environments allow the current values of variables at the time of the error to be inspected. Logical errors are more difficult to debug and occur where a syntactically and semantically correct program does the wrong thing, producing incorrect output. The program will continue to execute after the point at which a logical error has been made. The programming language environment cannot stop the program at the point of the logical error because the computer does not know what the system is intended to do. The computer simply does what it is programmed to do without question. Where logical errors have been made, temporary variables can be used to assist debugging. This involves outputting values of temporary variables, allowing the student (software developer) to understand where a subroutine has made an error and why. The student may need to trace how the values of given variables change during the execution of a program to determine why an incorrect output has been produced. One thing that students must be careful about is remembering to remove temporary code that was introduced for the purpose of debugging. One way of doing this is to use a specific form of comment to highlight where program instructions have been included for the purpose of debugging. These can then be easily identified and removed from the program once it is functioning correctly.

101

Evaluation

The development project is not just a technical task but also an academic one which requires an evaluation of the system or process that has been developed. The purpose of evaluation research, in contrast to scientific research, is to inform decision makers (McGuire, 2016). This requires indepth summative and formative evaluations of achievements, process improvements and costs (McGuire, 2016). A system may be executing correctly with respect to its specification. However, we still need to validate that it meets the users' requirements, is useable and is useful. The International Organisation for Standardisation (ISO) lists six areas of evaluation for software systems (ISO, 1991): functionality, reliability, usability, efficiency (performance), maintainability and portability. Functionality is concerned with the correctness of the system; does it perform as intended? This might not be straightforward as requirements may be vague, as is the case with the challenge analysis example. Reliability of any product is concerned with faults developing and impacting on system availability. The system may be functionally correct, but the interface also needs to be usable. Feature analysis can be used to evaluate both the system's functionality and usability (Pfleeger, 1998: 457). Efficiency can be evaluated during experimental approaches. For example, neural network systems can be set up with different learning rates and different sizes of middle layers, allowing alternative architectures to be compared. This can also be combined with evaluation of correctness, where we may discover a trade-off between learning performance and correctness for a neural network system. Maintainability is not actually a user requirement, but it is very important for developers who may need to enhance products over time. Systems should be developed systematically and documented sufficiently to assist maintenance, especially if those maintaining a system may be different individuals than those who originally produced it. Portability is the extent to which a system can run on different hardware and under different operating systems. Portability is also concerned with use of alternative data protocols. For example, the player movement data used in the challenge analysis example may have come from one particular technology/system, but we would like the challenge analysis system to be capable of working with player movement data from a full range of technologies.

Evaluation methods include feature analysis, surveys, case studies and formal experiments (Pfleeger, 1998: 456–460). Feature analysis and experimental approaches were mentioned in the previous paragraph. Surveys allow user feedback to be gathered and analysed to gauge satisfaction with the system's functions, operation and usability. A case study could be used to contrast a situation when the system is applied to the same situation when the system was not applied. For example, we could use an alternative video analysis system involving operator input to identify challenges and compare this to the automatic challenge identification system using a single match.

The most appropriate evaluation technique for the challenge analysis system would be a validation of actual challenge events that would be identified by an expert human observer watching a match video. As mentioned earlier in this section, the system could be evaluated when applying four different sets of criteria (neither of Criteria 6 or 7, just Criterion 6, just Criterion 7 or both Criteria 6 and 7). Tables 4.1(a) to 4.1(d) summarise the type of evaluation results that could be found. They show the agreements and disagreements between the software system and expert human observation. Not considering space created by the receiving player is the most encouraging version of the system because there is only one false negative case: where the human observer recognises a potential challenge but the system does not show it. False negative cases are more serious than false positive cases because any

Table 4.1 Validation of the automatic challenge identification system when four alternative sets of criteria are used

(a) Space for receiving player is not analysed.				(b) Receiving player finds space with respect to nearest opponent.			
Software	Human Observation			Software	Human Observation		
	No	Yes	Total		No	Yes	Total
No	26	1	27	No	110	34	144
Yes	111	36	147	Yes	27	3	30
Total	137	37	174	Total	137	37	174

(c) Receiving player finds space with respect to challenged opponent.				(d) Receiving player finds space with respect to nearest and challenged opponent.			
Software	Human Observation			Software	Human Observation		
	No	Yes	Total		No	Yes	Total
No	117	34	151	No	125	35	160
Yes	20	3	23	Yes	12	2	14
Total	137	37	174	Total	137	37	174

challenge identified by the software that a coach would not consider to be a challenge can simply be ignored when preparing feedback for squads. Admittedly, there are 111 false positive cases, which was far greater than when the other three sets of criteria are applied. However, not being able to see the overwhelming majority of actual challenges identified by human experts in the system output renders these other three versions of the system of little assistance to analysts, coaches and players.

The evaluation should not be an entirely quantitative experiment, and students should also evaluate processes and systems using richer qualitative analyses. Considering the example of the challenge analysis system allows us to recognise the types of things that could be discussed within evaluations. Of critical importance is that video times of challenge events are stored, allowing relevant video footage to be examined. A potential enhancement to the system could be to create an XML file of challenge events that could be incorporated into the timeline of a video analysis package using an appropriate lead time before the dribble commenced and an appropriate lag time after the ball was received by a teammate. The outcome of the challenge event is also recorded, meaning that challenge statistics can be generated for a team as a whole or for individual players. The graphical output showing player movement during challenge events could also be evaluated: would coaches use this, or would they stick to using the relevant video sequences? Reusability of system components in further systems is also worth discussing within system evaluation (Pfleeger, 1998: 478). For example, the subroutines for determining distances between players, identifying nearest opponent, drawing the pitch and initialising event and movement data structures within the challenge analysis system could have been isolated for use with other tactical analysis systems. There may be application area–specific issues that are worth discussing. For example, a by-product of the challenge analysis system is that the false positive cases represent other important events where the distance between dribbling player and the nearest opponent reduces, such as the defender pressing or tracking the dribbling player.

SUMMARY

This chapter has discussed enterprise projects and development projects that can be undertaken as an alternative to a traditional scientific research project. The vocational nature of sports performance analysis makes such projects attractive options for many students. The projects are applied practical exercises within an academic evaluation. Typically some process or product is developed. In the case of the enterprise project, the evaluation involves market research and the development of a business plan. The emphasis of the project is on the enterprise idea as a business concept. Development projects, on the other hand, are concerned with the effectiveness of the process or product that has been developed. Evaluations typically focus on improvements made to practice by the product or process. The reporting of these two types of project is covered in Chapter 9.

REFERENCES

Bangsbo, J. and Peitersen, B. (2004) *Offensive soccer tactics: how to control possession and score more goals*. Champaign, IL: Human Kinetics.

Barrow, C., Burke, G., Molian, D. and Brown, R. (2005) *Enterprise development*. Mitcham, Surrey: Thompson Learning.

Bolton, J.E. (1971) *Report of the committee of enquiry on small firms, Cmnd. 4811*. London: HMSO.

Bridge, S. and O'Neill, K. (2013) *Understanding enterprise, entrepreneurship and small business, 4th edn*. London: Palgrave Macmillan.

Burns, P. (2016) *Entrepreneurship and small business, 3rd edn*. London: Palgrave Macmillan.

Bygrave, W.D. (1989) 'The entrepreneurship paradigm (I): a philosophical look at its research methodologies', *Entrepreneurship Theory and Practice*, 14(1): 7–26.

Di Salvo, V., Gregson, W., Atkinson, G., Tordoff, P. and Drust, B. (2009) 'Analysis of high intensity activity in Premier League soccer', *International Journal of Sports Medicine*, 30: 205–212.

Drucker, P. (1999) *Innovation and entrepreneurship*. London: Butterworth-Heinemann.

Dyer, M. (1985) 'Software verification through statistical testing', in T. Anderson (ed.), *Software requirements specification and testing* (pp. 127–138). Oxford: Blackwell.

Finklestein, A. and Fuks. S. (1989) 'Multi-party specification', in *Proceedings of the 5th International Workshop on Software Specification and Design* (pp. 185–195). Pittsburgh, PA: Association of Computing Machinery (ACM).

Fonseca, S., Milho, J., Travassos, B., Araújo, D. and Lopes, A. (2013) 'Measuring spatial interaction behavior in team sports using superimposed Voronoi diagrams', *International Journal of Performance Analysis in Sport*, 13: 179–189.

Gregson, W., Drust, B., Atkinson, G. and Di Salvo, V. (2010) 'Match-to-match variability of high-speed activities in Premier League Soccer', *International Journal of Sports Medicine*, 31: 237–242.

ISO (1991) *Information Technology – software product evaluation: quality characteristics and guidelines for their use, ISO/IEC IS 912*. Geneva, Switzerland: International Organisation for Standardisation (ISO).

Jain, R. (1991) *The art of computer systems performance: analysis, techniques for experimental design, measurement, simulation and modelling*. Chichester, UK: Wiley.

Jones, C. (1985) 'Specification, verification and testing in software development', in T. Anderson (ed.), *Software requirements specification and testing* (pp. 1–13). Oxford: Blackwell.

McGuire, M. (2016) 'Evaluation research', in N. Gilbert and P. Stoneman (eds), *Researching social life, 4th edn* (pp. 161–179). Thousand Oaks, CA: Sage.

Pfleeger, S.L. (1998) *Software engineering: theory and practice*. Upper Saddle River, NJ: Prentice Hall.

Pyle, I., Hruschka, P., Lissandre, M. and Jackson, K. (1991) *Real-time systems: investigating industrial practice*. Chichester, UK: Wiley.

Sommerville, I. (1992) *Software engineering, 4th edn*. Wokingham, UK: Addison-Wesley.

Williams, S. (2013) *The financial times guide to business start-up*. Harlow: Financial Times/Prentice Hall.

CHAPTER 5

THE RESEARCH PROPOSAL

OVERVIEW

Research proposals are used at a variety of levels, from undergraduate students planning research projects to proposals for funded research being made by experienced researchers. The research proposal allows readers to understand the research to be done and make decisions about it. This chapter, like the rest of the book, is aimed at university students doing research projects leading to dissertations. Producing a research proposal is important because it enables students to firm up their research project and enables university staff to scrutinise research proposals and allocate supervisors to students. The chapter discusses the process of considering research topics, selecting a topic, learning about it, identifying a research project that is needed, turning this into a specific research question and writing up the research proposal.

There is a bone of contention, a veritable chicken-and-egg conundrum if you like: What comes first – the generation of the research question or the investigation of academic literature? In the experience of the authors, it can be either. One supports the other. The generation of a question may initiate from something we hear from a pundit on the radio that piques an interest. This question may then be researched further by investigating previous literature in the area. Thus, the students will be well informed about the relevant theoretical and methodological aspects. This is merely the initial stage of the process; however, a considerable amount of project effort depends on directions set at this point. If there is an initial poor selection of research question, this may not be detected until the hypothesis is being drawn or, worse, when drawing conclusions and recommendations.

107

SELECTING A RESEARCH TOPIC

The qualities of a good sports performance analysis research project listed by O'Donoghue (2010: 55–68) are that it should be

- Relevant to the student's programme of study
- Interesting to the student
- Topical
- Important
- An area with practical application
- Relevant to the student's career aspirations
- An area where university staff have expertise
- Covered in performance analysis literature
- An area of student strength
- Feasible and workable

Students from many different degree programmes can do dissertations in sports performance analysis; these include sports studies, physical education, coaching, sports and exercise science and specialist performance analysis programmes. Students should do a project that is relevant to their programme of study which is a named award. Sports performance analysis dissertations are relatively unproblematic in this respect for the types of programmes listed.

The project should be interesting to the student and interesting in general. It is particularly important that the student is motivated to maintain progress on the project over a period of six or seven months. The student is more likely to be able to do this if they are doing a dissertation in a problem area that they have a passion for and are genuinely curious about what the research will find. Media coverage of sports helps identify topical areas to study in sports performance analysis. There are weekly discussions of sports in addition to some interesting speculations made by commentators.

The importance and practical relevance of an area are what make it interesting in general. A question that students should ask themselves is, "What is useful to know about my sport that we don't know at the minute?" Is there something that would be useful to the student as an athlete or coach that has never been studied in the sport? There are tactical options, choices of techniques and a range of work-rate strategies that are used in sports performance that have not been scientifically

108

assessed to see whether they improve performers' chances of winning. If a research study could contribute such knowledge then it has practical application in that decisions can be made based on that knowledge. For example, if a study finds that a certain tactical option leads to successful outcomes more than alternative options, then players can choose to adopt this tactic more often and make the necessary preparations in order to be able to apply it.

As students approach the final stages of their degree programmes, they will be thinking about what they will be doing after their degree is completed. Some may have particular career paths in mind and may, therefore, choose to undertake a research project in that area. This helps the student add relevant experience or study to their curriculum vitae which will improve their chance of taking career opportunities in their chosen area. For example, a student may wish to be a practicing performance analyst in a coaching context and, therefore, takes performance analysis modules as well as gaining relevant work experience as an analyst. They can choose to do an enterprise project or an empirical research project in which they work as an analyst and evaluate the performance analysis service they provide. Chapter 4 of the current text book covers such projects.

If a student undertakes a project in an area where the university has relevant expertise then it will be easier for the student to find an appropriate supervisor. Ultimately, the research project is an independent piece of research undertaken by the student. However, the feedback and support given by the supervisor will be much better informed if the supervisor has knowledge and experience in the area. The criteria listed by O'Donoghue (2010) for a good project idea are not independent, and some have priorities over others. If a student has a feasible and interesting idea for a sports performance analysis project but the academic staff at the university focus their research on other areas, the student should still do the project they wish to do and are motivated by. Staff research interests should be looked at where students know they wish to do a performance analysis dissertation but have still not decided on a particular research problem. Staff web pages list their research interests and publications. There may be an area that a member of staff has worked in that leads to students identifying related areas that they are interested in.

Coverage of an area in academic literature is an indication that it is recognised as important and relevant. Students will be able to review the literature relating to their chosen research topic area, identifying gaps in the existing research that they can address through their own research project. Some ideas are more original than others, and this may mean that there is less existing literature on the idea. However, it is most unlikely that there will be no relevant literature at all on the area. If the project is to examine the effect of some factor on some area of performance, there will be literature on broad areas of performance (tactics, techniques or work-rate) that is relevant. The literature used does not have to come exclusively from sports performance analysis, and a rationale for a performance analysis project can be justified making use of literature in coaching, psychology and physiology. For example, momentum in a sport of interest to the student may not have been addressed in previous research. However, there is literature on momentum in other sports within performance analysis and psychology literature.

Areas that students are interested in are usually areas where their work also merits higher marks. Before deciding what type of performance analysis dissertation to do, students should consider whether they should do a dissertation in performance analysis or in some other area. If students are uncertain about what career they are aiming for and are equally interested in performance analysis and other disciplines then they should undertake a dissertation in an area where they perform well. This will increase their chances of a good mark on the dissertation, which will keep more career options to them if it helps gain a higher degree classification.

It is essential that the research project is feasible. The student needs to think through what is involved in the research. Is the data collection feasible? Is it possible to collect data about the variables of interest? Are the behaviours observable? Can they be recognised? Can data collection be done without pausing videos of performances or do events have to be viewed on multiple occasions to classify behaviours of interest? Does the project require any resources or support that are not realistically possible? It is not possible to analyse data, produce and discuss results and draw conclusions without any data. The student also needs to consider access to the types of research participants they are proposing to study. Will these individuals have time to participate, and will they be willing to participate? The student needs to imagine the process of recruiting participants and gathering data, honestly considering all of the difficulties involved and whether or not these difficulties can be addressed. Supervisors are able to assist early on in this respect as their experience of supervising student projects helps them identify areas that are not feasible quite quickly.

A final quality of a good research question is that it should be possible to address it with a simple research design. This may involve comparing samples of matches or correlating performance variables. Some students may feel that this is not very ambitious and may wish to analyse a larger pathway of performance variables. However, studies with intermediate-level variables between independent and dependent variables can become unmanageable. A project investigating the effect of some factor (e.g., venue effect or positional role) on some set of dependent performance variables can result in a high mark if done to a high standard. The purpose of the study will act as a framework for the answer to the research question and be linked to the design of the study. The student will have a good understanding of what they are doing, why they are doing it, how they are going to undertake the research and how the analysis will provide an answer to the research question.

LITERATURE REVIEW

As previously discussed (O'Donoghue, 2010), it is necessary to select an interesting, important and feasible research problem. Though the initial interest in the topic may have been derived by other means, the importance of the topic should be supported by a review of relevant literature. Gratton and Jones (2004: 51–52) suggested some additional purposes of undertaking a literature review, which include demonstrating knowledge of the research area, understanding relevant theoretical concepts and determining the extent of previous research. Indeed the process of consulting with relevant literature will have probably started while the student was still deciding on the research topic. The research proposal includes a section on the background which is shorter than the literature review that will be produced in the eventual dissertation report. The background section needs to focus on providing the rationale for the given study, having reviewed the main research in the area. The student should be critical in reviewing existing literature as this is expected more in level 5 work than in level 4 work. The limitations recognised in previous research help the student identify a project and justify a rationale for it. The process of exploring and reviewing literature therefore continues after the research proposal has been completed.

111

There are systematic ways of reviewing literature using electronic databases with selected keywords. The databases can include PubMed, SPORTDiscus and Web of Science. Given that there is less research done in sports performance analysis than in other disciplines of sports and exercise science, students should also do manual searches of journals that publish sports performance analysis research. The *International Journal of Performance Analysis in Sport* is the main journal catering to research in the area, but students should also review the sports performance section of the *Journal of Sports Science*. The proceedings of World Congresses of Performance Analysis also contain research that may be relevant to the student's topic area; the most recent one of these was published after the 2012 conference (Peters and O'Donoghue, 2013). There also may be key review articles on sports, aspects of performance or methodological issues relevant to the student's research. These secondary sources may be published as book chapters or as review papers within journals. They identify the main primary sources of research in the given areas within the review article. The *Routledge Handbook of Sports Performance Analysis* (McGarry et al., 2013) contains review chapters, some of which may help students start their literature reviews. As has already been mentioned in this book, there is overlap between performance analysis and other disciplines of sports science. Therefore students should also consult with relevant journals in other disciplines of sports science that are applicable to their research topic. There may also be sources that are specific to the sport of interest to the student's research. For example, the series of Science and Football and Science and Racket Sports books published by Routledge contain sections on performance analysis within those sports.

The student should record details of articles that are read so that these can be used within the eventual review of literature chapter. These details may include the article or chapter title, author(s), journal/book title, publisher name and location (for books), volume and issue (for journals), page numbers and year/month of publication. The student should also summarise what was done and what was found by the authors. The process of summarising previous research in the student's own words helps develop better understanding of the research. Any relevant references used by the paper should also be noted where electronic database and other manual searches have not identified them. The process of reading secondary and primary sources and identifying further sources

112

of literature continues until saturation, when no further useful papers are being identified (Gratton and Jones, 2004: 59).

When reviewing previous literature, the student should be critical, identifying strengths and limitations of previous research. The strengths and weaknesses of previous research studies are identified by examining the methods used. There may be limitations of a previous research study based on the currency, volume or type of matches included. There may also be limitations in the reliability and validity of the variables used in the study. The design of the study and the data analysis techniques used may be open to criticism. Some papers will be reviewed more comprehensively than others depending on the relevance of the paper to the student's own research topic.

The write-up of the research proposal is covered later in the current chapter. This focusses on the background literature coverage done by the student, which needs to be organised. The student can use a notebook and a word-processing file containing the details recorded from previous research. The information recorded will be in an unstructured form until the student decides on a paragraph structure for the background section of the research proposal. The student needs to arrange the background section to make an argument justifying the need for their own study. This argument needs to be made using completed sentences and paragraphs rather than the note form initially used when recording literature.

SPECIFYING THE RESEARCH QUESTION

Structuring the problem

The first thing that the student should do is restrict the scope of the study. Consider the student wishing to compare the effectiveness of alternative tactics used in a given sport. They will not be able to do this for all levels of competition in the sport, and so they should restrict the study to a given age group, gender and level of the sport. There are also temporal, geographic, contextual and methodological ways of restricting the scope of a study (Gratton and Jones, 2004: 43). There may be many different tactics that can be applied within the sport, so a further way of restricting the scope of the investigation is to restrict it to a subset of tactics where there is debate about which alternatives are the most effective.

The research problem is given structure by developing a conceptual model of sports performance that acts as the basis of what is being studied. This conceptual model could simply be some aspect of sports performance and factor(s) that may have an impact on it. These will eventually form the dependent and independent variables, respectively, of the research design. Alternatively, the conceptual model may be a set of sports performance variables that may be related. These will eventually be defined as variables to be included in a correlation study. The links and associations between elements of the conceptual model under consideration are hypothetical at this stage. The purpose of the research project will be to determine whether they are linked or not.

Conceptual modelling involves abstraction and reasoning. Abstraction is a means of representing complex areas of sports performance (such as possession tactics in a team game) in a simpler and more concise way (for example the number of passes per possession). The concept of 'possession tactics' involves an infinite amount of information that can be derived from a match video. A fingerprint of variables including number of passes per possession reduces the volume of information to a manageable set of values that focus on those things that distinguish between different tactics.

The potential links between elements within a conceptual model can be identified through reasoning; this may be a combination of inductive and deductive reasoning, considering knowledge from previous research as well as speculation using alternative forms of knowledge. Deductive reasoning combines general theory to create specific testable questions. For example we may speculate that teams who keep the ball longer in team games may have better technical ability and thus do not lose the ball as much. We may also speculate that these teams will therefore have longer possessions in terms of the number of passes per possession. Deductive reasoning leads us to question whether the number of passes played per possession is different between teams of different abilities.

Inductive reasoning combines specific observations and experiences in the real world of sport to form testable research questions. For example, over the past decade Barcelona and Spain have been successful soccer teams. There is also speculation that these teams play with an elaborate buildup style, retaining possession of the ball longer than other teams. Combining these two pieces of knowledge within an inductive reasoning

114

process can lead us to question if teams of different abilities have differing numbers of passes per possession. No matter which approach has been used to derive the basic research question, the question is still vague. We need to consider what we mean by team ability and whether passes per possession is a good indication of tactics used in a team game. A team may attempt to adopt such a buildup possession strategy but have a low number of passes per possession because they lose the ball through technical errors rather than applying a direct possession tactic. The process of abstraction is used to determine a set of variables that could represent the broad concept of tactics as well as a classification variable to distinguish between teams of different abilities.

Defining variables

The conceptual model of a research problem identifies the broad variable classes that form a research question. The next step is to operationalise the research question by defining these variables. In our example of effectiveness of possession tactics in a team game, we need to be clear about team ability and how we distinguish between successful and unsuccessful teams. We could define successful teams as those that end up in the top half of the league in the season the matches took place with remaining teams classified as unsuccessful. We could use winning and losing teams within matches to represent successful and unsuccessful teams but this would rule out any drawn matches. In a hybrid tournament of a round robin stage followed by knockout stages for teams qualifying from the round robin stage, the qualifying teams could be deemed successful, and the unsuccessful teams would be those eliminated before the knockout stages.

A set of variables could be defined to represent possession tactics. Areas of the pitch could be classified to allow us to record the areas of the pitch where possession was obtained. The percentage of a team's possessions that commence in each area would then form a set of dependent variables. The number of passes per possession could be recorded, allowing summary indicators such as the mean number of passes per possession to be calculated for a performance. Similarly, the number of players involved in each possession could be recorded so that the mean number of players involved in a possession could be calculated for a given performance.

Forming hypotheses

The first thing to say about formal hypotheses is that they are not always appropriate. Where the student is proposing to do a qualitative research study, formal hypotheses in terms of operationally defined variables are not appropriate. Instead proposals for such studies should set out aims and purpose in more natural text form. Formal hypotheses can be used in traditional notation studies where a quantitative approach is to be used. There is usually a null hypothesis (H_0) and an alternative hypothesis (H_A) which are mutually exclusive as well as being the only possible outcomes of the study. The alternative hypothesis is sometimes referred to as the research hypothesis because it is the outcome where the study concludes a link between the concepts of interest. The null hypothesis is a potential outcome reflecting no association or link between the concepts of interest. The hypotheses must be testable so that they can be rejected or confirmed based on the research to be done. Well-formed hypotheses are a logical framework for the study that then guides the design of the study, the data collection and the analysis methods (Newell et al., 2010: 116). The hypotheses for our study of possession tactics employed by successful and unsuccessful teams could read as follows:

H_0: There is no difference between teams in the top and bottom halves of the league for any of (i) the mean number of passes played per possession, (ii) the percentage of possessions commencing in any defined area of the pitch or (iii) the mean number of players involved in a possession.

H_A: There is a difference between teams in the top and bottom halves of the league for one or more of (i) the mean number of passes played per possession, (ii) the percentage of possessions commencing in a defined area of the pitch or (iii) the mean number of players involved in a possession.

DESCRIBING METHODS

Having established a rationale for the proposed research and identified a specific research question, the student needs to consider how the research will be done. In the case of a traditional empirical performance analysis project, a system needs to be developed to gather the necessary data. The development process involves creating the system, which is covered in Chapter 7 of the current book, pilot testing the system and testing the system for reliability. The system can then be used in the main research study. The student needs to state the type and number of matches being used as well as the criteria for inclusion and exclusion of matches. The data analysis methods can be specified if the research question has been specified well. The description of methods within the research proposal is not as detailed as in the eventual dissertation report. The student does not need to develop the system until they are undertaking the dissertation. At the proposal stage it is good enough to identify the main performance variable classes and state that observational methods will be used. The student needs to show awareness of the system development process by stating that pilot testing and reliability assessment will be done. The student will also gain marks for explaining the data analysis methods to be used.

COMPLETING THE RESEARCH PROPOSAL

As covered in this chapter, developing a research proposal involves identifying a research topic, surveying relevant literature, proposing a specific research question, justifying the research question and devising methods. The proposal is typically completed during a stage of a student's programme that precedes the dissertation project itself. This allows a supervisor to be identified and the project to be discussed and amended if necessary. In many universities, the research proposal is assessed within a research methods module, and thus the preparation for the dissertation project is actually a secondary purpose of the proposal. The research proposal's primary purpose is to assess the student's knowledge of research methods. In order to be able to write the research proposal, the student needs to demonstrate an understanding of alternative research methods, including their strengths and weaknesses, and be able to design a research study and justify the proposed methods.

The role of research ethics within the proposal depends on the practices at the student's university. Some universities will insist on ethics applications being made at the time the research proposal is submitted, while other universities will separate these two activities. Hopefully, the student's research proposal will receive a pass mark and the project will be given the go-ahead to commence subject to ethical clearance. However, it is possible that a good research idea might be presented poorly within the research proposal. The student may need to resubmit the proposal in order to pass their research methods module and be able to undertake a dissertation. It is also possible that a very well-written research proposal might pass but the research idea is not feasible within the time constraints or with the facilities available at the given university. In a situation like this, a formal proposal does not need to be resubmitted, but the student will need to satisfy the staff that they have changed their plans for the dissertation sufficiently to allow a project to commence. The worst case scenario is where the research proposal fails and the proposed project will not be allowed to commence. This is usually because the project is unethical, is not substantive enough, is not of the required academic level or is outside the scope of the student's degree programme.

The proposal for a scientific research project contains an introduction, background to the topic, statement of the purpose of the research and description of methods. The introduction states the aim and overall purpose of the research up-front so that the reader is able to read the remaining sections with a good general idea of what the project is all about. The background to the research topic contains a critical review of relevant literature and provides the theoretical underpinning of the project. In identifying gaps and limitations in previous research, the background section also provides a rationale for the proposed project. In stating the purpose of the research project, the student articulates the research question, establishing the scope of the study. It is not always possible to specify a precise research question using operationalised variables. However, in stating the purpose of a quantitative study, the student should at least provide a conceptual framework for the study. This should identify the broad aspects of performance that are of interest and any factors hypothesised to influence those aspects.

The methods section should identify how the research is to be done. In the case of a quantitative observational analysis project, the methods section should identify data sources and whether computerised performance analysis systems will be used or whether the project will rely on manual notation methods. It should be written in sufficient detail to allow practical and logistical issues with the project to be considered. Unlike in the eventual dissertation, the methods section of a research proposal is written in the future tense.

118

Kumar (2005: 188–189) also recommended that a research proposal contain a section on ethical issues in the research, a timeframe and a structure for the eventual dissertation report. A plan should identify all of the data collection work, data analysis tasks, literature survey and write-up tasks, as well as anything else in the project that requires time. The amount of time needed for each task needs to be understood along with any temporal ordering of activities. The plan is a useful mechanism for management of the eventual research project. Figure 5.1 is an example of a project plan for an undergraduate research project in sports performance analysis.

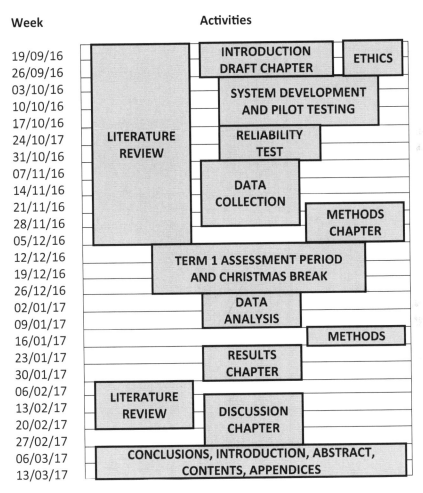

Figure 5.1 Research plan

There are similarities between proposals for scientific research projects, enterprise projects and development projects. Proposals for enterprise projects still require a description of background, purpose and methods. However, in the case of an enterprise proposal, the rationale for the project is an applied commercial rationale rather than a need to contribute to theoretical knowledge. The purpose of a development project is to produce and evaluate some product or process. Therefore, the project proposal needs to reflect this, and the project plan needs to include such activities as requirements gathering, specifying the product, design, implementation and testing, rather than describing the methods of a scientific research project. The proposal for a development project should articulate the need for developing the product or process, consider the feasibility of the project and identify resources required.

SUMMARY

This chapter has described the process of producing a research proposal. There is a lot of work to be done before the student actually starts writing the proposal. Most importantly, the student must select a viable and interesting research problem area. They need to explore the literature in that area to help them identify a project that they can do that will fill some gap in the knowledge. The student then needs to formalise a specific research question. This develops a conceptual model for the project and acts as a framework for the study. It is at this stage that the data gathering and analysis methods can be considered. The research proposal itself includes background to the research problem, a statement of the purpose of the study, which may be expressed as formal hypotheses, an outline of the methods, a project plan and a section on ethical issues in the research.

REFERENCES

Gratton, C. and Jones, I. (2004) *Research methods for sports studies*. London: Routledge.

Kumar, R. (2005) *Research methodology: a step-by-step guide for beginners*. London: Sage Publications Ltd.

McGarry, T., O'Donoghue, P.G. and Sampaio, J. (2013) *Routledge handbook of sports performance analysis*. London: Routledge.

120

Newell, J., Aitchison, T. and Grant, S. (2010) *Statistics for sport and exercise science: a practical approach*. Harlow: Prentice Hall.

O'Donoghue, P.G. (2010) *Research methods for sports performance analysis*. London: Routledge.

Peters, D. and O'Donoghue, P.G. (2013) *Performance analysis of sport IX*. London: Routledge.

CHAPTER 6

ETHICS

OVERVIEW

Chapter 5 of O'Donoghue's (2010) *Research Methods for Sports Performance Analysis* textbook covered ethical issues that are relevant to sports performance analysis research projects. It started out by discussing how the seven sources of scientific dishonesty listed by Shore (1991, cited in Thomas et al., 2011: 79–85) are also issues within sports performance analysis research. Therefore, this aspect of research ethics will not be repeated in the current chapter. The current chapter will cover ethical principles, ethical dilemmas in sports performance analysis research projects and ethics policies and procedures. These issues were discussed in O'Donoghue's (2010) chapter on ethical issues in sports performance analysis. The rationale for the current updated chapter is that sports performance analysis research is expanding in scope with studies combining performance analysis with other methods. Ethics processes are maturing, and many scholars in the area of sports performance analysis still lack a full understanding of ethical principles that are relevant to their research. The chapter commences with a section on ethical principles, followed by a section on ethical dilemma in sports performance analysis and a discussion of ethical policies and procedures.

ETHICAL PRINCIPLES

Origins of modern research ethics

Ethics has been defined as "norms for conduct that distinguish between acceptable and unacceptable behaviour" (Resnik, 2015) and "widely agreed moral principles for what is right and wrong" (Tinkler, 2013: 195). With respect to research, ethics are concerned with the recruitment and treatment of participants and with avoiding risk of harm to researchers, participants, organisations and the general public. Research ethics have evolved over the centuries, and some practices in research in the past would not be acceptable or even be legal today. The roots of modern research ethics can be traced back to the Nuremberg Code of 1947. The Nuremberg Code was established as part of the verdict of the Nuremberg Medical Trial (Weindling, 2001). The code contains the following ten principles of legitimate medical research:

1 Voluntary, well-informed consent of the human participants in a full legal capacity is required. The participants should have a good understanding of their role in the research and of any benefits and risks involved.
2 The research should have potential positive benefits for society that cannot be achieved by other means.
3 The research should be justified by previous knowledge that establishes a need for the study.
4 The research should be managed in a way that avoids unnecessary physical and mental discomfort and harm.
5 The research should not be conducted if it implies a risk of death or disabling injury.
6 The risks of the research should be proportional to its expected humanitarian benefits.
7 Preparations for the research study and facilities used within the study must be adequate to protect participants from risks associated with the research.
8 The research must be conducted by staff who are properly trained and qualified.
9 Participants must be free to withdraw from the research at any point.
10 Researchers must stop any research activity when situations arise where participants are in danger.

The Helsinki Declaration is a set of ethical principles developed by the World Medical Association that has undergone several revisions since first being made in 1964. The Helsinki code (Helsinki Declaration, 2013) contains thirty-three points covering risks, benefits, publication of results, vulnerable populations, informed consent, privacy and confidentiality, use of placebos and research ethics governance. The origins of the Nuremberg Code and the Helsinki Declaration are in the medical field. Neither is legally binding, but they have established ethics principles that have been adopted and developed by professional bodies, universities and research institutions. We will now cover the main ethical principles that are relevant to sports performance analysis research.

Voluntary informed consent

People who participate in research studies should do so voluntarily. This means that they participate of their own free will, rather than being coerced into participation. Researchers should avoid situations where people participate in studies as a result of power relations between the researcher and the participants. For example, consider a coach researching the impact of some coaching methods on athlete performance. If the participants are coached by the researcher, then they may fear being deselected from the team if they do not participate in the study. People may also feel pressurised into participating in studies where researchers use 'gate keepers' who have influence over the participants. For example, coaches and performance analysts may be approached by researchers seeking to gain access to athletes. Firstly, this can be uncomfortable for the coach or analyst who may feel that making such a request to the players might jeopardise their own relations with the squad. Very often they refuse to act as gate keepers, preferring researchers to approach squad management directly. Secondly, where the coach or analyst does play a role in recruiting participants, the athletes may feel obliged to participate in the study, especially if the researcher and the coach or analyst are connected. A related issue to voluntary participation is the use of incentives. Some may participate in studies because they are vulnerable and in desperate need of money rather than because they wish to participate in the study.

Participants who consent to participate in the study should provide evidence of their consent in writing. It is very important that participants are fully informed about the study and what their participation involves. Participants cannot be considered to consent to participation if they do not fully understand what participation involves or how their data will be used. This means that participants should be provided with complete information about the study in language they can understand. The information provided may use images or links to video material on the internet that provides demonstrations of tests or interventions that will be involved. These photographs and video sequences help potential participants make a more informed choice about whether they wish to participate in the study. The information should include the purpose of the research, the source of funding for the study, what participants are required to do, the amount of time involved and the locations of testing and other data gathering processes. It is essential that participants are aware of any risks that are involved in participation. These risks may include physical pain, strenuous exertion and psychological stress. Information about the research should also cover the extent to which anonymity and confidentiality will be preserved. The researcher should not promise anything that cannot be delivered. For example, there may be information provided by participants that researchers are obliged to report to other authorities for legal reasons, professional reasons or out of a duty of care for the participants. These possibilities should be mentioned in the information provided to participants. Participants should be fully informed of how data are being recorded and stored, how the data are secured and for how long they will be stored. For example, in performance analysis investigations, participants should be advised if their performances are being video recorded and how the video data will be stored and used.

Where participants have consented to their data being used in a particular investigation, their data should not be used in further investigations without gaining consent from the participants for this additional use of their data. If researchers can see the potential for data to be analysed in multiple studies, they should gain consent from the participants for multiple use of the data, explaining as fully as possible the ways in which their data could be used and providing assurances about ways in which the data would not be used. Gaining consent to use participant data in multiple studies is best done when gaining consent for the original study. This saves researchers from having to contact the participants some time (perhaps years) after the original study. The participants may have moved and changed contact details, making it difficult to locate them in the future. Furthermore, the participants may prefer for their data to be stored without personal identification details.

The information about the study should be provided to participants in the form of an information sheet (this could be electronic or on paper). Researchers should provide contact information to enable potential participants to contact them if they have any queries about the research. Participants should sign a consent form stating that they understand the research study, understand what their participation involves, agree to participate and acknowledge that they have the right to withdraw from the study at any time without prejudice.

Young people cannot legally provide consent to participate in research studies; in the UK the age at which consent can be given to participate in research depends on the interpretation of various rulings. However, universities typically consider people under eighteen years of age to be young people. Researchers should obtain consent from parents, guardians, coaches or teachers responsible for the young people. As well as obtaining consent from the parents, guardians or teachers responsible for the children, the researchers should also gain assent from the children themselves. There may be situations where a parent, guardian or teacher is happy to grant consent for a child to participate in a study but the child does not wish to participate. Consent from an adult responsible for the child should not be used to coerce the child into participation. The wishes of the children should be respected and they must be able to assent to or dissent from participation. The study should be explained to the child to give them some understanding of it even if it is not possible for the child to fully understand the study. The information provided to the children should be appropriate to their age, maturity and experience and should explain any inconvenience, effort or discomfort required from the children. Conflicts of interest must be avoided where the researchers are undertaking studies in schools where they teach, especially if they are also assessing the children they wish to recruit as research participants. Researchers who wish to include young people as participants must provide evidence that there is no legal reason preventing them from working with children. In the UK, the Disclosure and Barring Service (DBS) certificate has replaced the former Criminal Records Bureau (CRB) certificate. The DBS certificate shows 'unspent' criminal convictions. Convictions are 'spent' once any sentence and rehabilitation period is served. Serious offenses leading to lengthy prison sentences are never spent. Some universities only need to see researchers' DBS certificates before studies commence, while other universities may insist on updated DBS forms every twelve months if studies are conducted over longer periods.

Public and private behaviour

Observational research can study both public and private behaviour. Public behaviour is behaviour that people would expect to be observable to others. The main difference is that studying private behaviour requires the permission of the participants. Studying publicly viewable behaviour is the main research method used in sports performance analysis, and so this will be discussed more within the section on ethical dilemmas in the area. There are some more general concerns about the distinction between public and private behaviour that are worth mentioning in the current section.

There has been much debate about whether different types of social media data are public or private (Stevens et al., 2015). For example, one might expect that openly viewable data in non-password-protected forums can be used in research studies without permission from forum users. Data placed on unprotected social media may be public domain according to the terms and conditions of the particular social media platform. However, researchers should not take advantage of users who may not fully understood the terms and conditions. There have been different rulings in court cases with respect to social media users' reasonable expectations of privacy (Moreno et al., 2013). Therefore, researchers need to consider the terms and conditions of social media platforms and whether these are likely to be understood or even viewed by the particular population groups of interest to the researchers. There are also some difficulties in distinguishing between private and public data on some social media platforms. For example, publicly available Twitter accounts may have retweeted material from other accounts that have since become protected (private) accounts. Therefore, researchers should only use data placed on social media directly by users, rather than indirect data such as retweets.

Privacy is a serious matter, as many countries have laws governing what can and cannot be disclosed about the behaviour of individuals. For example, the UK has the Human Rights Act, which protects people's private and personal information from misuse. The 1998 Data Protection Act is a further UK Act of Parliament that must be complied with by anyone holding data about individuals. Personal data must be accurate, kept up-to-date, used fairly and lawfully and not retained longer than necessary. The data stored about individuals should be those data that are relevant for the given lawful purpose the data are being used for; excessive personal data should not be stored. Those holding data are responsible for protecting the data from being accessed and processed unlawfully. The act details criminal offenses, such as processing personal information without registering as a data controller and gaining unauthorised access to personal data.

Sports performance analysis researchers need to ensure that any personal data held are covered by their organisations and that they comply with policies and processes within their organisations. Video footage should not be maintained longer than necessary, and steps must be taken to prevent video footage falling into the wrong hands. Memory cards used with cameras should be cleared once video files have been copied onto the disks where they are to be stored.

Anonymity and confidentiality

There is a distinction between anonymity and confidentiality. Anonymity means that participants will not be identified, whereas confidentiality means that information provided by research participants will not be disclosed. Typically research leads to findings derived from participant data to be reported in dissertations or papers. Therefore, it is important that researchers inform participants about the purpose of the study and what information will be reported. Some studies identify participants, especially if the studies are in non-sensitive areas or the participants are well-known public figures. There are other studies where participants require anonymity. Participants should be provided with sufficient information about the extent to which and how their anonymity will be protected. The researchers should not make any promises in this respect that cannot be delivered. For example, if illegal activity is disclosed, the researcher may be required to report it to the appropriate authorities. Anonymity is usually protected in quantitative investigations by reporting sample averages rather than individual participant data. Where interview studies have been conducted and excerpts of raw interview data are reported in the findings, pseudonyms should be used to protect participant identity. This still allows readers of research papers to distinguish between sets of quoted interview data belonging to different unknown participants. Researchers using data from social media such as Twitter should not quote tweets directly if they wish to protect participant anonymity. Tweet content can be found very easily using search engines, thus identifying the participants.

Deception

Covert research is considered where participant knowledge of the research study might compromise the findings. For example, in an observational study, the participants might behave differently than their usual behaviour if they are aware they are being studied. Covert research in sensitive areas can involve risks to 'participants'. The quotes are used quite intentionally here because those being studied will not have given consent to be studied and will not have been informed that a research study is even taking place and so will certainly not have been fully informed about their "participation" in the research or how their data are going to be used and reported. Where informed consent is going to be obtained after data collection, granting participants the right to be excluded from the study, there are still risks. People do not like being deceived, it may make them feel they have been made fools of. This could lead to complaints or more serious reactions. Therefore, any use of deception in university research needs to be justified by the importance of the study, the benefits to society and a lack of alternative ways of studying the given topic.

There is a range of deception that can occur within research projects depending on the topic being investigated, participant characteristics and data-gathering processes. An example of a non-contentious use of deception was a study of relative age effect (Edwards and O'Donoghue, 2014) that compared the lived experience of international netball players born in different halves of the academic year. The researchers were concerned that interview responses might be influenced by knowledge of the purpose of the study; therefore, the precise purpose of the study was concealed from the participants until the interviewer asked what month the participant was born at the end of the interview. This was done to help uncover the truth about differences in experience of netball between those born in the first and second halves of the academic year. The general aim of the study – to investigate the lived experiences of international netball players, including selection and participation – was explained to the participants at the beginning of the study. The precise purpose of the study was explained at the conclusion of the interviews, and participants were given the right to withdraw from the study if they wished to.

Sensitive aspects of participant behaviour

Sensitive aspects of participant behaviour include confidential, risky or illegal activity by participants. There are aspects of participant behaviour that may be sensitive in studies of sports performance analysis. For example, in reflective studies done by practicing performance analysts, the coaches and athletes may fear that the way they use the information provided by performance analysis as well as their wider preparation may be scrutinised and criticised. One concern is that successful performers and coaches may not wish their practices to be publicised for rival performers and coaches to learn about. Therefore, researchers and participants should agree in advance what aspects of performance analysis work and the wider coaching context can be described in the ultimate research report and what areas should not be presented publicly.

Risk and harm

Active participants in research studies may undertake tasks for the purpose of the research study that are similar to tasks that they would perform in their normal lives, or the tasks may be less familiar. These tasks may include participating in interviews or focus groups, completing questionnaires or completing laboratory or field-based tests. The studies may also involve interventions, such as training regimes or dietary interventions. There are different types of risk involved with these activities that participants need to be aware of and that researchers need to manage responsibly within research studies. The nature of potential discomfort or harm may be psychological or physical. Interviews may cover topics such as injury experiences or deselection from squads that participants may find upsetting to talk about. Researchers should not only make participants aware of the possibility of psychological stress that may occur as a result of interviews but also have arrangements in place with counselling services if required.

Where participants do strenuous exercise, physical activity readiness questionnaires (PARQ) should be completed and acted upon where necessary. This requires researchers to specify criteria for exclusion from studies based on PARQ contents. Exercise testing and measurement should be administered by appropriately qualified personnel, and if any substances are being produced to be ingested by the participants, these should also be prepared by trained and qualified personnel. The typical process of obtaining ethical clearance for such research is discussed later in this chapter.

130

Vulnerable populations

We have already mentioned the issues involving young people in research studies within the section on voluntary informed consent. There are other vulnerable populations that some research studies may be interested in. These include the elderly and people with learning or physical disabilities. Researchers should consider issues in including these types of participants within studies. In particular, the ability of the participants to understand the research and consent to participation should be considered. Specific risks applying to the participants should also be acknowledged and managed within the research.

Studies without human participants

There are studies of sports performance that do not require passive or active human participants. These are typically theoretical studies of performance using probabilistic models. For example, the probability of a tennis player holding serve is given by an equation in terms of probability of the serving player winning a point, which is assumed to be independent of previous point outcome and score within the game (Hsi & Burych, 1971; Croucher, 1986; Newton and Keller, 2005). A simulation study could manipulate this equation to study momentum effects on the chances of winning service games (Newton and Aslam, 2006). Morris (1977) did a similar theoretical model of tennis that determined the most important points in tennis for various values of the probability of the server winning a point.

ETHICAL DILEMMAS IN SPORTS PERFORMANCE ANALYSIS

Sports performance analysis does not involve the same ethical issues as socio-cultural research into sensitive areas or laboratory-based medical studies. However, there are investigations that combine performance analysis methods with methods used in other disciplines of sports and exercise science. These require the general ethical issues discussed so far in this chapter to be addressed. Many descriptive sports performance analysis studies do not involve invasive methods. The main ethical issues involved in such studies relate to filming, analysis of vulnerable populations, the use of publicly available data, using sensitive information, anonymity of participants and access to performance data.

Filming

Filming by spectators at sports venues is often prohibited due to contractual agreements between sports governing bodies, clubs and commercial broadcasters. Clubs and governing bodies may also sell video recordings of performances, and it is necessary to protect valuable material from piracy.

Where filming of sports performance is necessary within a research project, the filming must be carried out in an ethical manner, complying with child protection policies of venues, obtaining permission to film, respecting the privacy of individuals and using equipment responsibly. Before seeking permission to film from sports organisations, the researcher should examine regulations regarding filming at particular venues, competitions, sports clubs and governing bodies involved. The principle of voluntary informed consent applies to filming just as it applies to other data collection methods. Researchers must describe the purpose of the investigation so that those granting permission to film will be fully informed about the purpose of the study and what is being filmed. Assurances must be given about the use of the video footage being restricted to the research project. Filming must be done in a way that minimises risk of damage to the equipment and harm to the researcher, players and other spectators. Equipment must be certified as safe to use at the venue. Electricity cables must be taped down to avoid people accidentally tripping over them, and filming must be done from a location approved by the venue. Researchers must co-operate fully with staff at the venue and comply with child protection procedures.

Performance analysis support

Chapter 4 discussed enterprise and development projects, which include projects where service provision could be evaluated. The purpose of this section of the current chapter is to raise awareness of ethical issues within such research. The researcher may already be working as a performance analyst with a squad and wish to undertake research into

132

the effectiveness of current practice or some innovation they wish to introduce. The project needs to be of the correct academic level and sufficiently interesting to maintain the student's motivation throughout. Undertaking a project based on work a student is already doing should not be seen as a short cut to completing a dissertation. Where the student's main rationale for doing so is to 'kill two birds with the one stone', there is a danger that there might not be a workable, interesting and substantive project to be done. The process of applying for ethical clearance plays an important role in establishing what the purpose of the study is by stating the research question and identifying where the data will come from. Students and supervisors need to use this process to develop a feasible and interesting research problem and a research question to investigate. Once a research question is established that can be investigated during a service provision study, the ethical issues involved in the project need to be identified and managed. The first issue is that the research requires voluntary informed consent from the squad, both coaches and players. The squad may have been happy working with the researcher as a performance analyst, but the new situation of a research study taking place may be uncomfortable for some of the squad. They may be happy to use performance analysis services but not wish to be participants in the research study. The researcher needs to devise methods that do not require squad members to participate in the study if they do not wish to. The squad members should not feel pressure to participate in the study and their position in the squad should not be affected by whether or not they participate.

Where a researcher wishes to join a squad as a performance analyst in order to investigate the viability or effectiveness of service provision, there may be tensions arising from the purpose of the researcher. The squad members are primarily interested in performance analysis support to improve their performance in competition, while the researcher is primarily interested in the research being done. Everyone involved needs to have a full understanding of the scope, duration and nature of the collaboration between the researcher and the squad. This will hopefully be a mutually beneficial exercise that helps the squad improve and provides excellent research data to be analysed. The researcher and supervisor need to avoid a situation where the researcher and university software and hardware are being exploited by the squad to obtain performance analysis support without having to resource it. One risk of a researcher joining a squad as a performance analyst is that they may be perceived as a threat to the coach, players and indeed any existing performance analysts already working with the squad. The athletes may fear that analysis of their performances could lead to deselection from the squad. Ultimately, the role of sports performance analysis in its coaching context is to help players improve. However, player misperception of the role is possible, and the associated risks are an ethical issue that needs to be managed. The coach may feel that tactical decisions that they are making will be scrutinised within the project in a way that may harm their reputation. The researcher wishes to uncover the truth about the use of performance analysis by coaches and players and report this fully. However, the coach and players will require some details of preparation to remain confidential. This can risk tension between the researcher and the squad, and so it needs to be acknowledged as a risk in the ethics application and considered by all involved in the project at the earliest time. Any existing analyst(s) within the squad may see the researcher as a threat who is providing a performance analysis service at a lower cost. When the researcher is a student, one of the motives for undertaking such a project is to gain relevant experience to improve their employment prospects. The student needs to be open about such motives and avoid working in a way that undermines existing analysts.

Irrespective of whether the researcher was already working with the squad prior to the project, there is a risk that some participants and the researcher may feel uncomfortable in interviews discussing the effectiveness or viability of the service provided. Some may feel unable to say what they really think of the service for fear of upsetting the researcher. The researcher needs to establish ways of helping participants provide complete and accurate information during research interviews, avoiding unnecessary discomfort to the participants. The findings need to be truthful while also avoiding undue reputational harm to research participants. A further issue that needs to be considered is that the researcher may be leaving the squad at some point once the research is finished. They need to have an exit strategy in place to avoid uncomfortable situations of feeling like they have let the squad down by ceasing to provide performance analysis support at the end of the study.

Anonymity is a problem with projects done by students who are already working as performance analysts within squads. The eventual dissertation can be written up concealing the identity of the squad, coaches and players. However, it may be common knowledge in the given sport and in the university that the student is working for the given squad.

134

Therefore, the student and squad need to be realistic about the prospects of maintaining anonymity. Some coaches and athletes agree to being identified within papers written about the research. They also have the opportunity to check findings and make suggestions to alter these if they feel studies do not represent their views accurately. There may be other studies where coaches and players agree with researchers what areas can be written about publicly and what information is not to be published.

One way of overcoming issues of anonymity is for the researcher to study an analyst's experiences and display the findings as a storytelling narrative that conveys the important findings about the experiences without using any information that could identify the analyst, coaches, players or organisations involved. It is recommended that performance analysis scholars undertaking such a project would need to have also studied socio-cultural issues in sports as well as ethnographic methods. The best example of this is Huggan et al.'s (2015) paper about an early-career analyst needing to develop micro-political literacy when working in a professional soccer environment. The research involved a series of four interviews with a real soccer analyst identified as an information rich case.

The storytelling approach (Smith and Sparkes, 2006; 2009) allows the findings of a study to be discussed without identifying the case. In the example of Huggan et al.'s (2015) study, the story was discussed in relation to social theory about micro-political learning but within specific sports coaching environments (Potrac and Jones 2009a/b; Thompson et al., 2015). The story covered key incidents within the analyst's career in detail rather than trying to reflect day-to-day work. These incidents included selling his skills after graduating, learning about the professional soccer environment and dealing with change. All students considering any type of reflective analysis study or intervention study should read this paper.

Using public domain data

There is a wealth of sports performance data available to the public which have potential benefits for research. These data include video recordings of sports performances provided on broadcast, satellite or internet channels as well as match statistics provided on the internet. Let us consider the ethics of using such data in research. Professional players are paid by their clubs or receive appearance money or prize money from events they compete in. Amateur athletes competing in competitions that are being televised, or where results appear on event internet sites, will be aware of the public exposure of their performance when they choose to enter the events. Those who organise sports events are paid by broadcasters who in turn receive money from the subscribers to the given media channels. It may, therefore, be argued that athletes agreeing to participate in televised events have given their consent for information about their performances to be made public. For this reason, academic researchers do not need to obtain voluntary informed consent to use publicly available video images and other publicly available data about performances within research investigations. Furthermore, it can be argued that athletes competing in events covered by publicly available media channels have also entered such events in full knowledge that they are not performing anonymously. Some universities consider research using data in the public domain to be exempt when it comes to ethical approval. Others consider the athletes portrayed in publicly available video and statistical data to be 'passive human participants' within the study; that is, they are not actively doing anything that they would not otherwise be doing if the study was not taking place. There are some ethical issues relating to investigations involving passive human participants. The presentation and discussion of results of some studies could cause unfair risk or social, psychological or financial harm to athletes, coaches or referees. This could result in legal action being taken against universities responsible for such research.

There are other ethical issues in using publicly available material that should be recognised by sports performance analysis researchers. Broadcast material is often provided commercially and, therefore, researchers or their universities must subscribe to the given media channels that provide the material. Pirated copies of the material should not be used, and copies of the material should not be passed on to other researchers who may not be subscribers of the given media channel. The source of the data, whether a media channel or an internet site, may specify terms and conditions for the use of any material they provide publicly. For example, some internet sites may insist that they have not granted permission for data to be used for research purposes and that permission must be granted by the individual athletes of interest. Researchers must comply with the conditions of any data sources they are using.

136

While athletes may be identified during media coverage of performances, there are situations where their anonymity must be preserved. Some research journals and professional bodies prohibit the naming of individual participants within research papers and other research outputs. Others require participants to give permission to be identified within the paper. Where journals prohibit the identification of athletes, researchers should choose alternative outlets in which to publish their research if their papers identify any athletes.

Pre-existing data sets

Descriptive studies of sports performance typically involve sustained data collection activity, processing of data and statistical analyses related to the research question of interest embedded within an academic research process. Some students may have access to pre-existing data sets, meaning that they do not need to collect data; for example data may be provided by commercial organisations, squads or governing bodies for use in research studies. This leads to two issues which must be addressed early within projects. The first issue is that some students may consider it to be unfair that classmates do not need to collect data, and there is a perception that the data processing and analysis done on pre-existing data sets takes no more time than the same activities when performed by students who have had to watch matches and collect their own data. The second issue is related to the first in that students who do not make a sustained independent effort during research projects risk failing the dissertation module. Therefore, supervisors need to ensure that studies involving pre-existing data sets are justified with sufficient challenge in the data processing and analyses aspects as well as the theoretical development involved. It is also useful for students undertaking such projects to independently analyse a subset of the matches to demonstrate the validity of the data source being used. Projects involving pre-existing data sets are easier to justify at the master's level, where students have previously undertaken data collection activity in undergraduate study. At the master's level, there is an expectation of more sophisticated data analysis and theoretical development than at the undergraduate level. Undergraduate students, on the other hand, are expected to undertake projects where they collect data. The experience of data collection is beneficial at this level because students can observe the data in context and consider potential methodological and theoretical issues for discussion at a later date.

ETHICS POLICIES AND PROCEDURES

Research ethics governance

Research undertaken at universities and other academic institutions needs to be conducted to the highest ethical standards. Ethics governance within these organisations takes the form of ethics committees who take responsibility for research ethics. Typically, a university research ethics committee maintains research ethics policies and procedures while also being the main contact for external bodies who may wish to inspect audits of university research. The main business of scrutinising research proposals is conducted by faculty or departmental research ethics committees. The university ethics committee disseminates policies and procedures to the faculty ethics committees as such policies and procedures are developed. For example, in recent years research has been conducted on and using social media. This has led to ethical concerns that have had to be considered and addressed within ethics policies (Moreno et al., 2013; Stevens et al., 2015). A university ethics committee is typically made up of personnel from each faculty so that a full range of research can be represented when developing new policies and procedures. The process of developing policies and procedures can also involve consultation with experts within faculties who are not members of the university's research ethics committee.

University ethics committees ensure as far as possible that there is consistency of practice with respect to research ethics across different university faculties. This means that ethics forms and guidance for completing them are typically developed at a university level. Individual faculties can then produce additional material that is relevant to the specific types of research problem areas that they cover. This material includes faculty-level policies and procedures that build on the more general university policies and procedures. Research ethics are covered during research process modules within taught programmes, and faculty research ethics committees have a role in developing the materials used during sessions on research ethics. The materials are typically provided through virtual learning-support environments.

138

Faculty research ethics committees are responsible for the ethical conduct of research within individual faculties and provide project status reports to the university research ethics committee so that all university research can be audited. Staff and students seek ethical approval for research projects from their faculty ethics committees. This can be done directly or indirectly. There are ethical issues that necessitate some research proposals needing to be scrutinised directly by faculty research ethics committees. These include projects involving participants under eighteen years of age and other vulnerable populations, research into sensitive aspects of behaviour, deception of participants, use of human tissue and invasive measurement and testing beyond what would normally be experienced by the participants. The indirect approach is where research that is uncontentious is recommended for approval by supervisors before being formally approved by the faculty research ethics committee. Thus, supervisors provide details of the research they have approved, the students involved and the process of recommending approval. The ethics form describing the research project must be stored for the duration of the project so that there is a record of the research that has been approved. In many universities, faculties have moved to electronic means of storing ethics documentation. This prevents material from being lost and also prevents multiple versions of ethics forms causing confusion. The electronic storage of ethics documentation allows students, supervisors and faculty ethics committees to understand exactly what was approved and how. Research that is sent to faculty research ethics committees may be approved by the committee when first considered or after necessary amendments have been made. Some research projects may not be approved due to serious ethical concerns or lack of detail.

Completing the ethics form

Researchers need to complete the ethics form in detail to allow an ethics committee or supervisor to make a decision on whether the project can be approved. The duration of the project, when it starts and completes and who is undertaking the research is needed. In describing who is doing the research, it is not simply a matter of entering the name of the researcher and any supervisor. The researcher needs to identify who will be doing the various tasks within the project and what relevant experience and qualifications they have in relation to their roles within the project. The purpose and rationale for the research should be included.

The methods should be sufficiently detailed in order to permit an ethical decision to be made. It is generally accepted that deciding on performance variables to analyse and developing an observational analysis system are part of many sports performance analysis projects. It is still possible to provide sufficient detail about the types of variables and the type of observation that will be done without going into detail of code windows and operational definitions of variables. The researchers should describe where the data will come from and who the participants will be, including their age, level, and gender, as well as the number of participants. The types of performances to be analysed should be identified, and the broad area of performance (tactical, technical or work-rate, for example) should be stated. If there is insufficient methodological detail for those considering the application to approve the project, it may be possible to conditionally approve the project. This happens when the committee or supervisor have a good idea of what the student intends to do but the form is vague in some areas of concern. The person(s) dealing with the form can state a condition, such as the project is approved subject to only adult participants being studied or the project can only use public-domain video material. This is a condition the researcher must comply with during the project. If the researcher feels that the project has been misunderstood and the condition is too stringent and compromises the research, they will need to reapply, providing more detail.

Any risks associated with the project should be listed along with the ways in which those risks are going to be managed during the project. Where the form uses different sections for risks and risk management, it is a good idea to number the risks so that the same numbers can be used to show which risks are addressed by each risk management process. Finally, the student should include any participant information to be used during recruitment, the consent form to be used and any risk assessment forms along with the ethics application form.

Students should view research ethics as an on-going process that continues for the duration of the research project. The ethics form is a legal document about how the research will be conducted that has been agreed to by the researcher (whether a student, member of staff, or research degree student) and the university. The research must be conducted according to what has been approved.

140

Awareness and training

Students and staff need to be acquainted with research principles, policies and procedures. Students will cover research ethics within research process modules. Typically this is done prior to the final year of undergraduate programmes or, for master's students, before students need to submit dissertation proposals and ethics applications. University staff also need to engage in continuous professional development in the area of research ethics. This is because conducting ethical research not only requires research ethics policies and procedures to be in place and a good understanding of ethical principles in research, but also requires staff to understand how policies and procedures are to be enacted. Staff have responsibilities for applying for ethical approval for their own personal research as well as assisting dissertation students to make ethics applications. The staff also have responsibilities to store ethics forms for the purposes of research auditing as well as retaining data and consent forms for periods required by ethics policies.

Therefore, members of faculty research ethics committees should meet with subject teams to provide staff development opportunities. These meetings should be held once per year and provide an opportunity for new procedures to be presented to staff, ethical dilemma in recent research studies to be discussed and guidance from the university's central ethics committee to be outlined. Scenarios with ethical dilemmas from the given subject area can be discussed. This helps members of the ethics committee gauge the staff's level of awareness of research ethics. The training days can also report on faculty auditing of research projects in the previous year. Were there any projects approved that should not have been approved? Were there any approved by supervisors that should have come to the faculty's research ethics committee? Were there any sent to the committee that could have been recommended for approval by the supervisor? Were there any with missing information on participant recruitment, methods, risks or supervisor signatures? Were there any uploaded into ethics repositories without the supporting participant information sheets, risk assessment forms or consent forms? Were there any projects that could have benefitted from existing protocols but failed to refer to these in the ethics application? Raising these errors with staff helps ensure that improvements are made at the operational level of research ethics management. This type of training helps maintain staff awareness of ethics principles, policies and procedures and is especially important where faculties have regular turnover of staff.

SUMMARY

Sports performance analysis typically involves observation of passive human participants competing in competitive sport. This type of research does have ethical issues to be managed, no matter whether the performances have been recorded from public domain media coverage or private videos have been used. Some projects may combine sports performance analysis with other methods that have greater ethical issues to be managed. There are other types of project that fall under the scope of sports performance analysis research, including enterprise and development projects. The ethical issues involved in these projects have been discussed within the current chapter. Finally, all research undertaken within universities needs to be approved directly or indirectly by a research ethics committee, ethical documentation needs to be completed and retained and the agreed methods must be complied with for the duration of the project.

REFERENCES

Croucher, J.S. (1986) 'The conditional probability of winning games of tennis', *Research Quarterly in Exercise and Sport*, 57: 23–26.

Edwards, L. and O'Donoghue, P.G. (2014) 'Relative age effect in netball: a qualitative investigation', *International Journal of Coaching Science*, 8(1): 47–68.

Helsinki Declaration (2013) 'Ethical principles for medical research', *The JAMA Network*, http://jamanetwork.com/journals/jama/fullarticle/1760318 (accessed 26 November 2016).

Hsi, B.P. and Burych, D.M. (1971) 'Games of two players', *Journal of the Royal Statistical Society – Series C*, 20: 86–92.

Huggan, R., Nelson, L. and Potrac, P. (2015) 'Developing micropolitical literacy in professional soccer: a performance analyst's tale', *Qualitative Research in Sport, Exercise and Health*, 4: 504–520. http://dx.doi.org/10.1080/2159676X.2014.949832

Moreno, M.A., Goniu, N., Moreno, P.S. and Diekema, D. (2013) 'Ethics of social media research: common concerns and practical considerations', *Cyberpsychology, Behavior, and Social Networking*, 16(9): 708–714.

Morris, C. (1977) 'The most important points in tennis', in S.P. Ladany and R.E. Machol (eds), *Optimal strategies in sport* (pp. 131–140). New York: North Holland.

Newton, P.K. and Aslam, K. (2006) 'Monte Carlo tennis', *SIAM Review*, 48: 722–742.

Newton, P.K. and Keller, J.B. (2005) 'The probability of winning at tennis', *Theory and Data, Studies in Applied Mathematics*, 114: 214–269.

O'Donoghue, P.G. (2010) *Research methods for sports performance analysis.* London: Routledge.

Potrac, P. and Jones, R. (2009a) 'Power, conflict and co-operation: towards a micro-politics of coaching', *Quest*, 61: 223–236.

Potrac, P. and Jones, R. (2009b) 'Micro-political workings in semi-professional soccer coaching', *Sociology of Sport Journal*, 26: 557–577.

Resnik, D.B. (2015) 'What is ethics in research and why is it important?' National Institute of Environmental Health Sciences, www.niehs.nih.gov/research/resources/bioethics/whatis/ (accessed 23 February 2017).

Smith, B. and Sparkes, A.C. (2006) 'Narrative inquiry in psychology: exploring the tensions within', *Qualitative Research in Psychology*, 3: 169–192.

Smith, B. and Sparkes, A.C. (2009) 'Narrative analysis and sport and exercise psychology: understanding lives in diverse way', *Psychology of Sport and Exercise*, 10: 279–288.

Stevens, G., O'Donnell, V.L. and Williams, L. (2015) 'Public domain or private data? Developing an ethical approach to social media research in an inter-disciplinary project', *Educational Research and Evaluation*, 21(2): 154–167.

Thomas, J.R., Nelson, J.K. and Silverman, D. (2011) *Research methods in physical activity, 6th edn.* Champaign, IL: Human Kinetics.

Thompson, A., Potrac, P. and Jones, R.L. (2015) 'I found out the hard way': micro-political workings in professional football. *Sport, Education and Society*, 20: 976–994. doi: 10.1080/13573322.2013.862786

Tinkler, P. (2013) *Using photographs in social and historical research.* London: Sage.

Weindling, P. (2001) 'The origins of informed consent: the international scientific commission on medical war crimes, and the nuremberg code', *Bulletin of the History of Medicine*, 75(1): 37–71.

CHAPTER 7

SYSTEM DEVELOPMENT

OVERVIEW

Whether students are designing a system to be used in an applied practical setting or to form part of a research project, the process of system development is largely the same. The key to good system design starts with students identifying what they require their system to do, namely what information the students want to obtain from the performances that they will be reviewing. If the students have not yet finalised this, then perusal of relevant literature and Chapters 2, 3 and 4 of this book might be a good place to pique some interest.

Whilst this book is oriented towards research methods, and therefore the specifics will be focussed towards this process, the fundamentals of system development remain the same, even when working in an applied practical setting. Discussion with the coaching staff about what they would like to see from the analysis is of utmost importance. Having knowledge about the sport and understanding the variables/information that students can get from observing the sport would help with driving the discussion of options. Many coaches will not understand the time implications of some of the relevant variables that can be collected, so students should always be mindful of the time that it takes to obtain and process the data for feedback purposes. This is not to say that students should use this as a delimiting factor of their involvement in the scenario, but rather as more a reference guide to ensure that whatever information they do obtain from the performances can be used in a timely fashion to provide feedback.

For academic research, students will need to obtain ethical approval for the research that they are undertaking. This will normally involve the completion of a form that provides enough information for the reviewer to understand the scope of the project and the sample and data collection methods. In order to be able to apply for this ethical approval, students will need to have a thorough understanding of what they will be researching, with clear aims and objectives specified and a proposed method detailed. This is covered in Chapter 6.

STAGES OF DEVELOPMENT

The process of designing, developing, refining and implementing an analysis system can involve several different stages from inception through to final implementation. Just because students have studied performance analysis for a few years doesn't mean that this is necessarily going to be a straightforward and quick process. To ensure the students' system provides them with all the necessary information, there will be a process of development from initial ideas to the final product. It is advisable to start this process as early as possible to ensure that students allow themselves adequate time for development, refinement, final data collection and data analysis. Figure 7.1 shows the process of system development for sports performance analysis systems.

RESEARCH AND PLANNING

Probably the most significant element of any system development remains the research into or discussion of the possible topic area; as mentioned in Chapter 5, this forms part of the initial scoping of the system in the research and planning stage. At this stage, students should formulate their research question and identify the specific aims and objectives of the research project. Normally this is done through initial discussion with a potential research supervisor and informed by knowledge from a literature search. These discussions will help to develop students' ideas from the embryonic stages into something that will satisfy the assessment criteria. Please note that these criteria are dependent on what level of research students are undertaking.

It is not possible to create a system without prior knowledge of the specific nuances of the sport and the research question that students are investigating. Refer to Chapter 5 for further steps associated with the research proposal and Chapter 6 for ethical issues when investigating in the area of performance analysis.

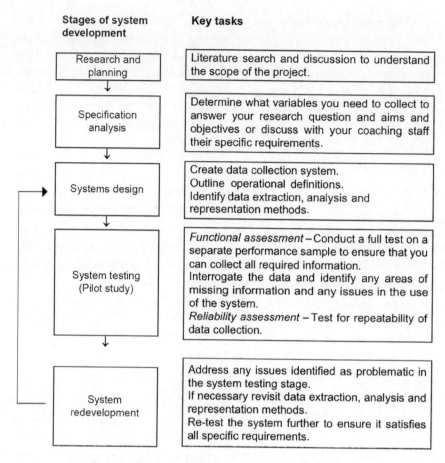

Figure 7.1 Stages of system development

When the research question has been outlined and the objectives have been identified, students will have a framework to identify exactly what it is that their data collection system needs to provide. Knowing the answers to the following questions will help students in the next stage:

- What is the purpose of the study?
- What are the aims and specific objectives of my research question?
- What information do I need know?
- What information do I not need to know?
- What do I expect to be the outcome of my analysis? What are my hypotheses?

146

SPECIFICATION ANALYSIS

The research question and specific aims and objectives of the project are now defined. With this information outlined students can work to select the relevant performance variables that will provide the necessary data. To successfully do this, students need to be sure that they understand the difference between action variables and performance indicators and how these contribute towards each other to answer the research question (for further information on this, see O'Donoghue (2015: 56–82)). Students might find that their performance indicators are loosely aligned to the specific research objectives that they have identified. To assist with this stage, a thorough exploration of the literature relevant to the research question is necessary. Reviewing the relevant literature will give students ideas of what data are obtainable and perhaps identify suitable processes of data collection. To help students in this process, they should now be able to answer the following questions:

- What data points can I collect?
- What process can I use to collection the information that I need?

SYSTEM DESIGN

This is potentially the most time-consuming part of the overall system development process, and something that is unique and specific to each student and their own research area. Using the action variables that students have identified in the previous stage (systems analysis), they can now create a data collection system. The same process can be followed whether students are using a hand notation system or computerised system or are undertaking biomechanical analysis of technique.

Operational definitions

With variables specified in a data collection sheet, it is now necessary for students to turn their attention to identifying exactly what they might mean when they collect the occurrences of these variables during the performance. The correct identification and definition of performance variables is one step towards ensuring a reliable data collection process. Whether students are acting as an individual researcher or as a group of analysts collecting data for a larger project, it is vitally important that

147

they take the necessary steps to ensure that the data collected are both valid and reliable. Not only will it help with ensuring that they will be consistent in their data collection processes, it will also assist when comparisons are made to findings from other similar studies (Williams, 2012).

Information derived from the review of literature should help students with writing these definitions in such a manner that they are clear and attempt to reduce any areas of confusion. Students should consider the operational definitions for technical effectiveness used by Hughes and Probert (2006), shown in Table 7.1. O'Donoghue (2010) acknowledged the level of subjectivity with terms such as 'slight pressure' and 'good technique' that are seemingly undefined, noting that there is no allowance for excellent technique being performed without pressure. Does this mean that this information is not collected? Or does this highlight a deficiency in the analysis system designed? Should the concepts of pressure and quality of technique be merged into a single scale?

Table 7.2 is an example of operational definitions of two variables in an equestrian study (Arundel and Holmes, 2013). It is worth noting that operational definitions do not always need to be denoted via text explanations. Depending on the research project it may be more suitable

Table 7.1 Technical effectiveness ratings for soccer (Hughes and Probert, 2006)

Rating	Operational definition
+3	Excellent technique performed under pressure
+2	Very good technique performed under slight pressure
+1	Good technique performed under no pressure
0	Average, standard technique
-1	Poor technique performed under pressure
-2	Very poor technique performed under slight pressure
-3	Unacceptable technique performed under no pressure

Table 7.2 Operational definitions of ground and flight times (Arundel and Holmes, 2013)

Performance variable	Operational definition
Ground time	Time between the fences, from when the back feet have landed on the ground after the fence to when the front feet leave the floor at the take-off of the next fence.
Flight time	The time over the fences, from when the front feet leave the floor at take-off of the fence to when the back feet touch the ground after the fence.

148

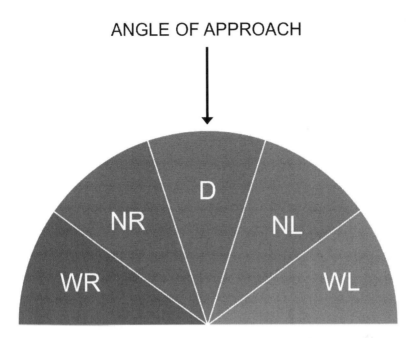

ANGLE OF APPROACH

Figure 7.2 Angle of approach definition (Arundel and Holmes, 2013)

to provide a diagrammatic view of delineation of variables collected (Figure 7.2), especially when students are identifying areas of an arena (Arundel and Holmes, 2013) or goal location (Alcock, 2010).

Recently Williams (2012) discussed how in other areas of sports there has been a move towards a consensus on operational definitions, however very little progress has been made on a standardisation of operational definitions within performance analysis. Williams (2012) noted that if a standard set of operational definitions were developed for individual sports, then replication of studies and comparisons of findings would be more meaningful. There, however, will always be the need for different operational definitions as game conditions and rules change and as individual research projects are designed to identify specific characteristics of the game.

Data collection system

Unless students' research questions involve the use of specific video sections of the performance, are related to time-based elements of performance or are technique-analysis based, then they are not restricted to using a computerised, video-based performance analysis system for their data collection. Whilst students have spent previous years learning how to master the data collection process within software packages such as Dartfish (Dartfish, Fribourg, Switzerland), NacSport (NacSport, Las Palmas de Gran Canaria, Spain) or Sportscode (Hudl, Lincoln, NE), use of these packages does restrict them to a specific location and time for their data collection. If they do not require the video footage or need to do further analysis with the timing elements of their data collection, then it may be easier for them to collect their data using a spreadsheet-based software such as Microsoft Excel or Apple Numbers.

Microsoft Excel allows students to add data into a spreadsheet based on a predetermined list of variables using a data validation list. By organising performance indicators and action variables into columns, students can work through the data collection process in a logical fashion and select the relevant items. Similarly, when using Apple's Numbers spreadsheet application, students can utilise the pop-up menu. In the creation of these systems, students should think about the logical order that they would see things as they occur during the performance. Then students can organise their variables to allow a workflow from left to right, ensuring that the data input process is systematic. This same design principle of a systematic workflow from left to right is also something for students to think about when designing a tagging panel, category template or code window within the performance analysis packages. Support in designing and utilising the relevant features within these packages can be found in O'Donoghue and Holmes (2015: 23–36). Students may also want to review the ergonomics of their data collection system. Unnecessary mouse movement or button clicks will only mean more work involved in collecting the data and will also mean there is greater chance of error. Lucy Holmes has used a software package (ioGraphica, BearOnUnicycle, Adelaide) that maps the mouse movements around the screen over time to identify any issues with design ergonomics.

Data extraction and analysis

Although students are not yet at the stage of having data from their data collection system, during this design phase it is also pertinent to understand how they are going to use the data that are collected. It is a

150

worthwhile exercise to collect some dummy data so that they can ascertain whether there is the need to make any changes to where the data are input into the data sheet or how the data are represented within the software. Commercial performance analysis software packages will have several options for accessing the data that they have collected; students can review O'Donoghue and Holmes (2015: 23–36) for some assistance.

Figuring out how to extract the data from the data collection system is something that many students neglect to look at during the system design and assessment. Failure to think about what they are going to do with the data they have collected can sometimes result in difficulty producing results and providing relevant information.

Data representation

Presenting the data that students' system provides is dependent in part on the audience that it is being presented to. If students are producing data for academic purposes, there are certain guidelines that they must adhere to; these will be outlined in their programme specifications or journal submission guidelines. If students are presenting this information to athletes or coaches, then speed of interpretation is a key consideration. O'Donoghue and Holmes (2015: 68–84) discuss the use of data dashboards to present data based on performances, identifying some key principles for dashboard design.

Of course, the other influencing factor in the data representation is the data themselves. Certain data lend themselves to being displayed and interpreted in tabular or graphical format. Students should always be cautious that data only be presented once. Some students fall into the trap of presenting the same data as both a table and a graph. Students also need to ensure that they are not producing too many graphs or tables. In Chapter 1 of the current book, the authors discussed the use of a grid of eight squares that outlined the results that are expected to be produced based on the aims and objectives of the research. Students should ensure that all of these are being satisfied with the data representations.

If students are producing results on a number of variables in relation to groups, then this could be displayed in one table. Table 7.3 and Figures 7.3 to 7.6 are representations of the same data. The decision as to

Table 7.3 Significant positional differences in performance variables (mean ± SD; post hoc Tukey with adjusted alpha) (Holmes et al., 2008)

	Defenders	Midfield	Forward
Total distance (km)[b]	7.84±0.72	9.56±1.40***	9.75±1.70***
Distance walking (km)[a]	2.10±0.19	1.80±0.25***	1.74±0.15***
Distance striding (km)[b]	1.72±0.72	2.28±0.39**	2.37±0.30***
Distance sprinting (km)[b]	1.32±0.53	2.20±0.88**	2.55±1.02***
% time spent walking[a]	49±5	40±6***	39±7***
% time striding[b]	12±2	17±3***	16±3***
% time sprinting[b]	3±2	12±6**	13±7***
% time low intensity[a]	82.1±4.5	71.7±7.8***	70.4±9.1***
% time high intensity[b]	17.8±4.5	28.3±7.8***	29.6±9.1***
Rest between sprints (secs)[a]	37.6±12.7	23.1±6.4***	19.3±4.0***
Total no of sprints[b]	132±76	177±45*	203±42***
No of RSA bouts[c]	5±4	12±8	16±9***
Frequency of Walk bouts[a]	533±32	499±29**	492±36***
Frequency of Stride bouts[b]	311±60	390±62***	409±47***
Frequency of Sprint bouts[b]	127±49	176±45***	201±42***
Work:Rest ratio[b]	4.98±1.68	2.78±1.03**	2.85±1.95***

[a]defenders > midfield and forward; [b]defenders < midfield and forward; [c]defenders < forwards

*$p < .05$, **$p < .01$, ***$p < .001$

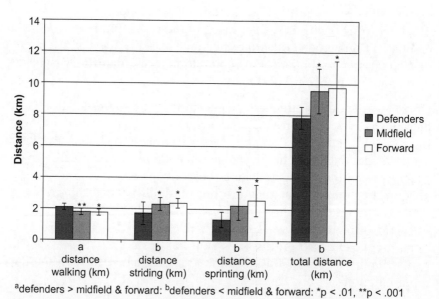

[a]defenders > midfield & forward: [b]defenders < midfield & forward: *$p < .01$, **$p < .001$

Figure 7.3 Significant positional differences in distance covered (Holmes et al., 2008)

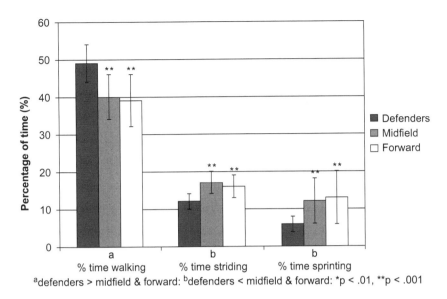

Figure 7.4 Significant positional differences in percentage of time spent in locomotion categories (Holmes et al., 2008)

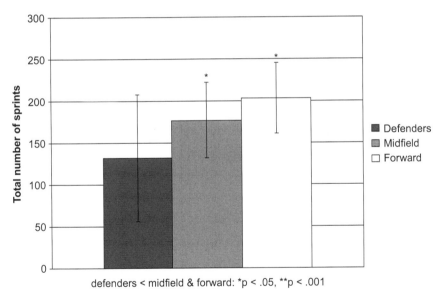

Figure 7.5 Significant positional differences in the total number of sprints (Holmes et al., 2008)

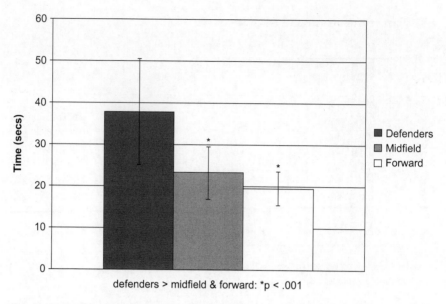

defenders > midfield & forward: *p < .001

Figure 7.6 Significant positional differences in the amount of rest time between sprints (Holmes et al., 2008)

the best form of data representation is somewhat personal. As the table and figures demonstrate, both formats show the same data and indicate the significant differences immediately. Some would argue that there may be too much information displayed at once within Table 7.3, whilst others would argue that the table gives a greater view of the exact data points, enabling a clearer view of the differences between the groups. Both are equally acceptable within an academic context; the table might be beneficial if students have other information that they want to display that is not in this grouping format.

Following completion of the design stage, students should now be able to answer the following questions:

■ Can I provide data to answer my research questions?
■ Is there any confusion between the data variables I am collection?
■ Do I know what format these data will be in?
■ How will I use these data to answer the research question?
■ What is the best form of data presentation to satisfy my research question?

154

SYSTEM TESTING (PILOT STUDY)

Functional assessment

Assessing the functionality of any system is highly important in both applied and research data collection processes. This should be done to assess whether the system allows for all data variables to be collected. Students might find that, as they use the system, they identify missing elements required for data collection. They might also realise that with very little extra work they can obtain some more information that might help further along in the data analysis process. These might be extra bits of data that assist with discussion elements that previously have not been thought about. As a note of caution, students should be careful not to add too much information in as an extra, as this can detract from the main body of their work, and the essential data then become lost in an array of other data.

This functionality test can form part of the required pilot study and therefore should be documented within the methods section as part of the system development process. When conducting this process there are number of things that students need to look out for:

- Does it provide all the necessary information to answer the research question and meet the project's aims and objectives?
- Is the process easy to use? Is it in a logical order?

Reliability assessment

The reliability of the data collection system could be the one thing that determines whether the data obtained from it are usable or not; from an applied perspective, it could also be the determining factor of whether someone gets to keep their job or not. After spending the time designing a system, analysing the performance and arranging the data for the coach(es) to interpret, the last thing that students want is to be giving them information that they are not sure is correct. Similarly, for a research project, students wouldn't want to make comparisons or general population assumptions based on incorrect data. As discussed previously, there are many things that can affect the reliability of the system design, its use and the information extracted, from operational definitions to system ergonomics to usability.

O'Donoghue (2012: 337–367) discusses reliability, measurement issues, types of reliability study, selection of relevant reliability statistics, and production of reliability statistics. For most undergraduate dissertations, students need to be thinking about intra-operator reliability: the consistency of the operator as part of the data collection to produce the same results on separate occasions. For a more rigorous level of reliability analysis, an inter-operator reliability test must be conducted. This requires another trained individual to use the data collection system and analyse the same performance independently. When comparisons of the two independent observations have been made, the reliability of the system can be gauged. This assessment might identify that all or some of the variables being assessed are unreliable. If this is the case, then further steps to rectify this would need to be taken. These steps might include adjustments to the overall data collection system, further training of the operator or adjustments in the operational definitions used. It is worth noting that precise operational definitions do not necessarily guarantee a good level of reliability. O'Donoghue (2010: 155–157) discussed a research project that had eight pages of detailed operational definitions, but following training and agreement of the definitions, reliability assessments identified serious limitations. For further information on how to use data to assess for levels of reliability, refer to O'Donoghue (2012: 337–367).

When conducting a reliability assessment of the data collection system, students should think about the following questions:

- Do I need to conduct intra- or inter-operator reliability assessment?
- How will I compare the two data sets?
- What reliability statistics am I using?
- What does the output of the reliability statistic mean for my system?
- How does this impact the use of my system going forward?

System redevelopment

This stage of the system development process is very much dependent on the outcome of the previous stage. Students should review their answers to the key questions that have been outlined in the functional

156

and reliability assessment sections above. Then they should ask themselves the following questions:

- Are there any changes that need to be made?
  If you answer YES to this question, return to the system design stage and make any relevant changes; then continue through to the system testing stage and assess the functionality and reliability of the system again.
- Does your system satisfy all relevant criteria?
  If you answer YES to this question, then your system is ready for full data collection.

SUMMARY

The stages of system development are in part a cyclical process. When students have decided what information that they want their data collection system to collect, it is the process of developing, refining and implementing the analysis system, following the progression through the stages. Following this process stage by stage should enable students to design and develop a useful data collection system for both academic research and practical applied purposes.

REFERENCES

Alcock, A. (2010) 'Analysis of direct free kicks in the women's football World Cup 2007', *European Journal of Sport Science*, 10: 279–284.

Arundel, S. and Holmes, L. (2013) 'Performance analysis of show jumping strategy during British eventing', in D. Peters and P.G. O'Donoghue (eds), *Performance analysis of sport IX* (pp. 183–189). London: Routledge.

Holmes, L.A., Peters, D.M. and Robinson, P.D. (2008) 'A time motion analysis of elite women's hockey – implications for fitness assessment and training', *Book of abstracts for the World Congress of Performance Analysis of Sport VIII*, Magdeburg, Germany.

Hughes, M. and Probert, G. (2006) 'A technical analysis of elite male soccer players by position and success', in H. Dancs, M. Hughes and P.G. O'Donoghue (eds), *Performance analysis of sport 7* (pp. 89–104). Cardiff: CPA Press, UWIC.

O'Donoghue, P.G. (2010) *Research methods for sports performance analysis*. London: Routledge.

O'Donoghue, P.G. (2012) *Statistics for sport and exercise studies*. London: Routledge.

O'Donoghue, P.G. (2015) *An introduction to performance analysis of sport.* London: Routledge.

O'Donoghue, P.G. and Holmes, L. (2015) *Data analysis in sport.* London: Routledge.

Williams, J.J. (2012) 'Operational definitions in performance analysis and the need for consensus', *International Journal of Performance Analysis in Sport*, 12: 52–63.

CHAPTER 8

DATA GATHERING AND ANALYSIS

OVERVIEW

This chapter describes both quantitative and qualitative analysis processes and how they should be linked to the research question and the interpretation of results. A selection of data analysis techniques from both qualitative and quantitative methods are outlined. There are two main types of quantitative study in sports performance analysis. The first compares performance variables between different samples of performances or matches. These could be independent or related samples. The second type of descriptive study correlates performance variables of interest. Although the vast majority of data analysis processes in sports performance analysis are quantitative in nature, qualitative methods may form part or all of the methods in a project. An example in which they may form part of the analysis is after the main quantitative study has been completed, the investigator may want to interview coaches or performers to discuss the value of the results. There are also different types of qualitative research that are distinguished by their theoretical positions (Flick, 2007: 11); the researcher should first justify the role of the particular type of qualitative method to be used within the project (O'Donoghue, 2010: 146).

Issues associated with initial study design are examined first in the chapter, as this subject has not previously been covered in detail (O'Donoghue, 2010). It is not always as simple as just applying the methods that have been described. There are two parts to a study; designing the study and then doing the study. Once the methods have been devised, there is still more to the research process than simply doing the research as intended. There are three key aspects of doing the research that are considered: management, ethics and recording. Ethics have been covered in Chapter 6 and, therefore, will not be covered here. However, issues related to the management of the dissertation and recording of data will be.

DATA COLLECTION METHODS

Once the project has received approval, the student should ensure that the research is conducted in the way that was approved. A signed ethics form should be regarded as a legal document. It is an agreement between the student and the university about how the research can be conducted (O'Donoghue, 2010: 147). More information regarding ethics procedures can be found in Chapter 6 of this book.

During the process of data collection, the student should keep a log-book of activity to record any problems or issues that may be of value to write up in the final draft of the dissertation. For quantitative studies, these issues are often in the form of a pilot study. Pilot studies play an important role in research by providing information for the planning and justification of a study design (Lancaster et al., 2004). This is especially true in performance analysis where we need to ensure that our system design is as valid and objective as possible. Results should be exported from relevant software and analysed to ensure the system produces the results that are expected. Pilot testing is also important for qualitative research where doing the research is more than merely following the research design (Flick, 2007: 39).

OBSERVATIONAL STUDIES OF SPORTS PERFORMANCE

Comparing samples of performances

The traditional type of undergraduate sports performance research project is a descriptive quantitative study of actual sports performance. These studies are still very popular and worthwhile. The studies observe real sports performances without any experimental manipulation of conditions and are, therefore, descriptive in nature. Descriptive studies do have disadvantages compared to experimental investigations when it comes to providing evidence of cause and effect relationships between variables. This is due to experimental control not being possible in such studies. However, descriptive research is a recognised type of research that does contribute to knowledge (Thomas and Nelson, 1996: 313–342). The traditional observational studies of sports performance have the advantage of ecological validity in that real sports performance is being studied rather than performance in controlled artificial settings.

The main type of descriptive study in sports performance analysis looks at the effect of some independent variable on some dependent performance variables. The independent variable is typically some categorical variable that allows samples of data to be formed and compared. The independent variable could distinguish between performers of different groups, such as male and female, different levels of player or different positional role. Performance variables can then be compared between these different types of performer. Alternatively, the independent variable could distinguish between different types of match. There is a subtle difference between comparing performers and matches, which is that studies comparing different types of match use dependent variables that represent both (all) competitors in the match. For example, a dependent variable such as rally length in volleyball or a racket sport is not just down to one of the performers in the match but depends on both players (or teams) in the match. Examples of independent variables in studies comparing different types of match are playing surface and type of match, as well as some of the variables already mentioned for comparing performers (such as gender and level of competition). This type of research design involves gathering data (dependent performance variables) for independent samples of performances that are to be compared. Independent t-tests or Mann-Whitney U tests can be used where two samples (for example male and female performances) are being compared (O'Donoghue, 2010: 178–181). One-way ANOVA or Kruskal-Wallis H tests can be used to compare three or more samples (for example professional, semi-professional and amateur-level performances). The independent samples t-test and the one-way ANOVA are parametric procedures, while the Mann-Whitney U test and the Kruskal-Wallis H test are non-parametric tests. Parametric tests are calculated using the values that were recorded for each performance variable. This makes parametric procedures more powerful than their non-parametric equivalents. However, parametric tests should only be used when the data satisfy the assumptions of those tests. These assumptions include dependent variables being normally distributed and the variance of each dependent variable being similar between the different samples being compared (O'Donoghue, 2010: 188–191). Non-parametric tests are often used in sports performance analysis because data tend to violate the assumptions of parametric procedures more often than not. Non-parametric procedures are calculated using ranks rather than actual values. This means that non-parametric procedures are distribution free and the distributions of dependent variables do not have to satisfy any requirements. However, the use of ranks rather than values does involve information loss, meaning that non-parametric tests are not as powerful as parametric procedures.

Descriptive studies can also compare samples that are related to a single set of performances. For example, we might wish to compare performance variables between the first and second halves of soccer matches or between the four quarters of basketball matches. Similarly, performance variables could be compared between different score-line states within matches, such as winning, drawing and losing. There are many other conditions experienced by performers that are interesting to compare, for example tennis points that are served to the deuce court and tennis points that are served to the advantage court. In this type of research design, two related samples can be compared using paired samples *t*-tests or Wilcoxon signed-rank tests, while three or more related samples can be compared using repeated measures ANOVA tests or Friedman tests. The paired samples *t*-test and the repeated measures ANOVA test are parametric procedures, while the Wilcoxon signed-rank test and the Friedman test are their non-parametric equivalents. As before, the parametric procedures are more powerful but should only be used if the data satisfy the assumptions of those procedures.

Effect sizes

In recent years, sports performance investigations have started using effect sizes as well as or instead of statistical significance. A difference in some performance variable between two samples of performances may be statistically significant while not representing a meaningful difference in real sport terms. For example, a set of ten sprinters may have 100m times ranging from 10.40s to 10.84s (mean±SD 10.61±0.14s), which are not significantly faster than the times of another group, which

162

range from 10.45s to 10.98s (mean±SD 10.74±0.18s) ($p = 0.103$). However, the average difference in finishing time of 0.13s suggests that the average member of the second group would have run 98.79m when the average member of the first group is finishing the 100m if the average member of the second group does the race at an even pace. We are aware that the 100m is not performed at an even pace because of the start. However, most involved in track and field athletics would recognise that 10.61s and 10.74s are noticeably different performances. For example, the UK men's rankings for the 100m in 2016 show that 10.61s and 10.74s would rank athletes 64th and 105th, respectively (www.thepowerof10 .info/rankings accessed 8 October 2016). As mentioned, the p value of an independent samples t-test comparing these two sets of ten athletes is 0.103. This is the probability that the difference is a chance difference due to the samples selected from the two relevant populations of sprinters being compared. It is more likely than not that the population from which the first group was drawn has a faster average time for the 100m than that of the population from which the second group was drawn. However, to be statistically significant, sports science studies typically insist on p values of less than 0.05 or sometimes less than 0.1. The p value is the probability of making a mistake when claiming the two populations are different based on what has been observed in the sample. The lower the probability of a sampling error, the more significant the difference. Note that while not being significant, the national rankings of 64th and 105th for the two groups' average times is meaningfully different. This is reflected better by an effect size measure such as Cohen's d. Cohen's d expresses the difference between the two groups as a fraction of pooled standard deviation of the two groups. In this example d = 0.78, which is interpreted as a large effect (Cohen, 2013).

Now consider the first group mentioned above performing the 100m after six weeks on an experimental training programme, with nine out of the ten improving their time. The average time of the group after the experimental training period is 10.57±0.12s. A paired samples t-test reveals that the improvement from before is highly significant ($p = 0.002$). This is because the average improvement of 0.037s is large in relation to the standard deviation of these pre to post differences (0.027s). Moreover, an improvement from 10.61s to 10.57s would move a sprinter from 64th place to 56th place in the 2016 UK rankings (www.thepowerof10.info /rankings accessed 8 October 2016). This is reflected by Cohen's d, which is 0.28 and interpreted as a small effect. Note that Cohen's d expresses the pre-post difference as a fraction of the pooled standard deviations of the two samples (0.142s and 0.119s) rather than using the standard deviation of the pre-post differences. So it is possible to have significance without a meaningful difference, but it is also possible to have a meaningful difference that is not statistically significant.

Using parametric procedures when assumptions of the tests are not satisfied

While we have identified three main subclasses of study that compare different samples of performances, these are not the only possible designs of such studies. There may be studies that look at more than one independent variable (for example positional role and level of player). Such studies may apply to independent variables that distinguish between different performances, repeated measures within sets of performances or a combination of both. Because the non-parametric procedures used in sports performance analysis include single independent variables, studies examining the effect of two or more independent variables use parametric procedures, usually factorial ANOVA tests. These tests not only determine the effect of the different independent variables in isolation but also examine their interaction. An interaction effect in sports performance is where the effect of one independent variable depends on the value of the other independent variable. For example, consider a study that examines the effects of gender and court surface on the time taken between a first and second serve in tennis. There may be an effect of gender if male players tend to move towards the net while playing a first serve. They will need to return back to the baseline in order to play the second serve in a way that female players may not need to. Similarly there may be an effect of court surface because more players of each gender move towards the net after playing a first serve on grass than on clay. An interaction effect is where the time between a first serve and second serve being played does not just depend on gender or on court surface, but depends on the combined effect of these two variables. Imagine a study that finds that female players have a mean inter-serve time of 11s on clay and 13s on grass and that male players have a mean inter-serve time of 12s on clay and 16s on grass. There is a gender effect, with men taking longer between the first and second serve than women. There is also a surface effect, with longer inter-serve times being observed in grass court matches versus on clay. The interactive effect is an additional

164

effect that the difference between inter-serve times on grass and clay differs between men's and women's matches. The increase in inter-serve time between clay and grass court matches for men (4s) is double what it is for women (2s).

Parametric statistical tests have assumptions that should be satisfied by the data they are being applied to, otherwise the p values produced may be considered invalid. We have already mentioned one situation where parametric procedures are used when data violate the assumptions of the tests; when multi-factor tests are applied, it is important to test the interaction of factors, and there are no equivalent non-parametric tests. Another situation in which we may use parametric procedures is when we have very small samples. Imagine a set of seven matches in which we are comparing some performance indicator between the first half and the second half of the matches. There are a limited number of combinations of ranked values if we use the non-parametric Wilcoxon signed-rank test. This makes it more difficult to achieve statistical differences than when a parametric paired samples t-test is used. The paired samples t test has more scope to find a significant difference because the actual values of the performance indicator in each half are used in the calculation of the test statistic.

Related samples in sports performance

A common mistake made by students doing sports performance analysis dissertations is that they use Mann-Whitney U tests to compare the performances of winning and losing teams within matches because there are two different sets of teams. These two sets of teams cannot be considered to be independent samples because the winning team's performance is directly influenced by the losing team and vice versa. Therefore, the winning and losing performances within matches should be compared using a Wilcoxon signed-rank test that recognises that they are related samples.

Units of analysis

There is more than one way of analysing data for a given research purpose, and the design of the study depends on a number of issues, including the volume of data that can be feasibly collected, whether we are comparing performers or performances and whether samples can be matched or not. For example, O'Donoghue (2010: 181–182) described four different ways that venue effect on performance could be considered. Firstly, paired samples *t*-tests could compare home and away performances within a set of matches. Secondly, paired samples *t*-tests could be used to compare mean home performances with mean away performances over multiple matches for a set of teams. The third approach uses independent samples *t*-tests to compare a set of home performances with a set of away performances where these two sets of performances do not come from the same matches and the two samples may contain different numbers of performances. The fourth approach described by O'Donoghue (2010: 181–182) is to use a chi-square test of independence to compare the frequency profile of events between a set of home performances and a set of away performances. This is the weakest approach in terms of statistical rigor because events from the same performances are not independent and the chi-square test is being tricked into thinking there are more data than there actually are; there may be over 1,000 events, but they may come from only four matches. Statistically, the chi-square test is dealing with these events the same way it would deal with sets of questionnaire responses from thousands of different people.

Correlation studies

The second main type of study is a correlation study that investigates relationships between performance variables. Typically, these studies correlate process indicators with some key outcome indicator(s) to see which are the most associated with outcome. For example, a set of event counts and percentage success rates for different events could be correlated with the number of points rugby teams score within matches. Correlation studies can also correlate process indicators with some ranking variable, such as league position or league points achieved.

Recent research has used regression analysis techniques to model the combined effect of different factors on match outcome (Gomez et al., 2016; Lago-Peñas et al., 2016). Gomez et al. (2016) investigated the effect of substitutions on match outcome and controlled for quality of opposition and match status using regression analysis. Lago-Peñas et al. (2016) used regression analysis to model match outcome (goal difference between teams) in terms of the time of the first goal and the quality

166

of teams playing in matches within Europe's five main soccer leagues. Multinominal logistic regression has been used to model categorical outcomes of events. For example, Almeida et al. (2016) modelled penalty kick outcome in terms of situational variables, player characteristics and details of the penalty performance. The situational variables included competition phase, match location, match status and match period. Characteristics of the penalty taker included footedness, playing position and age difference to the goalkeeper. Penalty performance factors included shot direction and goalkeeper's action. Vaquera et al. (2016) did a binomial logistic regression to model ball screen success in basketball on score-line, match period, court location and possession duration. García-Rubio et al. (2015) used both linear regression and logistic regression to model the impact of venue, opposition quality and scoring first on match outcomes in pool and knock-out stages of UEFA Champions League matches. There are other variants of regression models, for example evolutionary learning of globally optimal trees (evtree) have been used in volleyball to model the effect of relative player positioning on zones the ball is played to (Pérez et al., 2016).

QUALITATIVE RESEARCH IN SPORTS PERFORMANCE ANALYSIS

Types of qualitative research

There are two broad types of qualitative research that have been used in sports performance analysis: observational studies and interview studies. Observational studies tend to involve field notes, while interview data are recorded within transcripts. Given the choice of methods, researchers need to find a fit between the research question, the type of data involved and the methods. The various options should be considered before justifying the choice of method(s) to be used in a study.

Data from qualitative observation

Traditional notational analysis is an observational approach that attempts to manage the complexity of sports performance using a quantitative approach analysing events that can be classified, counted and timed. When human observers are involved in data gathering, there are subjective processes in classifying behaviour during sports performance (O'Donoghue, 2015: 46–48). However, the traditional notational approach remains a reductive one. Qualitative data has been used within performance analysis investigations where non-participant observation has been used. For example McLaughlin (2002) used unrestricted qualitative observation of children's behaviour in the playground to explain the work-rate patterns revealed by quantitative time-motion analysis. The time-motion analysis tended to study the children's work-rate in isolation, while the qualitative analysis of the same videos also considered the context of their behaviour as well as interactions with other children. In a sense, the quantitative part of McLaughlin's study described what the children did, while the qualitative part moved towards explanations of why they moved the way they did. This is an example of mixed-methods research that combines quantitative and qualitative techniques. It is also possible for mixed-methods research to use different types of quantitative methods or different types of qualitative methods (Alexander et al., 2016). Observation in sports performance analysis shares characteristics of other qualitative research: it takes place in a natural setting, focusses on context and is fundamentally interpretive (Marshall and Rossman, 2011: 3).

Non-participant observation is typically unobtrusive, and sports performers are used to spectators being present when they compete. This means that their behaviour is less likely to be influenced by the presence of researchers than human behaviour in other fields might be. A major advantage of qualitative research in sports performance analysis over qualitative analysis in many fields of social science is that match videos are available. Therefore, field notes will not be the only record of the behaviour being investigated. Nonetheless, researchers need to use field notes as part of the process of analysing the vast amount of information within match videos in order to produce concise and readable findings. The researcher should record details related to anticipated subtopics of the study as well as details about areas that may not have been anticipated prior to the analysis. This is necessary because qualitative research needs to be flexible to allow important new lines of enquiry to be followed if they emerge. Details of the physical setting (Silverman, 2005: 157–159), social environment (Flick, 2007: 30–31), context (Richards, 2010: 57) and interactions between people should be recorded. The researchers need to appreciate that the audiences of their research may not see the same video material and are, therefore, relying

168

on the researcher's written descriptions. Use of language is important to describe scenes, events, culture, terminology and non-verbal communication. Researchers should use detailed non-judgemental descriptions when reporting the findings of observational studies (Marshall and Rossman, 2006: 98).

There are different types of field notes, including short field notes, expanded field notes and journals. Short field notes are recorded as soon as possible during or after performances being analysed. Even though a video of the performance is being recorded, the researcher may have ideas during the performance which may be more difficult recall if these short field notes are not written up soon after the episode. Expanded field notes are written later and include more detail than can be recorded when writing short field notes. A journal is used to record problems that occur during field work. An advantage of qualitative observation over interviewing is that researcher may observe things that the participants are reluctant to discuss (Patton, 2002: 262–263).

Interview data in sports performance analysis

Interviews are used to obtain rich qualitative data from participants of interest in a given study. In sports performance analysis, self-confrontational interviews have been used to investigate unobservable mental processes that occur during actual sports performance (Poizat et al., 2013). Qualitative data include inner thoughts, attitudes, beliefs, emotions, intentions and experiences that cannot be directly observed by traditional notation methods. Language is used to convey a mental image of thoughts, attitudes, beliefs, emotions, intentions and experiences (Strauss and Corbin, 1998: 15). Interviews have also been used within mixed-methods approaches in studies analysing coach behaviour (Donnelly and O'Donoghue, 2008; Bowley et al., 2013). The Arizona State University Observation Instrument (Lacy and Darst, 1984) was used to describe the distribution of coaching time among a set of fourteen broad behaviours; this was a quantitative observational approach. The interviews with high-level coaches explained differences between the coaching behaviours used at different levels. The benefits of using quantitative and qualitative methods within such a triangulation is that they complement each other (Alexander et al., 2016). The studies of Donnelly and O'Donoghue (2008) and Bowley et al. (2013) used mixed methods in a sequential way, with the qualitative part used to explain the findings of the quantitative part.

There are different types of interview that are useful in the study of sports performance, including phenomenology interviews concerned with lived experiences of participants, ethnographic interviews concerned with society and culture and elite interviews with prominent experts in the given topic area (Marshall and Rossman, 2006: 105–106). The first task in any interview study is to convince critics that the research is valuable (Marshall and Rossman, 2011: 11). Indeed, this is an initial stage of all research and should be done before expending effort writing a research proposal. Interview studies may not be fixed designs to test some hypotheses that have been formally expressed with operationalised variables. However, an interview study should still have a topic area and purpose stated at the early stages to indicate areas of literature to be reviewed (Marshall and Rossman, 2011: 57). Once the research topic and specific research question are decided and justified, the researcher can make preparations for conducting the interviews. This involves deciding on the types of participants and recruitment methods and obtaining ethical clearance to conduct data collection (Richards, 2010: 44–45). The setting should be comfortable for the researcher and the interview participants, who should feel relaxed and at ease during interviews (Fielding and Thomas, 2016).

Students who may be doing interview studies for the first time should also prepare for these investigations by reading specialist texts on interviewing (Kvale and Brinkmann, 2009) and qualitative data analysis in general (Patton, 2002; Miles and Huberman, 1994; Silverman, 1993; Silverman, 2005; Strauss and Corbin, 1998). The preparation phase should lead to the development of an interview guide (Fielding and Thomas, 2016) which covers basic themes of the study. This is a guide to the interview rather than introducing restrictive control to interviewing (Patton, 2002: 343–344). The interview guide typically includes introductory, follow-up and probing questions (Kvale and Brinkmann, 2009: 134–138; Patton, 2002: 372–374). Introductory questions allow the participant to talk about the area raised, follow-up questions encourage elaboration, and probing questions are used to obtain more detail and rich data going into greater depth.

The next stage of the study is to gather data by conducting the interviews. During interviews, the researcher maintains rapport and uses open questions to learn from participants. Once the interviews are completed, transcripts are produced and the data are analysed. Questions should be as open ended as possible and should encourage respondents to communicate attitudes, beliefs, motives and values (Fielding and Thomas, 2016). The researcher needs to consider image management effects where participants may conceal information. The participants may be more forthcoming if they are confident that the interview is being conducted in a non-judgemental way. Probes should be used to encourage participants to elaborate on points of interest, providing fuller responses that allow rich, detailed data to be elicited (Fielding and Thomas, 2016).

Once the interviews are completed, they can be transcribed, and the data can be analysed. Analysis will have already started during the interviews as the researcher will have been keeping the conversation focussed on the main themes of interest and being alert to areas that needed to be probed in particular ways. A later subsection of this chapter will discuss the analysis of qualitative data.

Focus groups

Focus groups are a variant on interviewing in which several participants discuss the research topic together facilitated by the researcher or someone else appointed by the researcher for this purpose. The facilitator should show genuine interest in all participants and be a moderator rather than an additional participant (Cronin, 2016). The facilitator needs to be prepared to hear views that they might not agree with and keep the level of moderation appropriate (Cronin, 2016). Focus groups are used when we wish to understand differences in perspective and when the group is better than the sum of the individuals for generating ideas (Krueger and Casey, 2000: 24). Krueger and Casey (2000: 25) also recommended situations where focus groups should not be used. These include situations where a consensus is required, research that requires asking for sensitive information, environments that may be emotionally charged and situations where confidentiality is important. A focus group should include six to ten participants and last between 1 hour 30 minutes and 2 hours (Cronin, 2016). It should be conducted in a venue that is accessible to all participants, where there is a minimum amount of distraction and interruption and where all participants are able to see and hear each other (Cronin, 2016). Preparation is important, and the researcher should ensure that equipment such as writing pad and pen for the facilitator, name badges, flipchart and pens, remote microphones and copies of focus group schedule are available (Cronin, 2016). The main stages of a focus group are the introduction, the opening circle, introductory questions, key questions and ending questions (Cronin, 2016). The introduction states the topic of the focus group, and the opening circle allows participants to introduce themselves and share pertinent information about themselves. This allows the facilitator to assess the participants, identifying any experts, dominant talkers, shy participants and ramblers (Krueger and Casey, 2000: 111–112). Introductory questions are about the participants' understanding of the topic, while key questions drive the study and involve more in-depth discussion. The ending questions draw the focus group to a close and may involve lengthy discussion (Cronin, 2016).

Case studies

The volume of case studies done in research has increased in recent decades (Yin, 2014), showing that this is an accepted research method in many fields of enquiry. A case study does not necessarily have to involve qualitative methods, and in sports performance analysis there are examples of case studies based on purely quantitative methods (Linke and Lames, 2016). However, most case study research investigates the participant(s) of interest in great detail using more complex qualitative data. The design of a case study is improved if multiple sources of evidence are used in the study (Yin, 2014: 45). This may involve the use of complementary methods to help validate findings. A case study should investigate individuals, groups, organisations, communities, projects or situations of special interest (Yin, 2014: 8, 35).

In sports performance analysis, case studies could be done on particular analysts, coaches or performers in a given sport. A case may be chosen because it will provide rich information about elite-level sports performance that is of interest to many beyond the case who aspire to participate at this level of sport. Interviewing elite participants is challenging because they are busy and in-demand individuals. Marshall and Rossman (2011: 155–156) recommended using more open questions when interviewing elite participants to allow them to discuss issues they view as important.

172

QUALITATIVE DATA ANALYSIS

Qualitative research is labour intensive, requires skill and needs to be done by researchers with the necessary characteristics. A contrast with objective methods is that in qualitative research, the researcher interacts with the data, while in quantitative research the researcher attempts to draw conclusions supported purely by the data without any interpretation. Qualitative researchers should view phenomena holistically, systematically reflecting on who they are and the how they interact with the data (Marshall and Rossman, 2011: 3).

There are different methods of qualitative data analysis that are described in some of the main research methods textbooks (Miles and Huberman, 1994; Strauss and Corbin, 1998; Silverman, 1993; 2005; Patton, 2002; Marshall and Rossman, 2006). Côté et al. (1995) described a detailed method that uses an inductive approach that works in a bottom-up manner. At the bottom level, interview transcripts are read in detail to identify meaning units within the text. Meaning units are raw sentences within the interview transcript. Once identified, these meaning units are grouped into higher-order properties that they provide evidence for. At the top level of abstraction, properties are grouped into broader categories, which in turn are grouped into the main components of the theory. The hierarchical structure of components, categories, properties and meaning units can be displayed as a result of the analysis. Strauss and Corbin (1998: 101–161) used the terms open coding, axial coding and selective coding when describing qualitative data analysis. Open coding is where the researcher identifies categories and properties in the data, whereas axial coding involves structuring these categories and properties into hierarchies. Selective coding is where broad properties are linked to the main components of the emerging theory. The structure also guides the analysis of the qualitative data supporting broad directions taken when selecting quotes to include and the interpretations made. The analysis of components, properties, categories and meaning units does not have to be in a bottom-up inductive process, but could also be done in a top-down deductive manner when the research is investigating some pre-existing theory.

Data collection and analysis happen in parallel (Richards, 2010: 94); initially data are gathered in an open-ended manner that is flexible and explorative. Eventually, as themes emerge, the analysis becomes more deliberate in investigating those themes (Hodkinson, 2016).

There is a contrast between theory construction by induction and theory use by deduction. The former develops evidenced theory based on data from the social world, while the latter finds evidence in the social world that can be explained by the existing theory (Gilbert, 2016). Coding complex qualitative data helps researchers become familiar with the data and recognise patterns in the data (Seal, 2016). The process of coding is not a straightforward assembly-line process leading to an easily produced hierarchy of components, categories, properties and meaning units. There may be some codes that overlap (Fielding and Thomas, 2016) and meaning units that provide evidence supporting more than one component. A further issue is that while the data may largely support some theory that is being developed, there may be other meaning units that contradict the theory. Gilbert (2016) describes the process of falsification when researchers look for awkward cases throughout the analysis, revising the theory where necessary or acknowledging variations.

Reporting findings

The findings of qualitative research can be presented in numerous formats, including storytelling narratives (Huggan et al., 2015). The storytelling approach involves constructing a fictional story about the topic being studied that is realistic, is based on the data analysed and avoids ethical issues of identifying vulnerable participants. Alternatively, the findings can be presented as text that describes the topic in a factual way, with interpretations being regularly supported with direct quotes from interview data that characterise different components of the theory. These quotes should be attributed to participants using a simple signature scheme that conceals their identities (Kvale and Brinkman, 2009: 279–281). Irrespective of the format used, the researcher needs to present findings in an academic manner while also engaging readers by writing in a more popular form (Kvale and Brinkman, 2009: 266).

Earthy et al. (2016) discussed the use of storytelling narratives in research. There are stories that are told by participants and stories that are told by researchers based on interviews with participants. Stories written by participants may be biographies or accounts; these may be intended as factual, but the participant is portraying himself/herself in a way to convey a particular message to an intended audience. It is not possible to include all relevant information, and some things will be

174

covered in greater detail than others. Researchers consider why the participants are telling the stories and why they are telling them in the way they are. Despite being fictionalised, stories provide important knowledge about contexts and cultures (Earthy et al., 2016).

There may also be political motives where researchers tell stories rather than the participants themselves (Earthy et al., 2016). The story may have a role in encouraging others to act. A researcher constructing a story based on a case participant will use a series of interviews, giving time in between to allow both the researcher and participant to reflect on what has been discussed in previous interviews. This allows the level of detail to increase in subsequent interviews and provides the opportunity to clarify any inconsistencies in interview data that can be identified in between interviews (Earthy et al., 2016).

Trustworthiness of the interview data

In traditional notation, the term 'reliability' is used to represent the consistency with which a notation system can be used. When qualitative analyses are used, the researchers wish to ensure that data are recorded accurately and findings produced by the analysis are a valid portrayal of participants' views. This combination of reliability and validity of qualitative methods is referred to as 'trustworthiness'. There are a number of different ways of establishing trustworthiness. Firstly, researchers should have the necessary knowledge of the subject area so that they are able to recognise important areas to probe into when they are interviewing participants (Kvale and Brinkmann, 2009: 147).

Secondly, pilot work should be carried out under the supervision of senior researchers before the main data collection commences (Davies et al., 2005). For example, pilot interviews can improve the interviewing process of the researcher ahead of the main interviews being conducted with important participants.

Thirdly, researchers should be sensitive to personal biography, biases and beliefs and how these may shape the study (Marshall and Rossman, 2011: 3). Observational research can be influenced by highly selective human perception and bias (Patton, 2002: 264). Being aware of such biases will help to minimise their influence on the research (Holt and Mitchell, 2006).

Fourthly, collaboration with peer researchers can improve the rigor of a study (Creswell and Miller, 2000). This could involve peer debriefing after episodes in the field or gaining feedback from individuals familiar with the field. In an interview study, a peer can independently check the process of coding and properties, categories and components that have been identified and the way they have been structured (Davies et al., 2005; Horton et al., 2005). Do they identify the same meaning units? Do they group these meaning units into the same properties, categories and components? It is unrealistic to expect a 100 per cent match when two independent researchers analyse the same interview transcript. This is because there are multiple ways of interpreting text. One researcher may view a sentence in an interview transcript as not sufficiently important to be a meaning unit, while the other may include it as a meaning unit. A meaning unit may be read as being relevant to more than one property, and independent researchers may disagree about the property it most provides evidence about. The level of agreement in identifying meaning units, properties, categories and components as well as relating these to each other in a hierarchy is reported as evidence of the level of trustworthiness of the analysis process.

A fifth way of establishing trustworthiness is member checking, in which interviewees are provided with the conclusions drawn from their interviews (Holt and Mitchell, 2006; Salmela et al., 2006). This is particularly important where the purpose of the investigation is to determine how people interpret phenomena (Marshall and Rossman, 2011: 43). This provides interviewees with the opportunity to suggest how the findings can be amended to portray their views more accurately or to withdraw their data from the study.

Creswell and Miller (2000) list additional processes of establishing rigor and usefulness. Triangulation allows findings produced by one analysis technique to be validated by applying an alternative method. For example, findings from both interview and focus groups can give greater confidence in the findings than if just one of these techniques was applied. Prolonged engagement in the field also improves validity of the study as the greater exposure will be more representative of the field. This also allows rich data to be analysed to study changes over time (Marshall and Rossman, 2011: 43). Researchers should also develop audit trails to show how raw field experiences that are represented by field notes support different findings of the study.

176

INTERVENTION STUDIES IN SPORTS PERFORMANCE ANALYSIS

Intervention studies are ambitious and are rarely done by undergraduate students. One example of an intervention study that was done by two undergraduate students was Jenkins et al.'s (2007) work with a university netball squad. One of the students provided motivational feedback while the other provided instructional feedback over a series of eight matches. The effectiveness of the motivational feedback was evaluated using open-ended questionnaires in which players were able to identify strong points of the motivational videos as well as areas for improvement in them.

The instructional feedback was analysed by examining whether or not it supported decisions within the seven match-to-match preparation cycles. Field notes were recorded while providing the performance analysis service and observing squad meetings and training sessions. These field notes were analysed considering the following questions about the use of the feedback provided: Did the analysis identify areas for improvement? Did the coach address these areas for improvement in training? Did the aspects of performance requiring attention improve in the next match? There are many uncontrollable factors in an intervention study like this, especially the varying levels of opposition and players available to play. This makes it difficult to attribute any improvements in performance to the provision of performance analysis support. This particular study (Jenkins et al., 2007) was also difficult to generalise because it was a case study of one squad. However, these studies are important to contribute to the overall body of knowledge about the effectiveness of performance analysis support in coaching. Enterprise projects and development projects often involve providing a performance analysis service that is evaluated. Chapter 4 provides more detail of this type of research.

SUMMARY

This chapter has covered data gathering and analysis. The main point made about data gathering is that it is not merely implementing the methods devised and ethically approved for the study. There are ethical and practical issues that need to be addressed during the process of data collection. Quantitative data analysis is not a black-and-white issue, and there are choices open to researchers as to the approach they take. Reliability, assumptions of statistical procedures, significance and effect size are all important, but the most important thing to remember is the purpose of the study. A well-designed quantitative study links analysis to the hypotheses of the study. Students undertaking quantitative research are encouraged to read statistics books that cover non-parametric procedures. Qualitative research in performance analysis can use interviews, focus groups or non-participant observation. This chapter has covered data gathering, analysis and trustworthiness during qualitative research. Students undertaking qualitative research are encouraged to read specialist books in the area.

REFERENCES

Alexander, V.D., Thomas, H., Cronin, A., Fielding, J. and Moran-Ellis, J. (2016) 'Mixed methods', in N. Gilbert and P. Stoneman (eds), *Researching social life, 4th edn* (pp. 119–138). Thousand Oaks, CA: Sage.

Almeida, C.H., Volossovitch, A. and Duarte, R. (2016) 'Penalty kick outcomes in UEFA club competitions (2010–2015): The roles of situational, individual and performance factors', *International Journal of Performance Analysis in Sport*, 16: 508–522.

Bowley, C., Bodden, W. and O'Donoghue, P.G. (2013) 'Behaviour of academy soccer coaches during training sessions', in D. Peters and P.G. O'Donoghue (eds), *Performance analysis of sport IX* (pp. 32–36). London: Routledge.

Cohen, J. (2013) *Statistical power analysis for the behavioral sciences*. Burlington, VT: Elsevier Science.

Côté, J., Trudel, P., Baria, A. and Russell, S.J. (1995) 'The coaching model: a grounded assessment of expert gymnastic coach's knowledge', *Journal of Sport and Exercise Psychology*, 17: 1–17.

Creswell, J.W. and Miller, D.L. (2000) 'Determining validity in qualitative inquiry', *Theory into Practice*, 39(3): 124–130.

Cronin, A. (2016) 'Focus groups', in N. Gilbert and P. Stoneman (eds), *Researching social life, 4th edn* (pp. 301–317). Thousand Oaks, CA: Sage.

Davies, M.J., Bloom, G.A. and Salmela, J.H. (2005) 'Job satisfaction of accomplished male university basketball coaches: the Canadian context', *International Journal of Sport Psychology*, 36: 173–192.

Donnelly, C. and O'Donoghue, P.G. (2008) 'Behaviour of netball coaches of different levels', in A. Hokelmann and M. Brummond (eds), *Performance analysis of sport VIII* (pp. 743–749). Magdeburg, Germany: Otto Von Guericke Universität.

Earthy, S., Cuncev, A. and Cronin, A. (2016) 'Narrative analysis', in N. Gilbert and P. Stoneman (eds), *Researching social life, 4th edn* (pp. 461–483). Thousand Oaks, CA: Sage.

Fielding, N. and Thomas, H. (2016) 'Qualitative interviewing', in N. Gilbert and P. Stoneman (eds), *Researching social life, 4th edn* (pp. 281–300). Thousand Oaks, CA: Sage.

Flick, U. (2007) *Designing qualitative research.* London: Sage.

García-Rubio, J., Gómez, M-Á., Lago-Peñas, C. and Ibáñez, S.J. (2015) 'Effect of match venue, scoring first and quality of opposition on match outcome in the UEFA Champions League', *International Journal of Performance Analysis in Sport*, 15: 527–539.

Gilbert, N. (2016) 'Research, theory and method', in N. Gilbert and P. Stoneman (eds), *Researching social life, 4th edn* (pp. 25–42). Thousand Oaks, CA: Sage.

Gomez, M-Á., Gasperi, L. and Lupo, C. (2016) 'Performance analysis of game dynamics during the 4th game quarter of NBA close games', *International Journal of Performance Analysis in Sport*, 16: 249–263.

Hodkinson, P. (2016) 'Grounded theory and inductive research', in N. Gilbert and P. Stoneman (eds), *Researching social life, 4th edn* (pp. 97–117). Thousand Oaks, CA: Sage.

Holt, N.L. and Mitchell, T. (2006) 'Talent development in English professional soccer', *International Journal of Sport Psychology*, 37: 77–98.

Horton, S., Baker, J. and Deakin, J. (2005) 'Experts in action: a systematic observation of 5 national team coaches', *International Journal of Sports Psychology*, 36: 299–319.

Huggan, R., Nelson, L. and Potrac, P. (2015) 'Developing micropolitical literacy in professional soccer: a performance analyst's tale', *Qualitative Research in Sport, Exercise and Health*, 4: 504–520. http://dx.doi.org/10.1080/21596 76X.2014.949832

Jenkins, R.E., Morgan, L. and O'Donoghue, P.G. (2007) 'A case study into the effectiveness of computerized match analysis and motivational videos within the coaching of a league netball team', *International Journal of Performance Analysis of Sport*, 7(2): 59–80.

Krueger, R.A. and Casey, M.A. (2000) *Focus groups: a practical guide for applied research, 3rd edn.* Thousand Oaks, CA: Sage.

Kvale, S. and Brinkmann, S. (2009) *Interviews: learning the craft of qualitative research interviewing, 2nd edn.* Thousand Oaks, CA: Sage.

Lacy, A.C. and Darst, P.W. (1984) 'Evolution of a systematic observation system: The ASU coaching observation instrument', *Journal of Teaching in Physical Education*, 3: 59–66.

Lago-Peñas, C., Gómez-Ruano, M., Sampaio, J. and Owen, A.L. (2016) 'The effects of a player dismissal on competitive technical match performance', *International Journal of Performance Analysis in Sport*, 16: 792–800.

Lancaster, G.A., Dodd, S. and Williamson, P.R. (2004) 'Design and analysis of pilot studies: recommendations for good practice', *Journal of Evaluation in Clinical Practice*, 45: 626–629.

Linke, D. and Lames, M. (2016) 'Substitutions in elite male field hockey – a case study', *International Journal of Performance Analysis in Sport*, 16: 924–934.

Marshall, C. and Rossman, G.B. (2006) *Designing qualitative research, 4th edn.* Thousand Oaks, CA: Sage.

Marshall, C. and Rossman, G.B. (2011) *Designing qualitative research, 5th edn.* Thousand Oaks, CA: Sage.

McLaughlin, E. (2002) Children's recreational activity and health: a time-motion study. Ph.D. thesis, University of Ulster, UK.

Miles, M. and Huberman, A. (1994) *Qualitative data analysis, 2nd edn.* London: Sage.

O'Donoghue, P.G. (2010) *Research methods for sports performance analysis.* London: Routledge.

O'Donoghue, P.G. (2015) *An introduction to performance analysis of sport.* London: Routledge.

Patton, M.Q. (2002) *Qualitative research and evaluation methods, 3rd edn.* London: Sage.

Pérez, M.d.C.I., Ordóñez, E.G. and Gonzalez, C.T. (2016) 'Keys to Success in High Level Water Polo Teams', *International Journal of Performance Analysis in Sport*, 16: 995–1006.

Poizat, G., Sève, C. and Saury, J. (2013) 'Qualitative aspects in performance analysis', in T. McGarry, P.G. O'Donoghue and J. Sampaio (eds), *Routledge handbook of sports performance analysis* (pp. 309–320). London: Routledge.

Richards, L. (2010) *Handling qualitative data: a practical guide, 2nd edn.* Thousand Oaks, CA: Sage.

Salmela, J.H., Marques, M., Machado, R. and Durand-Bush, N. (2006) 'Perceptions of the Brazilian football coaching staff in preparation for the World Cup', *International Journal of Sport Psychology*, 37: 139–156.

Seal, A. (2016) 'Thematic analysis', in N. Gilbert and P. Stoneman (eds), *Researching social life, 4th edn* (pp. 443–459). Thousand Oaks, CA: Sage.

Silverman, D. (1993) *Interpreting qualitative data: methods for analysing talk, text and interaction.* London: Sage.

Silverman, D. (2005) *Doing qualitative research: a practical handbook, 2nd edn.* London: Sage.

Strauss, A. and Corbin, J. (1998) *Basics of qualitative research: techniques and procedures for developing grounded theory, 2nd edn.* London: Sage.

Thomas, J.R. and Nelson, J.K. (1996) *Research methods in physical activity, 3rd edn.* Champaign, IL: Human Kinetics.

Vaquera, A., García-Tormo, J.V., Gómez Ruano, M.A. and Morante, J.C. (2016) 'An exploration of ball screen effectiveness on elite basketball teams', *International Journal of Performance Analysis in Sport*, 16: 475–485.

Yin, R.K. (2014) *Case study research: design and methods, 5th edn.* Thousand Oaks, CA: Sage.

CHAPTER 9

WRITING UP THE DISSERTATION

OVERVIEW

This chapter analyses how sports performance analysis dissertations are written up. This is a critically important process that should not be neglected by students. The dissertation report needs to do justice to the research activity that has been done. The chapter covers the contents of the various chapters to be included in different types of sports performance analysis dissertation. The standard introduction, literature review, methods, results, discussion and conclusions chapters that would be included within scientific research projects are discussed. These chapters are also used within enterprise projects, with methods and results being more about what was done and found in a market research study than in a scientific research study. These chapters would also be included with MSc dissertations, with the difference being that they are describing master's-level research rather than undergraduate-level research. The contents of requirements, specification, design, implementation, testing and evaluation chapters that would be seen in development projects are also discussed. This chapter also covers other forms of research presentation, such as PhD theses, journal articles and conference presentations. However, research proposals are not included because they have already been covered in Chapter 5 of the current book. General guidance on presentation and producing tables, figures, charts and appendices is also provided in the current chapter.

CHAPTERS

Word count

Table 9.1 suggests the number of words to include in each chapter of various types of undergraduate dissertations. Typically, a word limit is set, for example 10,000 words, but this can vary from university to university. Students will be expected to produce a dissertation report within a certain percentage of the word limit. For example, if a 10 per cent limit is set, then a 10,000 word dissertation should contain no fewer than 9,000 words and no more than 11,000 words. There are often penalties for exceeding the word limit and possibly also penalties for not producing a dissertation of enough words. Students should check the assessment criteria for dissertations in their own universities and edit the dissertation appropriately to avoid losing marks because of the word count. Students should also check what the word count comprises. Are the contents of tables included? Is the abstract included? Is the reference list at the end included? It is unlikely that appendices would be included in the word count, but the student should check this to be sure. The word limits for individual chapters are just suggestions, and if students are outside these limits for any chapters when they are first drafted, the student should not add or remove words until they have drafted all of the

Table 9.1 Word distribution for different types of undergraduate dissertations

Chapter	Quantitative research	Qualitative research	Enterprise project	Development project
Abstract	100–200	100–200	100–200	100–200
Introduction	500–800	500–800	400–600	500–800
Literature Review	2,500	2,500	1,600–2,000	2,000
Methods	2,000–2,500	1,500–2,000	1,500	
Requirements Analysis				1,500–2,000*
Specification				1,000*
Design				1,500
Implementation and Testing				1,000–1,500
Results	1,000–1,500	2,000*	1,500–2,000	
Discussion	3,000	2,500–3,000*	2,000–2,500	
Evaluation				1,500
Conclusions	300–400	300–400	300–400	300–400
Total	10,000	10,000	8,000	10,000

* These chapters may be merged.

182

chapters. It could be that the students need more words in some chapters and fewer in others. Once the whole dissertation has been drafted, the student can consider where words need to be added or removed.

Abstract

The abstract is an overall summary of the project in 150 to 300 words. It should briefly state the purpose of the study, what was done and what was found. Students should imagine they are asked by friends or family members what they did in their dissertation. What would they say if they had to give an answer in less than a minute? This is the sort of thing that should be included in the abstract. For a sports performance analysis project, the abstract may need to address broad areas of performance rather than identifying and defining specific variables used. The key independent variable should be obvious to readers if the abstract has stated the purpose of the study well. It is sufficient to say that a computer-based match analysis system was developed and used to collect the data. Other methodological areas, such as reliability assessment, would be too detailed for the abstract. The project will have found several things based on the set of variables used; not all of these will be significant, and some findings will be more important than others. The student needs to select the one or two findings that make the greatest contribution to knowledge or most impact for athlete preparation. The abstract should conclude with a sentence or two stating the main implications of the study.

Abstracts for qualitative research, enterprise and development projects should adopt a similar approach. They should be an accurate but high-level summary of the purpose, what was done, what was achieved and the main practical and/or theoretical implications of the project.

Introduction

The introduction should set the scene for the project and generate interest in the problem area. The introduction of a project includes a brief background to the area, the purpose of the project, a justification of the need for the project, definitions of terms used throughout the project and the scope of the study. The background is not a literature review but a brief outline of the problem area. It could be a research topic that originated in a popular media discussion or an enterprise project originating from personal interest. There may be high-profile review papers that have identified certain areas as requiring research attention or economic reports suggesting a market for a given enterprise idea. Alternatively, knowledge of existing products or services may have led the student to propose a development project to overcome some limitation in existing products or services. Although the literature review often leads to gaps being identified in knowledge, the rationale for the project is needed in the introduction. By the end of the introduction, the reader needs a full understanding of what the project is all about and why it has been done. There is varying practice for when the introduction is written, with some supervisors wanting the introduction chapter to be completed before any other work commences, while other supervisors are happy for the introduction to be done in a draft form early during the project and then completed after the rest of the dissertation. The reason for the latter approach is that the introduction is introducing the reader to a project that has now been done, and there may be important details that need to be included in the introduction that could not have been known early in the research project. In introducing the reader to the project, it helps to have completed the project. In case readers are wondering, Chapter 1 of the current book was the last one to be completed.

Literature review

Dissertation students will have made a good start to this chapter having done a research proposal that covers background literature. The process of reading and reviewing literature has been covered in Chapter 5, and so the current section is concerned with presentation of the literature review chapter in the final thesis.

After the purpose of the project has been specified in the introduction, the literature review chapter provides critical coverage of relevant theoretical and methodological issues. In the case of enterprise and development projects, economic trends and technological issues, respectively, may also be reviewed. The review of literature needs to be presented in a logical structure, so students should carefully consider the subsections to be included. A common mistake in sports performance analysis dissertations is including a general section on the performance analysis discipline.

184

A student doing a physiology dissertation (for example) would not include a general section of the literature review on physiology. They would instead focus on literature that is relevant to the dissertation topic. A further mistake made by students doing quantitative performance analysis research studies is that they include a section on feedback and the use of performance analysis within practical coaching. Unless the student is undertaking an evaluation of feedback and the effectiveness of performance analysis support in coaching, such a subsection is not relevant to the literature review.

Literature reviews for quantitative research projects in sports performance analysis tend to commence with broad theoretical debates being covered before funnelling down to the literature which is most related to the student's specific research question. This might involve analysing relevant concepts in sports in general before focussing on literature about those concepts in the given sport of interest. An alternative structure is to have different subsections on the broad independent and dependent variables of interest. If the independent variable of a project into home advantage was venue, then there may be a section on venue effect on sports performance in general. If the project was interested in the effect of venue on work-rate, then there may be a second section on the alternative ways of evaluating work-rate, justifying the use of observational means. Whether the student remains focussed on their own sport or draws on literature from multiple sports depends on how much literature there is available for the sport of interest. For some popular and well-researched sports, the literature review may be able to cover papers solely addressing that sport. Where there is little or no research done on the given sport, it will be necessary for the student to review relevant concepts in other sports, identifying that there is a gap in knowledge relating to the sport of interest.

Qualitative research studies are still research studies, but they do not have formal hypotheses with independent and dependent variables. However, there will still be broad concepts covered in existing literature that need to be reviewed. For example, an interview study into coach perceptions of performance analysis support will include sections of the literature review on feedback within coaching processes and the role of performance analysis within coaching. These will discuss theory about feedback and communication in sport and the evidence relating to the effectiveness of performance analysis–based feedback. These sections would also be relevant to dissertations in which intervention studies have been done and performance analysis was evaluated based on student experience of service delivery.

The literature review chapter of an enterprise project establishes the theoretical underpinning of the project. There may be a broad section on the type of process or product at the centre of the enterprise idea. In the case of a performance analysis enterprise project, this could be a performance analysis service. Therefore, theory about feedback and communication in coaching contexts would be important. This shows readers that the student is familiar with the field of sports science support that they are entering. A second broad section of the literature review should cover relevant issues facing entrepreneurs in sports science support in general and performance analysis in particular. This section of the literature review should cover the skills of an entrepreneur, criteria for success in enterprise ventures, business types, small business policy, the given market type for the service or product and the economic environment. The literature review should conclude by combining the theoretical and entrepreneurship underpinnings of the project. For example, the need for performance analysis support services can be discussed within the budget constraints of squads in a sport of interest to make the case for a particular kind of affordable service.

The literature review of a development project would typically include a section on the given application area and a section on product development processes in the given application area. For example, consider the example used in Chapter 4 of a tactical analysis algorithm. One subsection of the literature could discuss player-tracking data and identify gaps in how it has been used. Current methods of recognising tactics without using automatic algorithms can be reviewed, critically highlighting the costs and limitations of such methods. If the project is developing a software system, the second broad section of the literature review might discuss software development processes. This might cover software development principles, prototyping and software quality issues. The issues of software quality are particularly important as these can be used as part of a framework for evaluating the eventual product.

Methods

The description of methods can be preceded by a justification for the methods used. This allows the student to demonstrate a knowledge of the

186

strengths and weaknesses of alternative approaches. One of the challenges of quantitative performance analysis dissertations is keeping the dissertation within the word limit while describing methods in a complete and replicable way. This is especially difficult when performance variables are unique to the project and need to be defined. Therefore, it is not always possible to include a justification of the methods used, and methods chapters in such dissertations can still stretch beyond 2,000 words.

The methods chapter of a traditional quantitative performance analysis project would include sections on research design, system development, reliability evaluation, matches or performances included and data analysis. The section on system development should include descriptions of the performance variables produced, action variables to be input, pilot work during system development and the final system and operating procedures. The operating procedures should describe the sources of any video data and the procedure for data entry into the system. The details of the matches (or performances) analysed in the study should include the tournaments the matches were played in and any criteria for inclusion or exclusion of matches from the study. The data analysis section should describe the processing of system outputs for individual matches to produce the summary variables for the complete set of matches and describe the different statistical tests that were used.

The reliability evaluation should describe the method and results of the reliability study and interpret the level of reliability in relation to the purpose of the study. Students should state whether an inter-operator or intra-operator agreement study has been done. They should be clear about the level of training the operators had on the given system, as well as the operators' knowledge of relevant concepts of the given sport. Students should inform readers about the data that reliability statistics are applied to: are they applied to input action variables, output performance variables or a combination of both? Any decisions about the application of the system within the study should be covered. For example, some variables may not be sufficiently reliable for analysis in the main study. The reliability results are included in the methods chapter so that the results chapter can focus on the results relating to the main purpose of the project. When the purpose of the project is to investigate the reliability of a system or alternative systems, then the reliability results would be presented in the results chapter.

Qualitative research projects in the broad area of sports performance analysis might use interviews, focus groups or field notes. The methods chapter of such a dissertation should include sections on research design, participants, data gathering, data analysis, data reporting and trustworthiness. The research design is included at the start of the methods chapter and provides an overall summary of the methods. In describing the participants, students should not merely describe their gender, level and age group characteristics but should also give details of squad culture, settings and situations of any field work. Data gathering should describe the procedures applied during interviews and focus groups, provide an interview guide, describe the settings and identify methods used to record raw data. Data analysis should describe any anticipated themes, emerging themes, the process of content analysis and the different types of coding used (Gratton and Jones, 2004: 220–221). The method of reporting findings may be merged with the data analysis section as these activities are highly inter-related. The student should describe whether and how storytelling approaches are used. When excerpts of raw interview data are included in the findings, students should describe the general process of selecting these in relation to themes and any steps taken to preserve participant anonymity when presenting the findings. The student should mention any ethical dilemmas arising during access to participants, entering the field, gathering data analysing data and reporting findings. Methods of establishing trustworthiness could include familiarity with relevant literature, member checking, independent coding, reflexivity and methodological triangulation. Reflexivity is where students acknowledge their own backgrounds, experiences, beliefs and attitudes that may impact on their interpretation of data and discuss the steps taken to manage these impacts. Triangulation is where a concept of interest is studied using more than one approach; for example, a study could combine a student's field notes of performance analysis experience with interviews with players and coaches.

The methods chapters of projects that combine quantitative and qualitative analyses within mixed-methods approaches should include relevant sections of each approach, which have already been described previously in this section. The research design section of such a project should discuss the complementary use of quantitative and qualitative methods within the study to ensure that these methods are used in an integrated, rather than a disjointed, way. O'Donoghue (2010: 234–237) discussed how different subsections of such a methods chapter should be titled based on their role within the particular study. For example, a performance analysis support service may be evaluated using

188

quantitative match statistics as well as qualitative data from interviews. These could be described within broad sections of the methods chapter such as 'Match Analysis' and 'Coach Interviews'.

The methods chapter of an enterprise project should describe any methods involved in implementing the enterprise idea as well as the methods used in the main market research study. In the case of sports performance analysis enterprise projects, the implementation of the enterprise idea could be the development of a performance analysis system and its operation within a coaching process. There are a variety of methods that could be used in the market research study, which have been covered in Chapter 4. The methods chapter of an enterprise project should justify the choice of the particular market research methods, explaining their validity for the given market research exercise. The methods chapter of an enterprise project should ensure that the methods are replicable in the same way that the methods chapter of a research project should.

Results/findings

The results chapter of a quantitative research study into sports performance typically has a low number of words, as many results are presented in the form of tables, graphs, pitch diagrams and specialist profile diagrams. The text of a results chapter should not merely repeat the results presented in tables, charts and other diagrams but should describe notable aspects within and across different results types. The results compare samples or illustrate relationships between variables using a reductive approach based on the whole sample of performances rather than showing results for individual performances. Therefore, samples should be described using means and standard deviations or, where variables have skewed distributions, medians and inter-quartile ranges. Inferential statistics are best augmented with tables and charts presenting descriptive results, although some inferential results can be presented in paragraph text instead. The results chapter should cover the different types of dependent variables in a concise manner. The student should not present the exact same result in both table and diagrammatic form. There should typically be between six to eight result types presented in such a results chapter. This is something that should have been designed into the study when specifying the research question. The student needs to maintain the focus of the results on the research question rather than analysing any relationship between variables that can be analysed. For example, if the purpose of the study was to compare the tactics of winning and losing teams in a team sport, then each result type should include team (winning vs losing team) as an independent variable.

The findings of qualitative research may be presented in a separate results chapter, or they may be combined with the discussion in a joint results and discussion chapter. The structure of categories, properties and themes identified during the analysis can be presented as an initial summary (Côté et al., 1995). The findings relating to each theme can then be presented in an interpretive manner. This could be in the form of a story or a series of stories that portray the flavour of what has been found. Alternatively, the results can include quotes from interviews that characterise what has been found about different themes. The quotes should be presented using a signature scheme that protects the anonymity of participants. Results derived from the analysis of field notes should describe settings and behaviour. Whatever form of presentation is used, the results should be derived from the data gathered and not based on unsupported student speculation. The presentation of qualitative results needs to engage the reader, and there is often a conflict between wanting to write scientifically and wanting to write in a more popular form (Kvale and Brinkman, 2009: 266). The results should be interpreted in relation to relevant theory, whether the analysis was to confirm or refute some existing theory or develop new theory. Where there are inconsistencies in data with respect to some elements of theory, any discrepant evidence should be acknowledged (Strauss and Corbin, 1998: 159–161).

The results chapter of an enterprise project should present the findings of the market research study. This may be a combination of qualitative and quantitative findings, depending on the methods used to do the market research. Relevant tables and charts should be included to present different aspects of the market research. The chapter should summarise customer preferences for products and services. The results chapter of an enterprise project can highlight where findings differ from known market trends. However, explanations as to why any results have been found should be deferred to the discussion chapter, along with the business plan made using the results of the market research.

Requirements analysis

Development projects involve the practical work of producing and evaluating a product or process. They are not scientific projects and, thus, do not include chapters on methods, results or discussion. Instead, development projects have chapters on requirements analysis, specification, design, implementation and testing and evaluation. Normally the documentation for a product does not include information about where requirements came from but instead simply specifies what the product does. The reason for including a requirements analysis chapter in a development project done at a university is because it is a learning exercise and assessors are interested in the process and what was learned about product development, as well as the final system specification. The requirements chapter would have broad subsections on requirements gathering and requirements analysis. The requirements gathering section covers the sources of requirements, viewpoints considered during requirements gathering, methods of requirements elicitation, recording requirements and methods of checking requirements with potential users. The various requirements are listed and described. In the case of a software product, these include functional requirements and non-functional requirements. As mentioned in Chapter 4, the functional requirements include inputs, outputs, data stores and system processes that directly or indirectly transform inputs into outputs. The non-functional qualities include system performance, system reliability and usability. The requirements analysis section discusses how any conflicting requirements are dealt with and decisions made. Methods of checking that requirements are complete are also included in this section.

Specification

The specification of a process or product is the end-product of requirements analysis; therefore, requirements analysis and system specification are often combined into a single chapter. The specification of a product should be complete, unambiguous, verifiable, consistent, modifiable and traceable. A complete, unambiguous and consistent specification is essential for the developer to understand what has to be developed before designing and building the product. In the case of

191

a development project for a dissertation, the student writing the specification is often the same person who will be designing and implementing the system. Nonetheless, the specification should be written as completely as possible because it is a good test that the student has understood user requirements and can act as a means for helping the user communicate with user groups to obtain more consistent and complete requirements. A complete, unambiguous and consistent specification also allows verification that the eventual product does what it was intended to do. Traceability is where requirements can be traced through the system development process to identify system components fulfilling particular requirements. This can be a bit of a bureaucratic exercise, involving a numbering scheme for requirements to assist discussing them later in the development process. These qualities of completeness, consistency, unambiguous specification, modifiability, traceability and product verification need to be considered realistically with respect to the type of product being developed. Specifications of software products can be made using formal mathematical techniques, and this may be justified in some safety critical application areas. However, this level of rigor requires time and capabilities that may be unrealistic for many. The level of detail should be sufficient to check the requirements and understand the product that needs to be developed.

The content of a specification chapter should include an introductory section, a user description, the main functional specification and product lifecycle information. A product specification would typically use the introduction to describe the background to the product and its intended environment and provide an outline of the structure of the specification. However, in a dissertation report, the background will have already been covered in an introduction chapter and possibly a literature review. The user description should describe what the product does and how it operates from the user's point of view. This should include the product's function, operation, performance details and constraints, as well as any skills and abilities required of users. The constraints may be particular hardware or operating systems required by the system. The main functional specification describes the main features of the product, how they are operated and what they do. In the case of a software product, this would include inputs, outputs, data stores, processes and a data dictionary. The data dictionary provides the structure and content of different data stores, input data and output information. Product lifecycle information can include arrangements for user support, end-user training, expansion details and documentation.

192

Design

The design stage of product development is essentially moving from what the product will do to how it will do it. This is not always straightforward, as there may be several different ways of satisfying the same product specification. The design commences at a high level of abstraction, showing the structure of the product in terms of its main components. These components can then be designed by introducing lower-level detail of how they work. The design is a useful step between system specification and implementation that allows the student to consider development problems and potential design solutions before commencing implementation. As mentioned in Chapter 4, some small-scale products, such as those developed in student projects, may be developed using prototyping where there is iteration between requirements gathering and analysis and implementation activities. However, there should be some product design activity with at least an overall product design being documented. This helps the developer trace requirements to particular components of the system and ensures that interfaces between components are well understood before individual components are developed. In the case of software product development, the interface and algorithmic detail can be considered once an overall architectural structure of the system is designed. The design chapter is also an opportunity for the student to adopt particular design approaches and justify why they were chosen for the given product development project. This demonstrates general learning about product development and wider knowledge of product development principles.

Implementation and testing

The implementation and testing chapter should describe any processes and tools used to implement the product. The implementation strategy may develop components of the system in a specific order. This chapter gives the student the opportunity to justify the approach taken and describe any issues that arose during component development, testing and integration. The selection of test scenarios should be discussed. Testing should deliberately set out to demonstrate that the product works as intended. Specific cases should be described, along with any deviation from intended system operation that needed to be corrected. There may have been benchmark data sets used to test the product, allowing performance to be compared with alternatives. The student should take the opportunity to describe the use of such benchmarks and specific actions taken to identify where the product needed to be corrected.

Discussion

The discussion chapter is usually allocated more marks than the results chapter because it is where the student explains why they have found what they have found, making reference to theory and supporting academic literature. The discussion might not take as long to produce as the results chapter, but the ability to produce a good discussion chapter requires the student to have developed knowledge and intellectual ability over the course of their degree programme. The discussion should not merely repeat the results but should explain the results and discuss the implications of the results when combined with existing knowledge. For example, the results of a time-motion analysis study can be considered along with the results from published physiology studies into intermittent high-intensity activity to make an argument about the energy systems utilised in the given sport. The discussion should be structured into broad areas rather than following a result-by-result format. The broad areas under discussion may be the aspect of performance represented by a set of dependent variables and the independent factor hypothesised to influence the chosen aspect. These areas should be discussed in a holistic way using the evidence from the study as well as relevant literature. The discussion should cover where the results support or challenge existing theory and offer potential reasons for any agreements and disagreements found. The use of literature to support arguments is particularly important, and so the student should ensure that each page of the discussion makes reference to literature and that the chapter is not over-reliant on one or two papers.

The discussion chapter of an enterprise project should briefly explain the findings of the market research study and, more importantly, discuss how the market research study has influenced the proposed business plan. The business plan should be outlined, discussing how each part of it is supported by different findings of the market research study; the business plan itself is usually included as an appendix. Some enterprise projects may emphasise different aspects of the business plan than others due to differing findings in market research studies, justifying different

194

choices being made. The discussion should also draw on relevant literature. For example, the market research may indicate a particular marketing strategy to be more promising than others. Relevant literature about the suggested market strategy should be used, along with findings of the market research study in explaining why such a strategy is included in the business plan. The market research may suggest particular sources and volume of business finance are required. The candidate options for financing the enterprise should be discussed in light of the findings and drawing on business finance literature. There may be particular entrepreneurial skills required to launch the enterprise that would require the student to subcontract some activities to relevant experts to ensure the enterprise benefits from all of the skills required. This is an opportunity for the student to demonstrate their knowledge of different characteristics of entrepreneurs and explain their importance in the context of the student's enterprise idea. The discussion should conclude by summarising the key decisions included in the business plan and briefly explain the viability of the plan.

The business plan (included as an appendix) should contain the following contents recommended by Williams (2013: 67–72):

- An initial summary – This should describe what the business is, define the market, assess the potential for the business, forecast profits, estimate the initial capital required and identify the prospects for investors.
- Management – This should provide information about the student, including the student's experience, strengths and weaknesses, and include a supporting curriculum vitae (resumé).
- The product or service – This should be a simple description, explaining why the product or service is distinct. A survey of the competition is also included here, with an explanation of how the product or service fits into the market place given existing products and services.
- Marketing – This should describe the size and potential growth of the market, identify likely customers, outline sales pitches and discuss pricing strategy.
- Operational details – These include location, suppliers, facilities, equipment and IT strategy.
- Financial analysis – This should forecast short-term and long-term monthly income, expenditure, profit and loss. There should also be a

predicted balance sheet for two years in the future, and any assumptions behind the forecasts should be acknowledged, explaining the risks involved.

■ Prospects – These are the short- and long-term prospects for the enterprise, estimating the finance needed and identifying prospects for investors if appropriate.

Evaluation

An evaluation chapter is an alternative to a discussion chapter that is used within development projects. The student will have already written chapters on requirements, specification, design, implementation and testing; these previous chapters are largely concerned with the development of the system. The evaluation chapter, on the other hand, is an evaluation of the final product. Chapter 4 of this book has discussed product evaluation processes, using an automatic tactical analysis system as an example. The purpose of the current section is to discuss the documenting of this evaluation activity within the dissertation report. One of the distinctions between the development project and the research project is that the evaluation chapter within a development project is an applied research study in its own right. The previous chapters of the thesis will have been used to discuss the background and development of the system. The evaluation chapter, therefore, will need to include the purpose, methods and results of any evaluation studies done on the system.

The chapter should cover in-depth summative and formative evaluations of the product as well as economic aspects (McGuire, 2016). The evaluation chapter should be structured into broad subsections, such as feature analysis, performance and case-study evaluation. Feature analysis combines functionality and usability (Pfleeger, 1998: 457). User feedback can be in the form of questionnaire responses or more in-depth interview data about the product. Where such studies have been done, the chapter should describe the evaluation methods as well as the results of the evaluation. There may have been specific criteria set out for the product which it can be evaluated against. This could be presented as a table showing the extent to which the criteria are met by the product and existing alternative products. A performance section can describe any experimental work done to measure product performance under different conditions. For example, system performance

196

when implemented on different hardware configurations or when dealing with different input loads may be of interest. The system may have different settings which can be adjusted, impacting on performance. Details of such effect on performance should be included in this section. A case-study evaluation is an in-depth evaluation of the product being used as part of a typical job in the application context. This should cover how well the product worked – good aspects as well as areas that could be improved. The case study should compare situations in which the given task was done with and without the product, identifying any advantages and disadvantages of introducing the product. Other aspects covered in the product evaluation, such as portability, adaptability and reusability of components, should also be covered in the evaluation chapter.

Conclusions

The conclusions chapter should concisely summarise the findings of the study, practical recommendations and areas for future research without further discussion. In a research project, the conclusions provide the answer to the research question. The student should report what was found so that the conclusions are based on the data rather than on personal opinion. The practical recommendations must also be supported by the findings of the study, and students should not make unsubstantiated claims that cannot be supported. For example, a time-motion analysis study will provide useful knowledge that conditioning coaches should be aware of. However, without an experiment being done, the study does not provide any evidence that manipulating work and rest periods in training as suggested will actually be effective.

Areas for future research should be presented as opportunities given what the student has achieved rather than things that were not implemented within the student's project. The scope and limitations of any research project give plenty of ideas for future study. Some common areas of future research listed in quantitative performance analysis dissertations are applying alternative methods, investigating different levels of performance within the same sport and performing follow-up experimental investigations.

The conclusions of an enterprise or development project should briefly review the major achievements of the project in relation to the stated aims presented in the introduction. Clear recommendations about the business plan and the process or product that has been developed should be made. Just as in a scientific study, these should be supported by what has been found in the project.

Completing the dissertation

Students need to allow a week to complete the dissertation once the chapters have been written. The title page, declarations, acknowledgements, contents and appendices all need to be included. Students should thoroughly proofread their dissertations to ensure they don't lose marks unnecessarily for presentation. The contents pages of the dissertation should include chapter and section titles, a list of tables and a list of figures. The page numbers for these should not be added to the contents too early, as content may move within the dissertation report as a result of proofreading and correction. Students should have been building their reference list throughout their projects. During the final changes of the project, students should check that all references used in the text are in the reference list and vice versa. Students should also ensure that the referencing is done in the chapters of the dissertation and that the reference list complies with the required referencing style for the given dissertation module. There will be a wealth of support material for dissertation students, giving guidance on writing up the dissertation report. Students should use all of this material when checking their draft dissertation with respect to these guidelines.

Appendices may include processed rather than raw data, the output from statistics packages, blank data collection forms, screen dumps of computerised systems and ethics documentation. However, much of the verification information is better provided to supervisors using electronic means.

Students should provide draft chapters to their supervisor in good time to allow chapters to be read and feedback given. Where a student's work is delayed until close to the dissertation submission date, the supervisor may not be able to provide the quality of feedback they could have if the draft was received earlier. There may be several other students providing the student's supervisor with multiple chapters in a short period of time close to the hand-in date.

Backup copies

Students should keep backup copies of their dissertation, and backups should be made regularly. Given the developments in cloud storage, external hard disks and memory sticks, there really is no excuse for not having backup copies of work. Simply emailing data and chapters to one's self is a simple way of backing material up.

OTHER FORMS OF REPORTING

PhD theses

Doctoral studies typically involve a series of three to five studies that investigate a research problem from different perspectives. It is possible to undertake PhD research where performance analysis is dominant (Boddington, 2002; Choi, 2008; Robinson, 2011), but also possible that performance analysis may be used in one study within the overall research programme (Shapie, 2011; McLaughlin, 2003). The contents of such a PhD thesis would typically include the following:

- Introduction
- Literature review
- Methodology
- A chapter for each study (each chapter would include purpose, methods, results, brief discussion and summary conclusions)
- Overall discussion
- Overall conclusions

A methodology chapter at this level would be expected to discuss ontological and epistemological aspects of the research. There may be some common methods used within all of the studies of the PhD project that should be described before the individual studies. A PhD-level project in sports performance analysis might include studies on the validity of performance indicators and their reliability, a study comparing samples related to some independent factors of interest and an intervention study where performance indicators are evaluated within coaching practice. Studies identifying valid performance indicators could use a combination of quantitative techniques and expert opinion. Intervention studies usually take a case study format, applying some approach developed during the research and evaluating its effectiveness using a combination of self-reported data, field notes and performance data.

Slides for a conference presentation

Sometimes students send their projects to scientific conferences and are invited to present the work as a podium or poster presentation. If they are to present the work as a podium presentation, they need to produce a set of slides. A podium presentation in an open session may be as short as ten minutes, with three to five minutes afterwards for questions. Therefore, the student should include key slides on the background, purpose, methods, results, discussion and conclusions. An overview slide saying that these sections will be included in the presentation is not recommended because the format is familiar to most conference delegates. An overview slide is only really useful if the student is presenting the material in a different order. Slides should not contain a large volume of unreadable text but should include key bullet points. Diagrams of code windows and images of equipment used can be included in the methods slides. Charts that clearly indicate what has been found should be presented in the results. The student should not read from a script during the presentation as this does not look good and can interrupt their flow. The student is the person who has lived and breathed the project from beginning to end, so they should be able to speak with authority on their work and talk naturally about it, only requiring prompting from bullet points or diagrams on the slides. If the session chair tells the student they have one minute left, the student should be able to sum up what they did, what they found and what it means in the remaining time. The student should not worry that they might forget to say something if presenting without a script. Only they know what they intended to say and if something important was omitted, it may come up in questioning.

Poster

As has already been mentioned, research can be presented in poster form at scientific conferences, or there may be posters on research studies done within the student's degree programme. The poster can include some more detail than would be presented on slides. The poster should

200

include key figures, tables and photographs to convey details of the methods, results and theoretical aspects. Posters can be viewed by conference delegates and discussed with the student informally. Some conferences give poster presenters three minutes to describe their research and answer one or two questions. If you see some of the keynote speakers at a conference checking posters and taking notes using a clipboard, there are probably prizes for the best posters.

Writing a journal paper

Some student research projects are exceptional, with the necessary originality, rigor and impact to warrant publication in a peer-reviewed sports science journal. The dissertation needs to be reduced in size and presented in the format required by the particular journal it is being submitted to. Usually, the full introduction and literature review are not required, and these two chapters are merged and cut down to an introduction section that covers the background to the research problem and justifies the need for the study before stating the purpose of the research. Students and supervisors thinking of publishing papers in sports science journals should check the author guidelines of the journal. They should consider the type and quality of papers that have been published in the journal in the last one or two years and understand the scope of the journal. The supervisor should assist in the development of the paper, especially if the supervisor is an active research member of university staff. It is also worth mentioning here that producing a paper should not be at the expense of other modules the student is doing that count towards their final degree classification. Therefore, the process of publishing a paper should commence after the student has completed their programme of study.

GENERAL PRESENTATION AND REFERENCING

Plagiarism

Many universities use plagiarism detection systems, such as Turnitin, to detect whether students have unfairly used material that they did not produce. The system is efficient and shows evidence of similarity to other work in a form that makes it easy to develop a case against a student who has engaged in such unfair practice. Students should not copy material from other sources in the first place. If they review previous literature in their own words, they can avoid a situation in which their literature review chapter contains identical sentences to previous work. Similarly, the student should refer to supporting literature in their own words when discussing findings. This not only avoids plagiarism being committed but also strengthens the argument the student is making to link their findings to existing theory. It is very easy for students to find themselves accused of plagiarism. They may copy material directly from the internet and have every intention of changing it into their own words at some point. However, if they are busy with coursework in other modules, they may forget which paragraphs of a chapter under construction they wrote themselves and what text came from elsewhere. The easiest way to avoid this situation is to not paste text from elsewhere into chapters under development. Furthermore, many universities allow students to use systems such as Turnitin to check whether there is any similarity between their work and the work of others. In this scenario, there really is no excuse for students submitting work that contains material copied from elsewhere.

Tables

Tables are used in research to summarise large amounts of material. For example, there are review articles in sports performance analysis where tables have been used to show different characteristics of previous research studies. Tables can also be used in methods chapters to summarise the participants or matches used within studies; good examples of this type of table are seen in research sports performance analysis research papers as well as in abstracts. However, tables are more commonly used to show the results of studies. Consider Table 9.2, which shows the results for the cutting movements and sprints performed in our fictitious study comparing home and away performances in soccer. This table can be used instead of two separate compound column charts. The table could even be extended to include other time-motion variables related to acceleration and deceleration, leading to a further reduction in the number of result types produced. The final column shows the p values produced by the statistical test used to compare home and away performances within matches (Either a Wilcoxon signed-rank test or a paired samples t-test). Augmenting inferential results with the

202

Table 9.2 The frequency of cutting movements and sprints performed by the mean outfield player within soccer matches (mean+SD)

Movement variable	Team		p
	Home (n = 62)	Away (n = 62)	
Cutting movements			
To the left	82.5+18.7	79.9+16.8	0.192
To the right	76.2+18.0	76.4+14.9	0.940
V-cuts	26.9+7.6	24.8+5.7	0.020
Total	185.7+41.4	181.0+33.9	0.293
Sprints			
Explosive	20.7+10.8	21.6+9.1	0.346
Leading	12.8+3.3	13.1+3.1	0.357
Total	33.4+12.3	33.7+10.3	0.242

descriptive results avoids having to use paragraph text to state which variables were significantly influenced by venue and which were not. A further way of making the most of tables and avoiding using paragraph text to present statistical results is to include post hoc test results within tables. For example, imagine if Table 9.2 contained three types of venue (home, away and neutral – obviously not related samples any more, as there are only two teams contesting each match). The p value in the right-most column would now come from a test of whether venue had a significant influence or not. Where there is a significant influence of venue on any factor, post hoc procedures are employed to determine which pairs of venue differ with respect to the given dependent variable. Symbols ($^$, \$, #, etc.) can be used to denote pairwise differences within the table, saving having to report these differences in paragraph text. Whether a table or separate charts are used depends on the importance of the variables and what has been found. In some studies, sprinting and cutting movements may be so important in their own right that they would not be combined within a single table. Tables should have a title and include any notes required to ensure the reader can understand the content. For example in Table 9.2, the title advises the reader that the main body of the table summarises the home and away performances using means and standard deviations. The row headings should include any units of measurements (e.g., metres or seconds) that apply to the variables, and the columns should show the number of cases within samples (e.g., $n = 62$). The style of presentation of tables included in dissertation reports should be consistent and follow the guidelines given in the handbook for the dissertation module. An example of consistency is the use of a consistent number of decimal places within columns. Table 9.2 uses one decimal place; this should be used even if the value rounds to a whole number. For example we have used 18.0 and 181.0 instead of 18 and 181, respectively.

Table 9.3 is an example of a cash flow forecast that is part of a business plan in an enterprise project. When students are producing tables for such projects, they need to use the standard formats that are applied in business and accounting to aid readers who are familiar with these formats. Table 9.3 is based on the format used by Williams (2013: 331), but the data are for a sports performance analysis example. In a business plan, the student should use tables to be informative to themselves and to potential backers such as banks. One of the things that was specifically done when producing this table was right justifying the numerical columns. This is because the columns contain monetary quantities that are being added and subtracted. Table 9.3 would be used to help the student decide whether to launch their business idea after their degree

Table 9.3 Cash flow forecast for an enterprise project (values are in £)

	Month					
	Aug '17	Sept '17	Oct '17	Nov '17	Dec '17	Jan '18
Opening balance		*3,400*	*3,661*	*4,522*	*5,433*	*4,444*
Sales		1,000	1,500	1,500	1,500	2,500
Expenses claims received			250	400	500	500
Capital	10,000					
Total cash received	**10,000**	**1,000**	**1,750**	**1,900**	**2,000**	**3,000**
Capital equipment	2,500				1,500	
Capital software	1,000				500	
Set-up fees	2,000					
Phone bill	50	50	50	50	50	50
Internet site	1,000	50	50	50	50	50
Travel expenses		250	300	300	300	500
Professional organisation fees	50					
Work-experience student expenses			100	200	200	350
Bank loan repayments		389	389	389	389	389
Total cash payments	**6,600**	**739**	**889**	**989**	**2,989**	**1,339**
Closing balance	3,400	3,661	4,522	5,433	4,444	6,105

programme finishes. The particular enterprise idea is providing a performance analysis service to volleyball squads and is provisionally planned to launch in August 2017. In this month, the student (by now a former student) would need to purchase computer and video equipment and the software package they are using. Other initial expenditures, such as professional organisation membership, business start-up costs and internet site development, have also been recognised. The business start-up costs include registration and legal requirements. There are some reasonably fixed on-going costs, including mobile phone usage, internet site fees and bank loan repayments. In the example shown in Table 9.3, £10,000 is initially borrowed and is paid back over a three-year period. This assumes that the loan fees, interests and capital repayments come to a total of £14,000 over the three years, which is just under £389 per month. The variable costs and the income are particularly important when deciding whether to launch the business. The sales are assumed to grow to a point where further capital expenditure is required in December 2017 to allow expansion of service provision. As the service sales grow, the related travel and support costs also grow. The business plan has factored in support from a single work-experience student initially, but this could grow in January 2018. The forecast assumes that expenses will be paid back the following month, which is something the student needs to be aware of to avoid a negative balance.

The main information in the table that helps the student make the decision about whether to launch the business is the difference between the opening and closing balance in January 2018 (£1,461). The student needs to consider whether this is a full-time or part-time venture and whether the personal earnings from this are sufficient. There may be further growth possibilities, meaning the forecast should be taken further than six months. After three years, the bank loan will be fully repaid, cutting down on the monthly costs of running the business. There are choices to be made if launching the business. For example, the student may decide that freely available social media are sufficient for marketing purposes. This allows the costs of purpose-built internet sites to be removed from the cash flow forecast.

Charts

Charts should be presented in a manner that conveys what has been found. The use of charts will be discussed using a fictitious example project in which distances covered by the home and away teams in a set of sixty-two soccer matches are compared. The data are for the mean outfield player on the home and away teams within the matches. For the sake of this example, we assume that there have been no dismissals during any of the matches and that the data have been gathered using automatic player-tracking technology. The first thing to say is that for any set of data, there is no one single way of presenting the results in graphical form. Indeed, while preparing the diagrams for the current chapter, we found ourselves wondering whether the scaling of chart axes could be distorting differences in a misleading way. We've left the charts as we originally produced them so that these issues in producing charts can be discussed using the examples. Charts should have titles, axis titles and a legend when needed to aid understanding. The first type of chart we shall use is a pie chart, which is used to show the distribution of some whole amount among different values. For example, the pie chart in Figure 9.1 shows the breakdown of 380 soccer matches by outcome. You will note that the chart shows match outcome types and values. This is due to the black-and-white format of the book you are reading. However, it may be possible for you to use coloured charts in your dissertation, especially if it is submitted and marked electronically. Pie charts can also be used to show the breakdown of time, distance and events. While pie charts are good for showing the breakdown of sample cases (or distance or time) into categories, they are not good at comparing samples

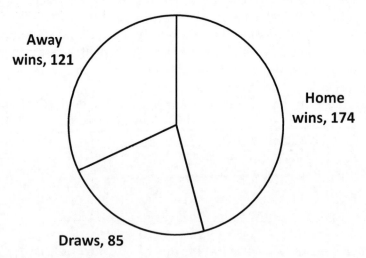

Figure 9.1 Distribution of match outcomes

of different sizes. Imagine if we used a pair of pie charts to show the breakdown of distance covered by the home and away teams within a soccer match. Each pie chart could have sectors representing movement of under 2 $m.s^{-1}$, 2–4 $m.s^{-1}$, 4–5.5 $m.s^{-1}$, 5.5–7 $m.s^{-1}$ and 7 $m.s^{-1}$ or faster. The issue here is the total distance covered by the average home team in a match might be greater than or less than the total distance covered by the away team. Pie charts of the same size might give a false impression that the total distance covered is similar between the two types of teams. In a situation where the breakdown of differing total amounts is being compared between samples, a compound column chart might be better, as it shows the total distance for each sample and the breakdown of that distance into movement at different speeds. There is an example of a compound column chart in Figure 9.3.

Figure 9.2 is a clustered column chart that shows the distance covered by the home and away teams during the first and second halves of matches. There is a cluster of columns for each team and a bar within each cluster for each half of the match. Note the use of the legend to distinguish the columns used for the first and second halves. The chart shows p values representing the significance of any differences in the distance covered between the first and second halves. Augmenting inferential statistics to charts or tables can help make the results more concise and avoid using

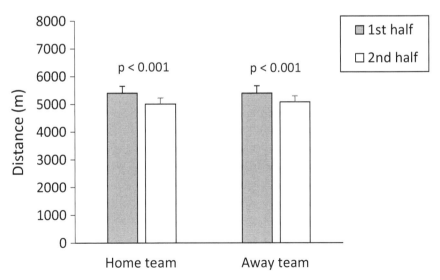

Figure 9.2 Distance (m) covered by players of each team in each half

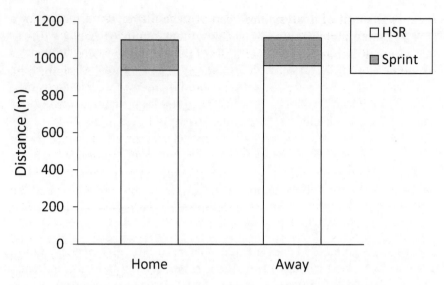

Figure 9.3 Distance (m) covered using high-speed running (HSR) and sprinting

unnecessary words in the results chapter. It may be necessary, however, to include some inferential results in chapter text if incorporating them within tables and charts becomes too cumbersome. For example, if there were a significant interaction between team and half of the match on the distance covered by the average outfield player, we might state this in paragraph text, along with the nature of that interaction effect. This chart is one of the ones we had to think about. Specifically we had to consider the scale on the vertical axis, which commences at zero metres. A lower limit of 4,000m might exaggerate the differences between home and away teams, and the differences between performances in the first and second halves of matches. The scale that we have used does make the values look similar despite the fact that there is a significant reduction in the distance covered from the first to the second half for each team. In selecting a range of values to be covered by an axis, we need to consider what is the meaningful range of values for the given variable. What is the lowest value we could ever expect for distance covered by the average outfield player in a forty-five-minute period of a soccer match? What is the highest value for this variable? We also need to have room to show any error bars. Another talking point about this example is that the error bars are very small. They actually represent the standard deviation. The reason why the four standard deviations shown are all less than 300 is

208

because the unit of analysis has been average player performance for a team within a match. This eliminates a great deal of variability due to positional differences and other inter-individual differences. The point of mentioning this here is to advise readers that methods describing data analysis should be clear about data pre-processing in preparation for analysis and clear about the variables that have actually been analysed.

Figure 9.3 is an example of a compound (or stacked) column chart. This is used to represent where the total of the columns are meaningful and we also wish to see the breakdown. In the specific example, the columns represent the distance covered using 'high-intensity activity' by the average outfield player in a team. This includes high-speed running (HSR), where a player is moving between 5.5 and 7 m.s^{-1}, and sprinting, where the player is moving at 7 m.s^{-1} or faster. Readers may be asking why we could not have used a compound column chart in Figure 9.2, as the total distance covered in a soccer match is made up of the distance covered in the first and second halves. The answer is that we could have used a compound column chart for that example as well. The reason for not doing so was that it might be difficult to see any differences between the second-half performances of the home and away teams if the part of the stacked columns representing second-half performances started at different places on the vertical axis for the two types of team. So it comes down to our judgement about what we are trying to show in the results. Do we wish to show the breakdown of distance covered in each half, or should a greater emphasis be placed on showing the difference between performances within individual halves of the match between home and away teams? Figure 9.3 is another example of a chart that raises questions about the best way to present the data. Error bars are problematic with a compound column chart, and so if the variance within samples is an important thing to show, we might need to use an alternative form of presentation. The distances covered using high-speed running and sprinting are so different that we would avoid using a clustered column chart because it would reduce our options for scaling axes. Where values are so different that it is actually difficult to see some of the stacked columns, a table might be a better option to show the data. One place where a column chart certainly should not be used is where the total of the stacked columns is not a meaningful total. Imagine a column chart showing the percentage of points won when the first serve was in and when a second serve was required. Imagine that the values of these are 65 per cent and 52 per cent respectively. The total of 117 per cent is not a meaningful percentage.

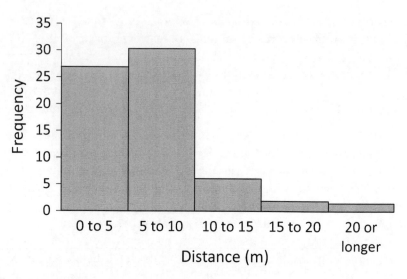

Figure 9.4 Number of sprints of different distances

The histogram is a column chart showing the frequency distribution of some continuous variable. Figure 9.4 shows the number of sprints of different lengths (m) performed by the mean outfield player of the home team. We would create an equivalent histogram for the away team. The histogram uses a column for each subrange of sprint distance value (0–5m, 5–10m, etc.) without any gaps between the columns. The lack of an inter-column gap reflects the fact that there are no values of the continuous variable (sprint distance) between the values of successive columns. Notice there is no legend; each column represents frequency of sprints performed, and the different lengths of sprint are already shown on the horizontal axis. This histogram could be shown with or without error bars.

Figure 9.5 is a line graph, which is used to show the distance covered during successive fifteen-minute periods of soccer matches by the home and away teams. A line graph is used to represent the influence of one continuous variable on another. Time within a football match is contin-uous so the use of a line represents continuity of this variable. It is dif-ferent to comparing distances covered by players of different positional roles; there is no continuum of positional roles going from defender to midfielder to forward. Positional role is a categorical variable, and so distinct columns should be used to represent each position in a chart. There are six fifteen-minute periods shown in Figure 9.5, but there is

210

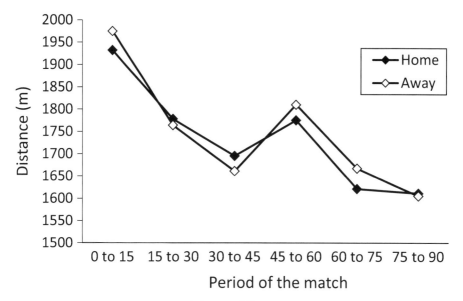

Figure 9.5 Distance (m) covered during different periods of the match by players of each team

continuity of time nonetheless. We are trying to show a trend of fatigue and need to consider the granularity of time. If we use periods that are too large (i.e., first and second half), it looks categorical, and a column chart would be better. If we use time periods that are too small (i.e., each minute from the 1st to the 90th) there will be a lot of noise in the line due to individual match effects. For example, there may be entire minutes in some matches when there is an injury break, meaning distance covered could be very low. Figure 9.5 was another one where we had to consider the scale of the vertical axis. The main issue here was that if we started the axis at 0m, then the two lines would appear almost indistinguishable. The restricted scale we have used might make the chart misleading as the differences appear larger than if a full scale were used. Researchers producing graphs like this need to consider the differences between samples (in our case between the home and away teams within matches). These differences may or may not be statistically significant, and we need to show the graph in a way that portrays what we have found. In biomechanical analysis of technique, line graphs are excellent for showing how displacement, velocity, acceleration, angle, angular velocities and angular acceleration change with time during the performance of a skill.

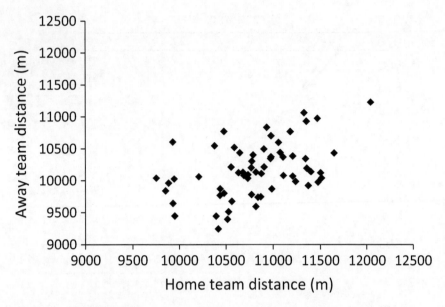

Figure 9.6 Relationship between distance (m) covered by mean player of home and away teams

A scatter chart plots two continuous variables against each other to display the strength of their relationship. There will be a marker on the chart for each case (whether a match, player or, in this case, an average team performance within a match). The marker is placed to show the value of the continuous variable on the horizontal and vertical axes. For example, Figure 9.6 shows the relationship between the distance covered by the home teams and opposing away teams within matches. Scatter charts can also have regression lines drawn through them and show the equation of the regression line if the relationship between the two variables is strong enough.

Playing surface diagrams

In sports performance analysis, a bird's-eye view of the playing area can be used to display the location of events. Hughes and Franks (2004a) showed examples of playing area diagrams for soccer, field hockey and squash, and Hughes and Franks (2004b) showed examples of playing surface diagrams for tennis, basketball and netball. Figure 9.7 is an example of a playing surface diagram for our fictitious study of the movement of

writing up the dissertation

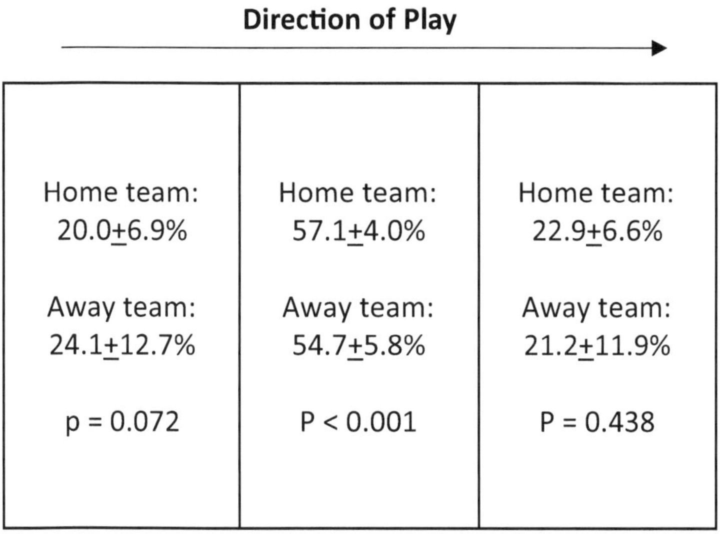

Home team: 20.0±6.9% Away team: 24.1±12.7% p = 0.072	Home team: 57.1±4.0% Away team: 54.7±5.8% P < 0.001	Home team: 22.9±6.6% Away team: 21.2±11.9% P = 0.438

Figure 9.7 Percentage of match time spent in different thirds of the pitch

home and away teams during soccer matches. There are three different thirds of the pitch, which should be clearly defined within the methods chapter. For example, many top-level soccer pitches are 105m long, and so the middle 35m could be used to represent the middle third. This allows matches played on pitches of different lengths to be included in the study. Figure 9.7 shows the percentage of match time that the average outfield player of each team spends in each third of the pitch. This is shown as the mean ± standard deviation, with p values of inferential tests comparing the two teams' values also shown on the same pitch diagram. These types of diagrams can be used for different types of playing areas in different sports to show the volume of events as well as the effectiveness of events. Some diagrams may be parts of playing surfaces; for example, in a study of penalty corners in field hockey it may only be necessary to show the attacking third of the field.

SUMMARY

There are various types of research reports that can be written for different audiences. The main report of interest to the current chapter is the dissertation report for sports performance analysis projects. The chapters of scientific, enterprise and development projects have been covered. Other types of reporting project work have also been covered in the chapter. These are PhD theses as well as podium presentations and poster presentations at conferences.

REFERENCES

Boddington, M.K (2002) The efficacy of visual feedback to enhance sporting performance, with specific reference to field hockey. Ph.D Thesis, University of Cape Town, South Africa.

Choi, H. (2008) Definitions of performance indicators within real-time and lapse time analysis systems in performance analysis of sport. Ph.D. thesis, University of Wales Institute Cardiff, UK.

Côté, J., Trudel, P., Baria, A. and Russell, S.J. (1995) 'The coaching model: a grounded assessment of expert gymnastic coach's knowledge', *Journal of Sport and Exercise Psychology*, 17: 1–17.

Gratton, C. and Jones, I. (2004) *Research methods for sports studies*. London: Routledge.

Hughes, M. and Franks, I.M. (2004a) 'How to develop a notation system', in M. Hughes and I.M. Franks (eds), *Notational analysis of sport, 2nd edn: systems for better coaching and performance in sport* (pp. 118–140). London: Routledge.

Hughes, M. and Franks, I.M. (2004b) 'Examples of notation systems', in M. Hughes and I.M. Franks (eds), *Notational analysis of sport, 2nd edn: systems for better coaching and performance in sport* (pp. 141–187). London: Routledge.

Kvale, S. and Brinkmann, S. (2009) *Interviews: learning the craft of qualitative research interviewing, 2nd edn*. Thousand Oaks, CA: Sage.

McGuire, M. (2016) 'Evaluation research', in N. Gilbert and P. Stoneman (eds), *Researching social life, 4th edn* (pp. 161–179). Thousand Oaks, CA: Sage.

McLaughlin, E. (2003) Children's recreational activity and health: a time-motion study. Ph.D. thesis, University of Ulster, UK.

O'Donoghue, P.G. (2010) *Research methods for sports performance analysis*. London: Routledge.

Pfleeger, S.L. (1998) *Software engineering: theory and practice*. Upper Saddle River, NJ: Prentice Hall.

Robinson, G.M. (2011) Establishing agility requirements and injury risk in elite soccer from automatically captured time-motion data. Ph.D Thesis, Cardiff Metropolitan University.

Shapie, M.N.M. (2011) Influence of age and maturation fitness development, trainability and competitive performance in youth silat. Ph.D thesis, Cardiff Metropolitan University.

Strauss, A. and Corbin, J. (1998) *Basics of qualitative research: techniques and procedures for developing grounded theory, 2nd edn*. London: Sage.

Williams, S. (2013) *The financial times guide to business start-up*. Harlow: Financial Times/Prentice Hall.

214

INDEX

215

216

217

219